H.D. and the Public Sphere of Modernist Women Writers, 1913–1946

Talking Women

GEORGINA TAYLOR

CLARENDON PRESS · OXFORD

OXFORD
UNIVERSITY PRESS

Great Clarendon Street, Oxford, OX2 6DP

Oxford University Press is a department of the University of Oxford.
It furthers the University's objective of excellence in research, scholarship,
and education by publishing worldwide in

Oxford New York

Athens Auckland Bangkok Bogotá Buenos Aires Cape Town
Chennai Dar es Salaam Delhi Florence Hong Kong Istanbul Karachi
Kolkata Kuala Lumpur Madrid Melbourne Mexico City Mumbai
Nairobi Paris São Paulo Shanghai Singapore Taipei Tokyo Toronto Warsaw

and associated companies in Berlin Ibadan

Oxford is a registered trade mark of Oxford University Press
in the UK and certain other countries

Published in the United States
by Oxford University Press Inc., New York

British Library Cataloguing in Publication Data

Data available

Library of Congress Cataloging in Publication Data

Data available

ISBN 0-19-818713-0

1 3 5 7 9 10 8 6 4 2

Typeset by Regent Typesetting, London
Printed in Great Britain
on acid-free paper by
Biddles Ltd,
Guildford and King's Lynn

Preface

THE AIM of this book is to investigate how traditional under-standings of modernism may have seriously misread projects involving women writers. This study contends that many women writers were not, as has been generally argued, at the margins of various previously understood modernist projects, but were often pursuing totally different issues and ideas in their work.

The idea of a 'public sphere' encompasses all the ways in which these writers shared their ideas and communicated with each other, forming an international network of writers. This will be explained in detail in Chapter 1. This study will locate H.D. at the centre of such a public sphere, and investigate how her various relationships enabled her to develop her ideas and how her ideas, in turn, formed a spring-board for others. It is possible to identify a body of writers who were publishing in the same sorts of places over time, corresponding with each other and had personal contacts with each other, and to study this over time despite individual writers leaving or becoming part of this public sphere.

The origin of this project was a feeling that existing accounts of modernism did not tell a plausible story of the way things were. Certainly there are excellent accounts of individual modernist women writers and small groupings, but there has been no challenge to the fundamental picture of modernism as comprised of various male-defined and male-dominated projects such as Imagism, Surrealism, Vorticism, and so on. It seemed unlikely that this was the end of the story, and that outside of these identified 'movements' there were simply writers 'doing their own thing' or hanging onto the margins of these projects. Many accounts of H.D. have understood her work largely in context of autobiographical information which may have influenced her: there has been very little consideration of what else may have been influencing her and, particularly, of who she was talking to.

I would like to thank everyone who has had a hand in this

work, both in its early life as a D.Phil. thesis and in its later development into this book. Thanks go in particular to Professor I. C. Butler, who supervised this work as a thesis.

G. T.

Acknowledgements

Copyright permission is gratefully acknowledged for the following:

Unpublished work by H.D. and Bryher, ©1914–1959 by Perdita Schaffner. Used by permission of New Directions Publishing Corporation, Agents.

'Mid-Day' and 'Pear Tree' by Hilda Doolittle, from COLLECTED POEMS, 1912–1944, copyright ©1982 by The Estate of Hilda Doolittle. Reprinted by permission of New Directions Publishing Corp.; also by permission of Carcanet Press Limited.

'Mannerisms of Free Verse' by Alice Corbin Henderson, by permission of the Estate of Alice Henderson Rossin.

'To a Steam Roller' (*The Egoist* 1915) by Marianne Moore by permission of The Estate of Marianne Moore. Reprinted with the permission of Scribner, a Division of Simon and Schuster from THE COLLECTED POEMS OF MARIANNE MOORE; copyright renewed ©1963 by Marianne Moore and T. S. Eliot; also by permission of Faber and Faber Ltd. (*Complete Poems* by Marianne Moore.)

Letters from Eliza Butler to H.D., Aug. 25, 1953 and June 30, 1953, held in The Yale Collection of American Literature, Beinecke Rare Book and Manuscript Library by permission of Sutton Publishing Limited.

Extract from letter from Ivy Compton Burnett to H.D., May 20 1944, held in The Yale Collection of American Literature, Beinecke Rare Book and Manuscript Library, by permission of The Peters Fraser & Dunlop Group Limited.

Extracts from the Harriet Shaw Weaver archive, by permission of Ms Hester Hawkes.

Permission to reprint is gratefully acknowledged for the following:

Grace Hazard Conkling, 'Spring Day' and 'The Little Rose is Dust, My Dear', Clara Shanafelt, 'Caprice', Margaret Fraser,

'Delicate Destruction', Alice Corbin Henderson, 'Mannerisms of Free Verse': all by permission of *Poetry*, copyrighted by The Modern Poetry Association, reprinted by permission of the Editor of *Poetry*.

Contents

I

A Theoretical Overview

. . . only through diversity of opinion is there, in the existing state of human intellect, a chance of fair play to all sides
of the truth.

John Stuart Mill[1]

The study of literature has usually tended to focus on the individual author. As Raymond Williams writes: 'We may know
that authors work within determinate social and cultural conditions, but we still emphasise the fact of individual production.'[2]
The study of H.D. has been no exception; indeed, the critical
consensus has been that she worked largely alone and had little
or no interest in a literary and critical exchange of ideas with her
contemporaries. Shari Benstock, for example, writes: 'Although
both Virginia Woolf and H.D. developed strong dependencies
on individual women . . . neither of them participated in a larger
community of women.'[3] Though several critics have commented
on H.D.'s exchange of ideas with specific close friends, and particularly with Marianne Moore, there has been a reluctance to
consider her work in relation to a diverse international group of
women writers. This study will demonstrate that H.D. can be
located at the heart of a network of women writers spanning the
Anglo–American divide; through discussion, and often through
disagreement, these writers came to challenge expectations of
women's writing and collectively to work on new ways of

---

[1] John Stuart Mill, 'On Liberty', *Collected Works*, vol. 4., 269, cited in Jürgen
Habermas, *The Structural Transformation of the Public Sphere: An Inquiry into a
Category of Bourgeois Society*, trans. Thomas Burger (Cambridge, UK: Polity Press,
1989), 135. Translation of *Strukturwandel Der Öffentlichkeit: Untersuchungen zu
einer Kategorie der bürgerlichen Gesellschaft* (Darmstadt: Hermann Luchterhand
Verlag, 1962).

[2] Raymond Williams, *Culture* (Glasgow: Fontana, 1981), 112.

[3] Shari Benstock, *Women of the Left Bank: Paris, 1900–1940* (Austin: The
University of Texas Press, 1986; London: Virago, 1987), 319.

expressing and exploring subjectivity, of engaging with socio-political reality and of stretching the possibilities of the literary form in new directions.

In examining the ways in which this network came into being and facilitated such an exchange of ideas, it will be considered in relation to the principles of a 'public sphere', a network operating according to certain clearly defined ideals of democratic exchange through which new opinion and thought is generated. By setting out the fundamental principles behind the operation of an ideal model of a public sphere it will be possible to understand some of the ways in which this grouping did and did not meet this ideal, and the extent to which it strove towards this. It will be argued that an examination of this public sphere of women writers can not only shed light on the work of individual writers within it, and particularly in this case the work of H.D., but must also challenge the way that 'modernism' has come to be understood.[4] An important discursive network has been all but eliminated from most accounts of the modernist period, and the work of many of the writers involved has therefore been marginalized. In attempting to 'set the record straight' this study will maintain a focus only on the women writers who were linked to H.D., and not on their male contemporaries who undoubtedly did play a role in the exchange of ideas. The reasoning behind this is to enable a focus on the specific ways in which these women writers were communicating and exchanging ideas, and to examine their work without an assumption that it can be slotted into previously identified networks and movements.

This chapter will begin by briefly outlining the basic theoretical principles behind the model of a 'public sphere'. Jürgen Habermas's seminal work, *The Structural Transformation of the Public Sphere* (*Structural Transformation*), will be discussed in

---

[4] These writers have been examined before as individuals and as small groups publishing in the same place, or living in the same geographical area, but no previous attempt has been made to look at the much wider network spanning a great number of little magazines and involving hundreds of women writers, stretching across the USA, Britain, and the Paris Left Bank. For studies of smaller groups see: Gillian Hanscombe and Virginia L. Smyers, *Writing for their Lives: The Modernist Women 1910–1940* (London: The Women's Press, 1987); Benstock, *Women of the Left Bank*; Kathleen Wheeler, *'Modernist' Women Writers and Narrative Art* (Basingstoke: The Macmillan Press, 1994).

order to draw out the essential principles of democratic exchange in an ideal model of group discussion and opinion formation. Though in some respects flawed, Habermas's model is crucial in setting out the basic principles of the public sphere, and its limitations usefully point towards some of the issues of concern for the study of this particular literary public sphere.

In *Structural Transformation* Habermas makes the claim that in the eighteenth century a sphere of discourse emerged between the state/economy (together the 'system') and the private (intimate) sphere. In this space, he claims, private individuals came together to discuss issues of mutual importance, not subject to the control of either state or economy. According to Habermas, the issues that were raised here were not issues of a purely personal and private nature (such as issues to do with family life), nor was the public sphere a forum for making political decisions (such as a parliament or smaller body of officials). The discussion within the public sphere was, in theory, able to create a climate of opinion that could influence official decisions without being constrained by the official interests of the state itself or of the economy. By standing apart from the 'system' it was in a position to observe and to offer critical opinion. Participation was open to all 'private citizens', that is, owners of property who were heads of households;[5] these men (women are relegated to the private sphere in this model) would be able to speak up for their private interests, but, so the argument goes, would also be motivated by a desire to serve the common good.

Habermas's model is primarily oriented towards the discussion of issues of broadly political interest and the ways in which consensus about such practical and ideological matters could come about. Crucially, however, he asserts that this public exchange was initially rooted in the literary sphere; the private citizen was able to read, reflect critically on what he read, and express a rational opinion.[6] Discussion groups in coffee houses and other public spaces emerged around the text, an informal 'criticism' where ideas could be experimented with and legitimated, or rejected, by public consent. As the public sphere developed, the literary text became part of a geographically dispersed exchange of ideas between rational bourgeois men, a true

[5] Habermas, *Structural Transformation*, 85.
[6] Ibid. 29.

'*publicität*' (publicness). The issues that emerged in the literary sphere were issues of aesthetic interest and of wider interest (such as issues of personal subjectivity), and the processes of opinion formation, influence, and development of new ideas that took place were rooted in a rational discourse and democratic forum through enabling structures such as the magazines, discussion groups, anthologies, friendships, and professional relationships.

The historical validity of Habermas's claims for the eighteenth century is not of primary interest here. What is important for the purposes of this study is that out of Habermas's historical account a model of an ideal (literary) sphere of democratic interaction emerges that can be used more generally to illuminate some of the ways in which ideas are exchanged and through which change may come about via discussion. His account is particularly useful in drawing attention to the kinds of institutions which might be significant in an exchange of opinions (the newspapers, journals, discussion groups), as well as the principles which must underlie an open sphere of exchange (such as an equal attention paid to the ideas of all participants regardless of their status, a willingness to be open to the opinions of others and the inclusion of all interested groups). New ideas emerge not only from the individual writer, but also out of the process of exchange itself, and 'truth' is discovered not because it is the property of one individual, but because all opinions are heard and reflected upon. In particular Habermas's model draws attention to the necessity of rational opinion formation as opposed to adherence to dogma or convention, and the requirement of the critical capacity to assess an utterance as far as possible on its own merits, regardless of the threat it might pose to the status quo or to existing ideology. The key factor in Habermasian public discourse, then, is this discursive rationality; language is used not to force agreement for the ends of a particular individual or group of individuals, but is motivated towards (though will not necessarily arrive at) a group consensus that will only emerge through a rational assessment of all contributions; Habermas writes:

This concept of communicative rationality carries with it connotations based ultimately on the central experience of the unconstrained, unifying, consensus . . . in which different participants overcome their merely subjective views and, owing to the mutuality of rationally motivated conviction, assure themselves of both the unity of the objective world and the intersubjectivity of their lifeworld.[7]

Finally, Habermas's model is useful in highlighting a principle of 'universality', whereby the interests of the public sphere are oriented around the interests of all, despite the fact that for various practical reasons not all will be able to participate actively in any individual discussion. The 'private subject' must, in Habermas's early formations of his theory, be a 'universal' subject able to bracket off his personal needs and act in the interest of all. Further, the public sphere as a whole will act in the 'universal interest' rather than the sectional interests of its particular constituency. The difficulties inherent in such an ideal will be discussed later in this chapter and throughout this study.

In considering modernist women writers as a 'public sphere' in a way broadly in line with the principles set out by Habermas, the focus will be on democratic exchange, the institutions that facilitated this, and the types of issues that emerged out of discussion. It will be demonstrated that a group of women writers between 1913 and 1946 did, to a large extent, have identifiable structures and an identifiable group of participants who were, broadly speaking, interacting in a democratic forum, a Habermasian 'public sphere', whereby new ideas emerged through a process of interaction. However, even to make this initial assertion is to encounter difficulties. Habermas's model rests very explicitly on an idea of one central sphere of discourse, *the* public sphere, which emerges alongside and offers a challenge to the official discourse of the state; his model does not take account of the possibility of rival networks each with their own interests, indeed to do so would contradict his own principle of 'universality'.

If we are to approach this network of women writers as a 'public sphere', then, an immediate modification must be made to the Habermasian model; the public sphere of modernist women writers must be conceived of as a 'counter-public sphere', that is,

---

[7] Jürgen Habermas, *The Theory of Communicative Action vol. 1: Reason and the Rationalization of Society*, trans. Thomas McCarthy (Cambridge, UK: Polity Press, 1984, 1987), 10. Translation of *Theorie des Kommunikativen Handelns* (Frankfurt am Main: Suhrkamp Verlag, 1981, 1987).

a non-dominant group whose interests are not necessarily compatible with those of the 'dominant' public sphere or with those of other competing counter-public spheres. Such a modification to Habermas's model has been made by Oskar Negt and Alexander Kluge, who write of an ideal of a proletarian counter-public sphere, an arena where workers come together in an exchange of ideas that is separate from the dominant bourgeois public sphere and emerges through different institutions.[8] Similarly, in Nancy Fraser's and Geoff Eley's 'competing publics' we find an idea of the marginalized group operating within its own discursive arena.[9] In both accounts the non-dominant group is able systematically to challenge the norms and values of the dominant public from which it is excluded, setting up the structures of operation—the magazines, publishing houses, discussion groups—which can replace, or run alongside, dominant structures. In fact, in Habermas's more recent writing he does acknowledge the possibility of alternative public spheres: 'It is wrong to speak of one single public . . . a different picture emerges if from the very beginning one admits the coexistence of competing public spheres and takes account of the dynamics of those processes of communication that are excluded from the dominant public sphere'.[10]

An application of a broadly Habermasian model of the counter-public sphere to this network of women writers allows for a detailed examination of the structures that facilitated their discourse, the discussion groups, letters, magazines, and anthologies that formed the basis for opinion formation and the challenge to literary and critical norms.[11] This public sphere

---

[8] Oskar Negt and Alexander Kluge, *Public Sphere and Experience: Toward an Analysis of the Bourgeois and Proletarian Public Sphere* (Minneapolis: University of Minnesota Press, 1993), 6 and throughout.

[9] Nancy Fraser, 'Rethinking the Public Sphere: A Contribution to the Critique of Actually Existing Democracy' and Geoff Eley, 'Nations, Publics, and Political Cultures: Placing Habermas in the Nineteenth Century', both in *Habermas and the Public Sphere*, ed. Craig Calhoun (Cambridge, Mass.: MIT Press, 1994), 116, 306.

[10] Jürgen Habermas, 'Further Reflections on the Public Sphere', trans. Thomas Burger, in *Public Sphere*, ed. Calhoun, 424–5.

[11] Such exchanges of ideas between groups of women through letters had of course taken place in earlier times. See, for example: Sharon M. Harris, 'Origins, Revolutions, and Women in the Nations', in *American Women Writers to 1800*, ed. Sharon M. Harris (New York: Oxford University Press, 1996), 165; Paula Bernat Bennett, ed., 'Introduction', in *Nineteenth-Century American Women Poets: An Anthology* (Malden, Mass.: Blackwell Publishers, 1998), p. xlii.

largely came into being because of the work of just three 'little magazines', all edited by women, which together offered women writers in Britain and the USA access to an unprecedentedly wide and diverse public. These were Harriet Monroe's Chicago-based *Poetry* (from 1912), Dora Marsden's London *The New Freewoman* (from 1913), and Margaret Anderson's *The Little Review* (from 1914), based initially in Chicago. Not only were these magazines edited by women, they attracted a large female readership and many female contributors, and expressed strong feminist points of view; they also operated according to often explicitly stated principles of democratic exchange, replacing the idea of a controlling editor with a model based around listening to the voices of as many (qualified) participants as possible, and allowing readers and contributors a more active role in shaping the course of debate. As Habermas argued for the eighteenth-century public sphere: 'The periodical articles were not only made the object of discussion by the public of the coffee houses but were viewed as integral parts of this discussion; this was demonstrated by the flood of letters from which the editor each week published a selection.'[12] The magazines were crucial to the operation of the public sphere of modernist women writers, and it was largely through their efforts that a core group of women writers came to conceive of themselves as a public, and to enter into discussion with each other within, and eventually well beyond, their pages.

The magazines, then, enabled a network of women to come together with no initial guiding manifesto or 'project' that would limit contributions, other than a stated belief in principles of democratic exchange and a broadly feminist ethos. Though many became involved at different junctures with certain more clearly defined projects, such as H.D.'s Imagism or Mina Loy's Futurism, these women writers generally stood at the margins of such projects, and were rarely involved in defining their own work within such narrow theoretical positions. In fact, such 'movements' become of little interest in a study of these writers as a group, where in place of rigid group ideology we find an openness to new ideas and a willingness to change and modify belief. Given the existence of this network with its own in-

---

[12] Habermas, *Structural Transformation*, 42.

dependent momentum and interests, the accounts given of modernism as a period, and of the important groups and guiding ideologies, must be radically revised. Crucially for this study, the work of individual participants within this network must be reassessed, and relocated not as marginal contributions to accepted modernist projects, but as central within a very different arena. Helen McNeil, for example, has written of modernism: 'The weak or timid—and almost all the women—fell by the wayside'.[13] These women did not, in fact, 'fall' anywhere; to publish in these magazines and to join the growing network of women writers was not to choose marginality, but to take an active stance towards a new public grouping with an enormous amount of dynamism and power to effect radical change not only in 'women's writing' but in the wider literary sphere. Women involved in this literary public sphere were, for example, among the first to experiment with 'stream of consciousness' narrative and with the application of psychoanalytic theories to literary work.

In studying H.D.'s work, then, it becomes apparent that a widespread critical belief in her isolation from her contemporaries is due to the fact that the vital structures and network in which she participated have not been previously identified. Once this network is located, it becomes clear that H.D. was not competing according to the terms of previously understood modernist projects, and that earlier critical evaluations of her work must be modified. Shari Benstock, for example, writes: 'As a woman [H.D.] experienced the sense of outsidership, the sense of difference from the masculine norms that all women face. But as a writer, she laboured under a double penalty: her expression had to meet the expectations of the male norm and had to "pass" as male writing'.[14] In fact, H.D.'s writing did not have to 'pass' as 'male writing' or meet a 'male norm'; her choices of publishing outlet, her correspondence with other women writers, her commitment to this particular network of exchange in numerous capacities that will be demonstrated over the course of this study, all demonstrate that she was not attempting to squeeze herself onto the margins of male-dominated modernist

[13] Helen McNeil, 'Introduction', in H.D., *Bid Me to Live* (New York: Grove Press, 1960; London: Virago, 1984), p. ix.
[14] Benstock, *Women of the Left Bank*, 332–3.

'projects', but was part of a group of women writers committed to finding their own way forward within a less rigidly delimited space.

This network was far from being only a minor force within modernism. Lawrence Rainey accuses H.D. of having written to a 'minute coterie'; he writes: 'Many of H.D.'s works, in other words, actively avoided contact with a wider public, not because H.D. was fearful of public reaction, but at least partly because she assumed that the public was unworthy of being addressed.'[15] In fact, the network within which H.D. participated was far from 'minute'. It grew rapidly after the early years and encompassed hundreds of women in Britain and the USA, and to a lesser extent the Paris Left Bank, over a thirty-three year time span. Several of the magazines that became important as its base had a large international circulation, and many of the writers involved travelled widely and were able to establish international contacts. H.D. not only felt others 'worthy' to be addressed, but entered into discussion in all possible areas, including criticism, theoretical writing, political campaigning, her own literary work, editing, correspondence with contemporaries, and later film work. Crucially, what distinguishes this grouping of writers from a coterie formation is its belief in itself as part of a wider communicating public, its engagement with issues that had a far wider impact than on a small grouping, its belief in itself as a real force for discussion and its willingness to open itself to new participants and new ideas.

In addition to the little magazines, then, other structures developed over time that facilitated exchange; many women came together in discussion groups and, increasingly, they worked together on shared projects such as anthologies, new journals, and magazines, and, later, projects connected with cinema. The base of the public sphere broadened to take in longer published works by writers who were becoming more established, and many of these women writers became involved in the world of publishing and editing. As the public sphere developed in confidence it became increasingly able to accommodate internal disagreement and to allow for heated argument

---

[15] Lawrence S. Rainey, 'Canon, Gender, and Text: The Case of H.D.', in *Representing Modernist Texts: Editing as Interpretation*, ed. George Bornstein (Ann Arbor: The University of Michigan Press, 1991), 105–6.

out of which new ideas and ultimately new literary forms and modes of expression emerged. It was also strong enough to be able to sustain periods of a loss of direction and to be able to find ways out of and through these.

One reason that this public sphere was so successful in generating new ideas was the participation of many not only as writers, but also as critics. There was not yet for these women a clear division of roles into 'writer' and 'critic'/'reviewer', or even any clearly established critical norms. As in the Habermasian idealized model of the eighteenth-century public sphere, so in this public sphere of modernist women writers all were able to participate as equals in a dynamic discussion that sprang up around the literary text. All participants, simply by virtue of being readers and writers, were qualified to write about socio-logical issues affecting women, about women's writing, history, and relation to tradition, without these being perceived as the domains of the sociologist, feminist theorist, or historian. Between these women a relatively free exchange of ideas could take place, based on the trust that all participants were able to read, understand, and make their own rational critical judge-ments, without the intervention of the critical 'expert' or any predetermined restrictions on opinion.

Habermas outlines the destructive effects of entering discus-sion with any unshakeable belief, or any uncritical adherence to tradition that would limit the ability of participants to reflect on a purely rational basis. For modernist women writers, the 'con-ventional' was challenged on all fronts, including any belief in woman as a purely 'private' subject, conventional religious beliefs and conventional ways of understanding human behav-iour and thought, and received ideas about the act of writing. The uncritical 'conventional' was increasingly replaced by a Habermasian 'postconventional' approach based on a critical interrogation of all ideas. This can help explain why the women involved in this network generally did not embrace any ideo-logical 'cause', perceiving the cause as the antithesis of true open debate; this included even the suffragist movement with which their interests were closely linked.[16] To accept a cause was to ·

---

[16] There were, of course, exceptions; those who were involved as young women with the suffragist movement included Alyse Gregory, Rebecca West, May Sinclair, Djuna Barnes, and Marianne Moore.

accept someone else's formulation of a problem rather than to view it as a complex issue requiring discussion and creative disagreement. Over the long period covered by this study, it is this attitude towards uncritical acceptance of any received ideology that is perpetually striking. As early as 1911, Dora Marsden writes of the suffragists: 'a political freedom secured at the price of forcing individual wills and consciences is more than just worthless. It is wicked, and we refuse to acquiesce in the uncritical attitude . . . of the public in general.'[17] Many years later Laura Riding writes: 'People who have allowed their public sensations to be formulated for them in terms of "causes" seem to have lost some of the energy necessary for a direct personal approach to public problems.'[18]

The Habermasian principle of 'universality' as a fundamental postulate of the public sphere is also useful in understanding some of the ways in which this particular public sphere operated. There were genuine attempts within this sphere of women writers to make the magazines and other networks open to as many as possible; the *Little Review*, for example, dropped its price in order to widen readership,[19] while *Poetry* built up a community of guarantors so that it could support writers by providing a secure site of publication, and could pay them for their work. Many of the most financially secure writers were able to offer support to others, such as Peggy Guggenheim's sponsorship of Djuna Barnes, Kay Boyle, Marianne Moore, Louise Bogan, Muriel Rukeyser, Eudora Welty, and Mina Loy. Bryher too endeavoured to help many women writers by establishing a foundation for writers in need.[20] To some extent, then, there was an idea that this public sphere should be open to all, and that by supporting the least wealthy they could be assisted to pursue a career as 'serious' writers rather than having to invest their energy in earning a living through more popular writing or alternative occupations.

However, there are several problems in attempting to carry

---

[17] [Dora Marsden,] 'Notes of the Week', *The Freewoman*, 1/2 (Nov. 30, 1911): 23.

[18] Laura Riding, 'Introduction', in *The World and Ourselves*, ed. Laura Riding (London: Chatto & Windus, 1938), 21.

[19] Anon., Announcement in *The Little Review*, 1/5: 67.

[20] Charles Molesworth, *Marianne Moore: A Literary Life* (New York: Athenaeum, 1990), 326.

over Habermas's principle of universality into a study of this public sphere of modernist women writers. Firstly, Habermas assumes a 'universal' subject who paradoxically is supposed to have a level of autonomy consistent with his status as propertied male, a freedom to meet others, access to networks of exchange, financial security and an absence from domestic ties that only a privileged minority will ever have, and historically have been available to far fewer women than men. Of the women writers involved in this particular network, it is certainly the case that the majority came from privileged backgrounds, either from the upper or upper-middle classes, and their interests were inevitably to some extent class specific.

There are, however, ways in which this class exclusivity can be understood not as an exclusionary attitude, but as a result only of the demand that participants be able to exercise a high level of creative and critical ability. Habermas writes not that the public sphere must include all subjects, but that underlying it will be an ideal of universality, a desire that all who are *capable* of participation should be able to do so. In his model of the eighteenth-century public sphere, then, the criteria of inclusion understood by these bourgeois men was not based on class or wealth, but on possession of the necessary education and intelligence—all must be able to exercise the necessary critical capacity. To some extent this idea can be carried over to the sphere of modernist women writers. Though in practice their sphere of discourse was relatively confined in terms of class composition, behind this lay a commitment to a high level of intellectual rigour that demanded that participants be well educated, with education related only contingently, not necessarily, to class. In addition the freedom to travel, the ability to make the right connections, the money to pay for publication of early work, and the leisure to be able to write rather than have to earn a living, all demanded a financial security that inevitably restricted access, without there being necessarily any intention to exclude. The mass of women would not have been able to leave home with little money and live independent lives, to have 'rooms of their own', in the way that Pound or Eliot were able to do, without a cushion of wealth behind them and an accompanying freedom from domestic responsibilities.

Nevertheless, it cannot be denied that this network of women writers was relatively blind to its own class composition, and demonstrated little interest in those women who lacked opportunities in education or who lacked the wealth necessary to pursue literary goals. Occasionally, some of the writers involved in this network did express an interest in widening educational opportunities, but most did not. Attempts to help those less well off in order to facilitate their participation, such as the sponsorships discussed above, were limited in scope, and were directed at the gifted few rather than towards any idea of giving the 'masses' access to the kinds of opportunities necessary to make their participation viable. The issues that emerged in this public sphere were not, generally, issues that would be central to the lives of working-class women, but were of interest primarily to the privileged few with the leisure time and wealth to take an interest in theorizing their own subjectivity, in consulting psychoanalysts, in travelling, and in reading periodicals and other texts.

Habermas's ideal of 'universalism', then, falls short of describing the basis of this public sphere. This is because his model rests on the ideal of a single public sphere which fails as a public sphere to the extent that it does not include all (men) who have the critical capacity to participate. Habermas writes: 'The public sphere of civil society stood or fell with the principle of universal access. A public sphere from which specific groups would be *eo ipso* excluded was not a public sphere at all.'[21] In fact, it becomes apparent that no public sphere could ever encompass the interests of all people, or be open to all, given uneven levels of wealth and education, of variant interests, and different demands. It is precisely by sharing certain interests and by positioning these against the interests of another group or groups, that a group can conceive of itself as a public sphere at all, and there is no reason to assume a limit to the number and types of groups that might emerge in this way. Once it is realized that any particular instance of a public sphere will necessarily to some extent be representing sectional interests (in addition to 'universal' interests) and will necessarily be limited in its participants, then it becomes possible to study this particular public sphere of women writers on its own terms. To begin to identify the types

---

[21] Habermas, *Structural Transformation*, 85.

of people able to participate in this public sphere (in general educated, reasonably wealthy, creative, broadly feminist women) is
to begin to understand the dynamics of this particular public
sphere, and to move away from an inadequate idealized universal model.

Another issue connected with Habermas's universalism which
must be considered, is that his 'universal' subject was not only by
definition bourgeois, but also male; indeed, his understanding of
the 'public' subject depends on there being a separate, private
sphere which is the domain of women. Habermas's theory is not
alone in a definition of the universal public subject as necessarily
male; Seyla Benhabib points out:

Universalistic moral theories in the Western tradition from Hobbes to
Rawls are substitutionalist, in the sense that the universalism they
defend is defined surreptitiously by identifying the experiences of a
specific group of subjects as the paradigmatic case of the human as such.
These subjects are invariably white, male adults who are propertied or
at least professional.[22]

The fact that the needs and positions of other groups have in
general been excluded from considerations of the 'universal'
subject does raise problems when such a model is brought to
bear on an excluded group. In this case, Habermas's model of
the public sphere assumes all participants to be able to bracket
off their life in the intimate sphere and become disembodied
minds in the public arena, leaving women to take care of the
private sphere. This both raises issues of woman's exclusion
from the public in this model, and also of woman's relationship
to the private, either as a space that she is 'confined' to, or which,
perhaps, she might choose to occupy.

That the private-intimate (domestic) sphere is women's
'natural' place has been a tenet of otherwise very different social
theories from Aristotle onwards. Before any public discussion
takes place then, women and women's concerns are excluded as
belonging to the private-intimate sphere. This is a commonly
observed problem in writing on women and the public sphere;
Mary Dietz's assessment of the problem is typical: 'In short, the

---

[22] Seyla Benhabib, 'The Generalized and the Concrete Other: The Kohlberg–
Gilligan Controversy and Feminist Theory' in *Feminism as Critique: Essays on the
Politics of Gender in Late-Capitalist Societies*, ed. Seyla Benhabib and Drucilla
Cornell (Cambridge: Polity Press, 1987), 81.

liberal notion of "the private" has included what has been called "woman's sphere" as "male property" and sought not only to preserve it from the interference of the public realm but also to keep those who "belong" in that realm—women—from the life of the public.'[23] By placing women's issues in this realm of the intimate sphere, so the argument goes, women are kept in a subordinate position, denied not only the legitimacy of their grievances but also the legitimacy of bringing these grievances into the public arena. Women's concerns are relegated to the 'lifeworld', that space concerned with private 'value' issues, a space that must be 'protected' from the intrusions of economy and state. In fact, as many of these theorists point out, this 'protection' is dubious, to do more with exclusionary mechanisms than with a desire to benefit women.

However, though there undoubtedly is a problem with a model which relegates women's interests exclusively to the private realm, it is far from clear that the 'private' is straightforwardly that into which women's needs and concerns are 'relegated', rather than also including a space which women might choose to occupy. The negative valuation of the 'private' realm is not necessarily one made by women themselves, and, in the case of many modernist women writers, was a space of strength and internal resources as much as it was a place of confinement. It is not necessarily desirable, then, simply to instate women into a Habermasian model as subjects able to occupy a public space by bracketing off their private lives and becoming disembodied minds. Nor can the answer to the difficulties raised by issues of the public and private, and women's historical association with the latter, be to collapse the categories of 'public' and 'private' altogether, as Iris Marion Young argues, as this is to remove the very basis for negotiation.[24] A more flexible interpretation of Habermas's model is called for, whereby we can allow that the private-intimate can be brought into the public sphere and questioned, redefining the limits of the intimate and public. For modernist women writers

[23] Mary G. Dietz, 'Context is All: Feminism and Theories of Citizenship', *Dædalus* 66/4 (Fall 1987): 4.
[24] Iris Marion Young, 'Impartiality and the Civil Public: Some Implications of Feminist Critiques of Moral and Political Theory', in *Feminism as Critique*, ed. Benhabib and Cornell, 59.

such questionings of the 'public' and 'private' as categories were central.[25]

In his recent writing Habermas faces up to the serious problem in his model as regards women's confinement in the 'private' sphere:

. . . the exclusion of women has been constitutive for the political public sphere not merely in that the latter has been dominated by men as a matter of contingency but also in that its structure and relation to the private sphere has been determined in a gender-specific fashion. Unlike the exclusion of underprivileged men, the exclusion of women had structuring significance.[26]

In his more recent *The Theory of Communicative Action* it becomes apparent that it is the context of the utterance which determines whether or not it will have public relevance. No issue is inherently public or private, and there can be movement in both directions across these definitions. So, for example, a choice of career may be for many people a purely personal choice, but becomes a public issue when Dorothy Richardson in *Pilgrimage* examines the constrictions on women's opportunities.

There is a further difficulty with Habermas's model that must be addressed in relation to its application to this sphere of modernist women writers. His model rests on principles of rationality that would seem to be more relevant to political debate than to the ways in which literature is read and discussed. This is particularly apparent when the subject of discussion is a network of women writers whose work became increasingly experimentalist and included avant-garde forms, 'automatic' writing, and Surrealist techniques. There would appear to be difficulties in applying a model so rooted in rationality to a sphere of exchange concerned with contributions including 'irrational' forms such as Elsa von Freytag-Loringhoven's Dadaist 'Mineself—Minesoul—and—mine—Cast-iron Lover'[27] ('Cast-iron Lover') or Mina Loy's 'Anglo-Mongrels and the Rose'.[28] Such work would seem

[25] These divisions were, of course, also addressed by nineteenth-century predecessors. See Susan Kingsley Kent, *Sex and Suffrage in Britain, 1860–1914* (Princeton: Princeton University Press, 1987; London: Routledge, 1990), 5.

[26] Habermas, 'Further Reflections', 428.

[27] Else Baroness von Freytag-Loringhoven, 'Mineself—Minesoul—and—mine—Cast-iron Lover', *The Little Review*, 6/5 (Sept. 1919): 6.

[28] Mina Loy, 'Anglo-Mongrels and the Rose', *The Little Review* [9/1–3] (Spring 1923): 16.

to contravene principles of clarity that are generally held to underlie rational discourse, as set out, for example, by H. P. Grice in his *Studies in the Way of Words*,[29] whereby a speaker who wishes to facilitate conversational exchange will attempt to present his or her utterance with the maximum clarity, truthfulness, straightforwardness, and relevance. In fact, Habermas asserts that the aesthetic validity claim is not of equal value to one dealing with 'truth' or 'rightness'.[30]

In reconciling the avant-garde form/women's writing in general with a model of public exchange rooted in rationality, it must be considered that these women writers did not, in general, ally themselves with specific avant-garde groupings, such as Futurism, but maintained a more open arena committed to a diversity of opinion. More fundamentally, it must be remembered that the central tenet of Habermas's theory in both *Structural Transformation* and *The Theory of Communicative Action* is that rationality is to do with the context of the utterance. There is no reason why the utterance itself might not, without contradicting this central tenet, have an irrational form, so long as it is intended as a rational contribution to discourse. As Steven Connor writes: 'Literary discourse is not merely non-serious—the other or mirror of seriousness—but that kind of language which permits and provokes the question of what constitutes the distinction between serious and non-serious language.'[31] The avant-garde or more experimental literary text, then, precisely by its deviation from the rational ideal of transparent speech, asks fundamental questions about that speech. In particular, the psychoanalytic encounter, in which many of these women writers participated, forms a model whereby the 'irrational' utterance, symptom, or recollection of dream, becomes part of a discourse rooted in bringing these into rational understanding. The irrational is not rejected in this model, but perceived as having an important contribution to make to a fuller understanding of the mind. As Habermas writes in *Knowledge and Human Interests*: 'The omissions and distortions that

---

[29] H. P. Grice, *Studies in the Way of Words* (Cambridge, Mass.: Harvard University Press, 1989), 26–30.
[30] Habermas, *Theory of Communicative Action vol. 1*, 20.
[31] Steven Connor, *Theory and Cultural Value* (Oxford: Blackwell Publishers, 1992), 127.

[psychoanalysis] rectifies have a systematic role and function
. . .The mutilations have meaning as such.'[32] In this way the
'irrational' avant-garde might be considered within the public
sphere as having something to contribute to an understanding
of a collective awareness of the historical epoch or collective
psyche, and be interpreted according to rational principles; the
public sphere becomes the 'psychoanalyst'.

It must also be realized that whatever the form of a literary
text, the discussion which springs up around it may operate
according to more obviously recognizable processes of democratic exchange, debate, and argument; it is crucial to the basis
of this study that these women writers were not only writing
literary texts which influenced each other and raised questions
about the literary form, but that the issues raised by their work
were explicitly canvassed in letters, reviews, criticism, and theoretical texts. The discussion that emerged around the work of
Freytag-Loringhoven, for example, as discussed in Chapter 3,
raised questions within this public sphere as to the limitations
and boundaries of art, the role of the unconscious in art, and
the connections between art and madness. The work itself facilitated a discussion of fundamental importance to the subsequent
direction of women's writing, and encouraged writers to think
about the processes involved in their own creativity. There was
nothing 'irrational' about such discussion, which operated as a
lively and rational dialogue oriented towards reaching a higher
understanding.

There is, however, a further problem with using an idea of
'rationality' as any kind of a basis for a study of women's writing, given that recent feminist criticism has tended to define
women's writing as antithetical to a 'constricting' rationality.
Rachel Blau DuPlessis writes, for example: 'The female perspective is holistic, synthetic, totalizing, rather than instrumental,
calculating, rational.'[33] This study will critically interrogate such
an idea, investigating the meanings of 'rationality' and the ways
in which these women writers respond to it as a concept. Instead

---

[32] Jürgen Habermas, *Knowledge and Human Interests*, trans. Jeremy J. Shapiro
(London: Heinemann, 1972), 217. Translation of *Erkenntnis und Interese*
(Suhrkamp Verlag, 1968).

[33] Rachel Blau DuPlessis, *Writing Beyond the Ending: Narrative Strategies of
Twentieth-Century Women Writers* (Bloomington, Ind.: Indiana University Press,
1985), 153.

of addressing this issue from the vantage point of contemporary feminist theory, the vantage point will remain throughout that of the writers involved; in this way the binary opposition of 'rational' (= male) and 'irrational' (= female) that seems to have been assimilated by much feminist theory, albeit with an increased valuation given to the latter, can be abandoned in favour of a more flexible approach to these issues.

There is one final problem inherent in any application of Habermas's model to a twentieth-century public sphere, since Habermas strongly asserts that he considers twentieth-century forms of publicity, and particularly the mass media (radio, film, popular press), to be antithetical to the operation of a public sphere. He makes the claim that the eighteenth-century public sphere began to decline as literacy rates rose without a corresponding increase in critical capacity, and that the mass media were harmful to any vestiges of critical discussion, since they encouraged passive reception rather than active engagement.[34] His views are very interesting in relation to this particular cultural formation; processes of commercialization and the growth of mass media in fact became an important subject of discussion as participants sought to balance their commitment to include the 'masses' in discussion with their equally strong desire to maintain the high levels of intellectual rigor that they felt were absent from popular culture. The cinema in particular became a site of heated exchange as these issues came to a head through the Hollywood film phenomenon, as will be discussed in Chapter 4.

Before moving on to a detailed analysis of this literary public sphere over a period of time, it is necessary first to briefly sketch out how this network is defined and identified, indeed what exactly is meant by identifying it as a 'public sphere' at all. The focus is certainly not on any 'fixed' group with a membership list or manifesto, but a changing network of female literary acquaintances of H.D. who together formed a dynamic 'public sphere'. H.D. was not at the centre of this grouping in the sense of having an organizational role, or having more of a controlling role than other significant figures. It would, in fact, be possible to start with any writer identified in this study and trace the web of

---

[34] Habermas, *Structural Transformation*, 163–80 and throughout.

contacts which emanates out from them over time, identifying a different 'centre' whose network of influences will be subtly different to that of any other writer. Nevertheless, around H.D. it is possible to see that there was a network of women writers who, broadly speaking, shared the same influences, were publishing in the same places and who shared certain common interests. It is particularly profitable to centre this study on H.D. since she travelled extensively and had a great number of contacts in the USA, Britain, and Paris.

Secondly, there is no fixed list of individuals who joined this network in the early years and remained part of it throughout; individual writers became part of this grouping and moved away from it over time, while other writers took part in later years. The current 'membership' is determined only by who was currently engaging in an exchange of ideas with H.D. and her contemporaries, who was publishing in the same places, engaging with the same issues, and potentially exchanging views in discussion groups and letters. For this reason the relevant participants as discussed in Chapter 5 will vary significantly from those discussed in Chapter 2. This is inevitable and does not point to a weakness in the idea of examining these writers as a public sphere, but points only to its living and changing nature over time. In the scope of this study it is certainly not possible to include biographical information on all participants or to chart exactly who was where and when: the reader who is interested in charting the careers of individual writers in detail must look to studies of individual writers or to a more biographically focused study.

In addition, it must be noted that this is not a comprehensive overview of all women's writing during this period. Any writer who had no direct influence on H.D., or her work on them, is excluded, however important in the literary world. For this reason, both Virginia Woolf and Anaïs Nin are virtually absent from this study, as is Leonora Carrington even when discussing the impact of Surrealism. Nor is this a comprehensive survey of the work done by little magazines, but only those in which H.D. published her work or which she was known to be reading. Many important little magazines of this period have therefore been omitted from this study.

Subsequent chapters will move on to a detailed consideration of the various interactions within this network between the years 1913 and 1946. Craig Calhoun writes of the counter-public sphere:

For any such cluster we must ask not just on what thematic content it focuses but also how it is internally organized, how it maintains its boundaries and relatively greater internal cohesion in relation to the larger public, and whether its separate existence reflects merely sectional interests, some functional division of labor, or a felt need for bulwarks against the hegemony of a dominant ideology.[35]

Such questions will now be asked of this particular 'cluster' of modernist women writers; this study will ask to what extent this network had a separate existence and identifiable objectives and interests from those of competing publics, and how specific structures facilitated a process of discursive opinion formation.

Most importantly, H.D.'s position within this network will be reflected upon, in a challenge to the dominant critical focus on her close private relationships and personal life. This study will attempt to demonstrate H.D.'s centrality in this international network of women writers by showing her involvement at all levels of discussion including criticism, theoretical writing, exchanges of letters, circulation of manuscripts, and, crucially, her commitment to her own experimental writing. By placing her work in this context it will be possible to discover which writers were influencing her creative processes and to what extent her ideas influenced others. It will also be possible to place both her periods of creative struggle and her periods of highest achievement into a context of the work of her contemporaries.

[35] Calhoun, 'Introduction', *Public Sphere*, 38.

2

The Genesis of a Public Sphere (1913–17)

It was as fit for one man's thoughts to trot in iambs, as it is for me,
Who live not in the horse-age, but in the day of aeroplanes, to
write my rhythms free.

Anna Wickham.[1]

At the start of 1913 H.D. was virtually unknown in the public
arena, but between 1913 and 1917, thirty-two of her poems
appeared in some of the most significant little magazines of the
time. Many were reprinted in collections such as the Imagist
Anthologies,[2] *The New Poetry*,[3] and her 1916 collection, *Sea
Garden*.[4] In this period she wrote and received her first reviews,
and edited her first magazine. Most importantly, she built
connections to other women writers that would sustain her for
the rest of her writing career. A network of women writers was
coming into being through these magazines and anthologies,
women who were reviewing each other's work, exchanging
ideas, working together on new projects, and entering into
private exchange via letters and personal contact. While these
writers have often been considered as individuals, or within
examinations of relatively small groups of individuals often
focusing on personal connections, what this chapter will begin
to establish is the development of a public sphere of women
writers in which hundreds of women were involved to a greater
or lesser extent, which spanned the Anglo–American divide, and
which far exceeded personal contacts.

---

[1] Anna Wickham, 'The Egoist', *The Contemplative Quarry* (London: The Poetry
Bookshop, 1915), 8.
[2] [Ezra Pound, ed.], *Des Imagistes: An Anthology* (London: The Poetry
Bookshop, 1914); [Amy Lowell, ed.], *Some Imagist Poets: An Anthology* (Boston
and New York: Houghton Mifflin, 1915, 1916 and 1917).
[3] Harriet Monroe and Alice Corbin Henderson, eds., *The New Poetry* (New
York: Macmillan, 1917).
[4] H.D., *Sea Garden* (London: Constable, 1916).

H.D.'s first taste of the publishing arena, outside of the minor American publications where some of her juvenilia had appeared, was through the American little magazine *Poetry*, edited by Harriet Monroe with Alice Corbin Henderson as assistant editor. *Poetry* had a significant circulation of up to three thousand copies,[5] and was able to attract vital advertising and sponsorship. Even in its early years it had a talent for discovering or accepting for publication the best new writing; it published many then unknown writers including H.D., Marianne Moore, Mary Aldis, and Clara Shanafelt, in addition to well-established writers such as Amy Lowell, Eunice Tietjens, Agnes Lee [Freer], Alice Meynell, Edith Wyatt, and Sara Teasdale.[6] Though *Poetry* expressed no specific commitment to women's writing as a separate category, it gave unprecedented public space to a great number of women writers, and on occasion produced women-only issues. By publishing their work consistently and by generating discussion about it, *Poetry* was central in the formation of a new network of women writers who were becoming aware of shared projects and influences.

Poetry, then, was located at the heart of an international network of women writers. Though most of its contributors were from the United States, with a particular and deliberate emphasis on local Chicago poets, there were nevertheless a significant number of English contributors or contributors living in England, such as H.D., Elizabeth Gibson Cheyne, Muriel Stuart, and Iris Barry, brought to the magazine largely through the influence of Ezra Pound as foreign correspondent. Readers of the English *The Egoist* were encouraged to become readers of *Poetry* and vice versa, bridging the Anglo–American divide. *Poetry* appealed for new subscribers in almost every issue, and placed advertisements in both the *Egoist* and the *Little Review*: 'We are trying to discover and develop the public for poetry which must exist in this country. But this public is hard to find.

---

[5] Frederick J. Hoffman, Charles Allen, and Carolyn F. Ulrich, *The Little Magazine, A History and a Bibliography* (Princeton: Princeton University Press, 1946), 44.

[6] It is beyond the scope of this study to include biographical information about each of the writers mentioned. However, *Poetry* included a brief introduction to each writer it published at the back of each issue, so for readers wishing to investigate the background of particular writers whose work appeared in *Poetry*, that is a good place to start.

Lovers of the art may never hear of the magazine unless our subscribers and other readers assist us.'[7]

Poetry was committed to fostering the ideal conditions of a public sphere where a free exchange and generation of new ideas could take place without other pressures, financial or ideological, intruding. By relying on guarantors to sponsor the magazine Monroe was able to print work that was not commercially viable, allowing the magazine to retain its openness to new ideas;[8] Monroe also insisted on paying contributors for their work in order to relieve writers of the need to publish less 'serious' but more profitable work. She was very supportive of the discussion groups that sprang up around the magazine, and encouraged contributors to visit her offices to discuss their ideas with her and with each other.[9] She felt that 'the magazine which expresses but one opinion is doomed',[10] and the literary content of *Poetry* was eclectic, from the traditional and 'sentimental' through to the avant-garde. Monroe's own tastes were always relatively conservative, but she was open to influence and suggestion from others, and included much work in the magazine with which she was not personally in sympathy.

The more avant-garde element within *Poetry* was largely due to the initially enthusiastic work done by Ezra Pound, whose ideas were strongly supported by Henderson. However, Pound's relationship with the magazine was tempestuous; he felt constantly frustrated that his own ideas were not given more weight and that rather than focusing on his own protégés, *Poetry* remained committed to the 'little fry'.[11] He wrote to Monroe in 1913: 'When you do finally adopt my scale of criticism you will, yes, you actually will find a handful of very select readers who

---

[7] Anon., appeal for subscribers. *Poetry*, 3/1 (Oct. 1913): unnumbered page at back of issue.

[8] It seems, however, that the magazine's guarantors did have some limited and occasional influence over its contents.

[9] See, for examples of such groups: Anon., 'Our Contemporaries', *Poetry*, 8/1 (Apr. 1916): 53; E.T. (Eunice Tietjens), 'Appreciation', *Poetry*, 9/4 (Jan. 1917): 199. H.D. does not appear to have been involved in a discussion group.

[10] H.M. (Harriet Monroe), 'Comments and Reviews: The Audience II', *Poetry*, 5/1 (Oct. 1914): 31–2.

[11] Ezra Pound to Alice Corbin Henderson, Oct. 14, 1913, in *The Letters of Ezra Pound to Alice Corbin Henderson*, ed. Ira B. Nadel (Austin: University of Texas Press, 1993), 56.

will be quite delighted'.[12] There was a clash of interests here, then, between Pound's laudable intention of bringing the highest possible quality of work to the magazine and excluding the derivative and traditionalist, and Monroe's equally good intention of encouraging promising unknown writers and those not affiliated to any group.[13] Though her policy resulted in much work of low quality, it also encouraged new writers to bring their work into the public sphere and thereby to expand their ideas and contribute to a much wider dissemination and exchange of new thought. H.D. appeared in the journal initially as a Poundian protégée, but was to maintain a connection with the magazine throughout her life, long after her break with Pound. Even in 1947 she was able to identify Helen Hoyt as having been one of the 'Poetry crowd', demonstrating that she had taken an interest in the 'little fry' as well as in the 'big names'.[14]

H.D.'s next published work appeared in the London magazine the *New Freewoman*, the successor to the feminist *Freewoman*. The *New Freewoman* (which became the *Egoist* from 1914) was edited by Dora Marsden, whose editorials reiterated again and again her absence of belief in all causes, morals, and group responsibility: 'The intense satisfaction of self is for the individual the one goal in life.'[15] Marsden's individualism alienated some of her readers;[16] it may well have harmed sales of the magazine, and certainly was a factor preventing the Imagist number being sold in the USA. Lowell wrote to Aldington in 1915:

. . . Ferris, Greenslet, Fletcher, and I thought it would be a mistake for us to distribute this number of 'The Egoist' over here. . . . In the first place, Dora Marsden's being on the first page makes it extremely

---

[12] Ezra Pound to Harriet Monroe, March 30, 1913, in *The Selected Letters of Ezra Pound 1907–1941*, ed. D. D. Paige (London: Faber and Faber, 1950), 18.

[13] Marsden's intention was not, however, to encourage the less able, only to widen the sphere of the 'gifted' and those showing 'potential'. This will be discussed further below.

[14] H.D. to Bryher, May 12 [1947], The Yale Collection of American Literature, Beinecke Rare Book and Manuscript Library, Yale University (henceforth referred to as 'Beinecke').

[15] [Dora Marsden], 'Views and Comments', *The New Freewoman*, 1/1 (June 1913): 5.

[16] See, for example, Alice Groff, letter to the editor, *The Egoist*, 2/2 (Feb. 1, 1915): 31.

doubtful whether anyone seeing the paper would care to buy it. To advertise it and attempt to sell it as an Imagist number when the most prominent thing about it is Dora Marsden's is almost certain to wreck it on the American market.[17]

However, in keeping with her individualism, Marsden was extremely hostile to unthinking collectivism; she encouraged free thought and debate throughout her involvement with the magazine and included many contributors whose world view differed radically from her own. Like Monroe she felt frustrated with a literary and philosophical environment grown stagnant: 'there are no thought-battles in England: no battles of ideas that is: no intellectual sport.'[18] Her magazine aimed to foster such sport, the free exchange of ideas characteristic of the public sphere. A circular announced: 'It will continue The Freewoman's policy of ignoring in its discussions all existing tabus in the realms of morality and religion. It will regard itself free to lay open any question to debate, and will in its open platform give as ready a welcome to capable adverse criticism as to support of expressed opinions, editorial or other.'[19] When Harriet Shaw Weaver took over the editorship in September 1914, she maintained this commitment to free thought outside of any group ideology: 'THE EGOIST is wedded to no belief from which it is unwilling to be divorced.'[20]

In common with Monroe at *Poetry*, such an open platform brought Marsden into confrontation with the more polarized vision of Ezra Pound, the literary editor. Marsden would not bow down to Pound's dictatorial desires, and he soon became frustrated at his lack of control; in 1914 he wrote to Henderson of *Poetry*: 'I have no special connection with the Egoist . . . I can't see that they can improve, and they seem to me rather a waste of energy under their present composition.'[21] Pound's desire for full control of the *Egoist* was thwarted when, during

[17] Amy Lowell to Richard Aldington, May 19, 1915, quoted in S. Foster Damon, *Amy Lowell: A Chronicle* (Boston: Houghton Mifflin, 1935), 306.

[18] [Dora Marsden], 'Views and Comments', *The New Freewoman*, 1/7 (Sept. 15, 1913): 123.

[19] Anon., circular for *The New Freewoman*, [1913], The Harriet Shaw Weaver archive, Add. MS 57355, British Library Department of Manuscripts.

[20] Harriet Shaw Weaver, 'Views and Comments', *The Egoist*, 3/1 (Jan. 1, 1916): 3.

[21] Ezra Pound to Alice Corbin Henderson, Dec. 21, 1914, in *The Letters of Ezra Pound to Alice Corbin Henderson*, ed. Nadel, 89.

Richard Aldington's absence from June 1916 until May 1917, H.D. was offered the assistant editorship with full editorial control. H.D. wrote to F. S. Flint: 'E. P. wrote! I think he expects to get R's job on the Egoist (in strict confidence)—But we did not answer his charming Machiavellian note!'[22] H.D. accepted the job and seems to have been highly committed to her editorship, yet discussions of this period generally view her role as having been merely to keep the magazine in operation for the sake of Aldington while he was away at the war. Barbara Guest, for example, writes: 'She was neither very good at the job, nor much interested in it, so eventually the job passed to the more competent Eliot.'[23] In fact, she seems to have seen this as an opportunity to get her own work better known in the public arena, and to develop the *Egoist* along her own lines, publishing work with which she felt a personal affinity. During this year her own work appeared on eleven occasions (compared to four times in the previous year and once in the following year), and included three reviews. H.D. published no other reviews in this period, but utilized her position as editor to experiment in a new genre. Two of these reviews concerned the work of writers in whom she took a personal interest—Marianne Moore,[24] whose *vers libre* was radically challenging expectations of poetic form, and the Imagist poet John Gould Fletcher—while the third concerned Charlotte Mew, an older English poet whose work H.D. admired. H.D. also included the work of the Imagist poets Fletcher, D. H. Lawrence, John Cournos, and F. S. Flint, as well as a serialization of Wyndham Lewis's *Tarr*.

Like the readership of *Poetry*, the readership of the *New Freewoman/Egoist* was international; the preliminary list of 128 people interested in, or already part of, the 'Thousand Club', a finance scheme to support the magazine, included 46 from the

---

[22] H.D. to F. S. Flint, Mar. 22, 1916, Beinecke.

[23] Barbara Guest, *Herself Defined: The Poet H.D. and Her World* (New York: Doubleday, 1984), 60.

[24] H.D. wrote to Moore following Moore's first appearance in the *Egoist*, to ask if she was the same person H.D. remembered from her Bryn Mawr days, and their friendship and exchange of ideas thus began through the mediation of this little magazine. See Margaret Holley, *The Poetry of Marianne Moore: A Study in Voice and Value* (Cambridge, UK: Cambridge University Press, 1987), 19, where Holley discusses H.D. to Marianne Moore, Aug. 21, 1915, Rosenbach Museum and Library.

USA, 78 from Britain, and 4 from elsewhere.[25] Like *Poetry*,
it had an extensive female readership and was central in the
development of a network of women writers across the three
magazines. The *New Freewoman* advertised itself in magazines
including *The Common Cause*, *The Suffragette*, and *The Vote*[26]
and the vast majority of Thousand Club members were women.
The *New Freewoman* was determined not to bow to pressures to
be more commercially oriented. Weaver sent out a letter to 'Dear
Madam', a general letter to all subscribers, announcing that
'the editorial staff will accept £1 a week until the finances of
the paper make more satisfactory terms possible.'[27] Marsden
appealed for all Thousand Club members to give £1[28] and
pleaded to the readers: 'The fact that practically all papers are
sold below cost is the reason why the English Press has to be
subsidised by advertiser or capitalist, and in consequence laid
open to corruption.'[29]

The third magazine in which H.D. published her work was the
Little Review, edited by Margaret Anderson, assisted initially by
Harriet Dean and later by Jane Heap. It was published first in
Chicago, moving to New York in 1917, and initially had around
two thousand subscribers.[30] Its enduring ethos, even more
explicitly than *Poetry* or the *Egoist*, was a forceful commitment
to dialogue, between writers, readers, critics, and the editors
themselves—all opinions were to be welcomed as contributions
in debate. Margaret Anderson was later to write of her motivations in setting up the *Little Review*: 'The thing I wanted—
would die without—was conversation. The only way to get it
was to reach people with ideas.'[31] Anderson's opening editorial
for the *Little Review* stated the importance of a critical and

[25] List of Thousand Club Members, The Harriet Shaw Weaver archive, Add. MS
57357.
[26] Anon., 'Minutes of Meeting of Directors held at Oakley House, Bloomsbury,
on Thursday, Sep. 10th 1913, after shareholders' meeting', The Harriet Shaw
Weaver archive, Add. MS 57358.
[27] Harriet Shaw Weaver to multiple recipients, [1913], The Harriet Shaw Weaver
archive, Add. MS 57354.
[28] Dora Marsden to Harriet Shaw Weaver, Feb. 25, 1913, The Harriet Shaw
Weaver archive, Add. MS 57354.
[29] Circular for *The New Freewoman*, [1913], The Harriet Shaw Weaver archive,
Add. MS 57355.
[30] Hanscombe and Smyers, *Writing for their Lives*, 184.
[31] Margaret Anderson, 'Editorial', *The Little Review* [no vol. no.] (May 1929): 3.

literary community for art—an ethos that was to stay with the magazine: 'Appreciation has its outlet in art: and art (to complete the circle and the figure) has its source in—owes its whole current to—appreciation.'[32]

The *Little Review* made its feminist ethos clear from the first issue, where Anderson proclaimed: 'Feminism? A clear-thinking magazine can have only one attitude; the degree of ours is ardent!'[33] The first issue also included 'M.H.P.'s' challenge: 'Who has given men the power and right to decide about woman's errand in the world? For lo! these many years we have been letting husbands, fathers, and brothers decide for us just what it were best for us to do; and if the new idea has any significance at all it is just this: that we feel able to decide for ourselves what we most want and need.'[34]

The magazine acted immediately as a practical forum for a critical women's community; of the twenty-six letters printed in the second issue, four times as many were from women as from men.[35] Most wrote in to praise the ethos of encouraging debate and an exchange of ideas. Katherine Tappert, typically, wrote: 'There are numerous points in the first issue that I should like to discuss with you; I must warn you that you are tempting your readers and must not be surprised if you are overwhelmed with letters, questioning, approving, and criticising.'[36] Again, Minnie Lyon wrote in to the *Little Review* to state what she believed its purpose to be: 'And it does not say: "Look, this is the only way" but "come all ye who have something to offer—only let it be sincere, true, unafraid." '[37] Like *Poetry* and the *Egoist*, the *Little Review* sparked a discussion group[38] and in September 1914 it introduced a new section, 'The Reader Critic'; here readers could write in and offer their own criticism or opinions, thus widening the scope of the forum and removing a division between 'experts' and 'non-experts'. Since traditionally there had been very few female critics, this was a particularly important step in empowering women to enter the critical arena and have their

---

[32] Margaret C. Anderson, 'Announcement', *The Little Review*, 1/1 (Mar. 1914): 1.
[33] Ibid.
[34] M.H.P., 'The Critic's Critic', *The Little Review*, 1/1 (Mar. 1914): 22.
[35] See *The Little Review*, 1/2 (Apr. 1914): 49–54.
[36] Katherine Tappert, letter to the editor, *The Little Review*, 1/2 (Apr. 1914): 50.
[37] Minnie Lyon, in 'The Reader Critic', *The Little Review*, 1/10 (Jan. 1915): 61.
[38] Anon., 'To Serve an Idea', *The Little Review*, 1/7 (Oct. 1914): 58.

voice listened to on equal terms with others in the public sphere. Like *Poetry* and the *Egoist*, the *Little Review* wanted to foster new ideas, not adherence to convention, and advertised itself as being 'not connected in any way with any organization or company; it is free from propaganda and outworn traditions; and has ideals and convictions which have already secured it a large, critical list of readers';[39] it was crucial to attract not just any readers, but 'critical' readers who were not passive recipients, but potential contributors. In order to stimulate new thought, the magazine printed articles that discussed contemporary issues in literature and thereby acted as a springboard for new discussion; from May 1915 Anderson announced: 'In each of the future issues of THE LITTLE REVIEW, beginning with June if possible, we shall have a special article attacking current fallacies in the arts or in life—getting down to the foundations.'[40] The editors were happy to publish views that challenged their own, and often modified their opinions in response to new ideas. Like *Poetry* and the *Egoist*, the *Little Review* had a principle of accessibility to its ideas, and certainly a desire that financial considerations should not be a barrier to entry into discussion; in July 1914 the editors announced a drop in its subscription price in order to make sure that even those who could not afford $2½ per year would still have access to the magazine.[41] In addition, though the editors were keen to attract financial backing, they refused to accept any money that had 'strings attached',[42] thereby protecting the magazine as a space for experiment and new thought. Instead, they chose to live temporarily in tents in order to save money, while Tietjens donated her diamond ring to the magazine's finances.[43]

[39] Anon., advertisement for *The Little Review*, *The Egoist*, 1/17 (Sept. 1, 1914): 339.

[40] Margaret C. Anderson, 'What We Are Fighting For', *The Little Review*, 2/3 (May 1915): 4.

[41] Anon., 'A Change of Price', *The Little Review*, 1/5 (July 1914): 67. This 'accessibility', of course, was a desire to reach more of those who were intellectually and educationally equipped to participate, not any wish to make the magazine 'popular'. This lowering of price would make the *Little Review* accessible to the struggling writer or impoverished artist, but not to those without the necessary educational background or unable to afford the reduced price.

[42] Anderson refused, for example, the offer of money from Amy Lowell, since Lowell expected in return to be allowed influence over the magazines. See Margaret Anderson, *My Thirty Years' War* (London: Alfred A. Knopf, 1930), 61.

[43] Ibid. 68.

The *Little Review* also had in common with both *Poetry* and the *Egoist* the editorial involvement of Ezra Pound. Though his involvement was highly beneficial to the magazine in securing subscribers and contributors, his role as foreign correspondent from 1917 led to the virtual eradication of women's writing. In 1915 Pound had written to John Quinn about the possibility of running a magazine together: ' "No woman shall be allowed to write for this magazine." It would be a risk. It would cause outcry, boycott, etc. . . . but most of the ills of american [*sic*] magazines . . . are (or were) due to women.'⁴⁴ Though his aspiration to edit his own magazine never materialized, this statement throws light on his work for the *Little Review*. In his first editorial he made his intention clear: 'I wished a place where the current prose writings of James Joyce, Wyndham Lewis, T. S. Eliot, and myself might appear regularly, promptly, and together'.⁴⁵ In this he was successful, temporarily changing the role of the journal from a space for diverse ideas to one expounding only the ideas of his own coterie. Following Pound's involvement, H.D. felt unable to continue to contribute to the magazine; she felt that Pound's 'antics' were amusing from a distance, but preferred not to get involved,⁴⁶ aware, presumably, of Pound's devastating impact on women's writing in the *Little Review* and his hostility to many of her contemporaries. Lowell also felt unable to contribute, and wrote to Anderson:

I have always had a strong feeling of friendship for you, and an interest in 'The Little Review', and I wanted to do all I could for it, but when you went over bodily to my bitterest enemies, although it in no sense disturbs the feeling of friendship nor my relations to you, it does disturb my relations to the magazine, and so long as you continue to give such prominence to these men, I don't feel like appearing in it.⁴⁷

Pound's involvement with *Poetry* and the *Egoist* was equally problematic, and he appears to have been playing the three magazines off against each other. He promised, for example, to

⁴⁴ Ezra Pound to John Quinn, 1915, quoted in Steven Watson, *Strange Bedfellows: The First American Avant-Garde* (New York: Abbeville Press, 1991), 385.
⁴⁵ Ezra Pound, 'Editorial', *The Little Review*, 4/1 (May 1917): 3.
⁴⁶ H.D. to Amy Lowell, August 10 [1917], typed transcript, Beinecke.
⁴⁷ Amy Lowell to Margaret Anderson, July 1917, quoted in Damon, *Amy Lowell*, 423.

give *Poetry* all his latest work,[48] writing to Henderson: 'I want you and H.[arriet]M.[onroe] to feel secure. in [*sic*] the moderately certain knowledge that I can annihilate anyone who gets in front of us. Simply I've got the artillery.'[49] Yet soon he wrote to Anderson of the *Little Review*: 'It may amuse you to know that ⟨our⟩ [authorial insertion] W. B. Y.[eats]'s poems are his newest & that the lot now with "Poetry" have been in reserve for some time—'.[50] He wrote to Anderson that if he could get her some more Yeats poems 'It will absolutely declass "Poetry" and we shall be THE IT.'[51] Yet Pound had written to Monroe of *Poetry* describing the *Little Review* as: 'A jolly place for people who aren't quite up on our level.'[52] Pound's desire to foster the work of a small group of favoured prodigies who conformed to his ideas of a 'movement' was always at odds with the views of the editors and stated ethos of the magazines. There was a clear divergence between the needs of the public sphere of modernist women writers to be as inclusive as possible and to allow in as many diverse ideas as possible, and Pound's commitment to a more competitive avant-garde, governed by manifestos and exclusive groups.

These, then, were the magazines where H.D. published her early work, the three working in effect together to assist the development of women's writing through the creation of an accessible arena where, in theory, all views were welcome and where a broad feminist ethos prevailed. Though there have been several important studies of these magazines and the work of their editors, these studies have not yet connected the magazines to their vital role in fostering a new public sphere of women writers;[53] the projects of these editors were in line with the great

---

[48] Ezra Pound to Harriet Monroe, August [18], 1912, in *The Selected Letters of Ezra Pound 1907–1941*, ed. D. D. Paige (London: Faber and Faber, 1950), 9.

[49] Ezra Pound to Alice Corbin Henderson, Jan. 20 [1913], in *The Letters of Ezra Pound to Alice Corbin Henderson*, ed. Nadel, 20.

[50] Ezra Pound to Margaret Anderson, [April 4, 1917], in *Pound/The Little Review: The Letters of Ezra Pound to Margaret Anderson*, ed. Thomas L. Scott and Melvin J. Friedman with Jackson R. Bryher (London: Faber and Faber, 1988), 25.

[51] Ezra Pound to Margaret Anderson, [May 7/8 1917], in ibid. 40.

[52] Ezra Pound to Harriet Monroe, Aug. 5, 1914, quoted in Scott and Friedman 'Introduction', in ibid. p. xxiv.

[53] See, for example, Jayne E. Marek, *Women Editing Modernism: 'Little' Magazines and Literary History* (Lexington: The University Press of Kentucky, 1995).

desire by many writers to enter into a literary exchange in a new kind of forum, to generate a new literary community that was able to interrogate fundamental tenets of the literary text, and to explore new areas of thought.[54]

Many writers published, as H.D. did, across all three magazines, including the established American poets Clara Shanafelt, Helen Hoyt, and Amy Lowell, and the English poet Alice Meynell, while many more published in two of the three. Appearing in both *Poetry* and the *Little Review*, for example, were Sara Teasdale (established American poet with several volumes to her name), Eunice Tietjens (Chicago poet), Mary Aldis and Florence Kiper Frank (both living in Chicago and publishing poetry and short stories), Edith Wyatt (a member of *Poetry*'s advisory committee), Marjorie Seiffert (American song writer and poet), and Elizabeth Gibson Cheyne (English poet). In both *Poetry* and the *Egoist* writers including Mary Carolyn Davies (American poet), Frances Gregg (story writer and poet, close friend of H.D.), and Marianne Moore appeared alongside each other. In addition, many of these women came together in various anthologies, such as Monroe's *The New Poetry* and the experimental *Others* anthology, which included Mary Aldis, Helen Hoyt, Mina Loy, Adelaide Crapsey, Mary Carolyn Davies, Frances Gregg, Alice Groff, and Marianne Moore.[55]

A crucial means of developing an exchange of ideas between these women was the act of reviewing, often by these writers themselves rather than by a 'professional' critic. H.D., for example, wrote reviews in this period of Marianne Moore and Charlotte Mew, while May Sinclair and Mary Aldis wrote reviews of H.D., and Lowell wrote about Fannie Stearns Davis and Eunice Tietjens. This arena did not yet possess any rigid critical norms or theoretical suppositions, nor had it separated the professional critic from the creative writer; writers were empowered to enter freely and equally into a sphere of criticism without having to conform to a recognized critical discourse. While this led to enthusiasm and fresh ideas, it did cause some

---

[54] Many of the women writers in this public sphere did, in fact, themselves become engaged in editorial work; these included, over the period of this study, Marianne Moore, H.D., Léonie Adams, Eda Lou Walton, Genevieve Taggard, May Sinclair, and Ruth Lechlitner.

[55] Alfred Kreymborg, ed., *Others: An Anthology of the New Verse* (New York: Alfred A. Knopf, 1916).

frustration, as these reviews tended to be overly impressionistic, reflecting only the personal likes and dislikes of the reviewer with little relation to a shared critical standard. Henderson complained: 'A type of criticism coming into vogue lately is of the subjective or pseudo-impressionist variety . . . it does not occur to them that it may make some difference whether the soul is, or is not, well qualified for the adventure.'[56] Reviews of H.D.'s work were highly susceptible to such personal and emotional responses, since her work had broken with any critical absolutes that might be applied, and in any case appealed to the reader on a deep and intimate level; Mary Aldis wrote that H.D.'s work 'vibrates to beauty as sensitively as a Greek Dryad'[57] while Monroe compared H.D.'s work to a 'butterfly's wing—fugitive, delicate, shot with color, visible a mere instant against the blue'.[58] At this stage much of the enthusiasm was manifesting itself as just that, with no critical terminology or terms of comparison yet in place.[59]

There was, however, a strong feeling of a need for a new criticism to accompany modern experiments in writing. May Sinclair felt that 'up till now [criticism] has been content to think in clichés, missing the new trend of the philosophies of the twentieth century'.[60] By this she meant both that critical discussion had not kept pace with new understandings in areas such as science, psychoanalysis, and cinema, and that critical thought was bound up in evaluative norms of an older generation. Sinclair expressed the dissatisfaction with critical norms that many were feeling: 'I find myself criticising criticism, wondering what is the matter with it and what, if anything, can be done to make it alive . . . it is absurd to go on talking about realism and

---

[56] A.C.H. (Alice Corbin Henderson), 'A Jitney-Bus among the Masterpieces', *Poetry*, 9/1 (Oct. 1916): 39.

[57] Mary Aldis, 'Some Imagist Poets, 1916', *The Little Review*, 3/4 (June–July 1916): 29.

[58] H.M., 'Reviews', review of *Some Imagist Poets: An Anthology*, *Poetry*, 6/3 (June 1915): 153.

[59] This, of course, was precisely what Pound had been reacting against. However, though he was undoubtedly right to point out the failures of overly impressionistic criticism, his desire to define more rigid principles of the poetic form was experienced as far too constricting.

[60] May Sinclair, 'The Novels of Dorothy Richardson', review of *Pointed Roofs*, *Backwater* and *Honeycomb* by Dorothy Richardson, *The Egoist*, 5/4 (Apr. 1918): 57.

idealism, or objective and subjective art, as if the philosophies were sticking where they stood in the eighties'.[61] In other words, a criticism that divided up thought into obsolete categories, such as belief in material objects as either subjectively constructed or objectively given, when these very categories were being challenged in literary texts, was bound to be inadequate in describing these texts. Criticism needed to take note of current developments of thought within philosophical systems, psychoanalytic theory and science, as well as within the literary texts themselves, and begin to construct new and more relevant critical categories. For this reason, the writer rather than the professional critic was in a privileged position, less weighted down by obsolete terminology. Gradually there became a greater sense of a shared critical vocabulary, as descriptive terms such as 'stream of consciousness' and 'polyphonic prose' emerged. Concepts from other fields such as the psychoanalytic 'complex' or cinematic 'montage' would gradually become current terms in critical discussion.

Many of these women writers used reviews in these early years as a way of supporting each other—the ecstatic praise in the reviews of H.D. discussed above was not unusual in its tone. Support between various members of this emergent network also manifested itself in many other ways, both practical and emotional. During the war Lowell wrote to H.D. to offer both encouragement and practical help, and H.D. was able to write to Lowell: 'I have had my last two month's [*sic*] allowance lost or stolen. We have waited and waited—cabled to my people etc.! . . . You once offered us some money—when I was ill.'[62] Lowell's offer of support caused H.D. herself to think of ways to help other writers in difficulty, and she wrote to Lowell: 'I think your spirit of generosity very beautiful indeed. I wrote you a day or so ago that it would help us so to have a little fund "for indigent artists" that we could draw on occasionally, a pound at a time. I will write you how it goes.'[63] This is one of the first examples of the desire to support each other as non-commercial artists, with the most affluent subsidizing the least affluent, and would be followed by other such projects. In a sense this repre-

[61] Sinclair, 'The Novels of Dorothy Richardson', 57.
[62] H.D. to Amy Lowell, Jan. 20, 1916, typed transcript, Beinecke.
[63] H.D. to Amy Lowell, Feb. 22, 1916, typed transcript, Beinecke.

sents a continuation of a tradition of philanthropy by 'leisured' women; however, in this case the motivation was less centred on 'doing good' in the abstract, and more on fostering a very specific community of writers; by offering help to writers in need, the financial donor would increase the number of those able to participate in this public sphere and thereby widen the discussion, benefiting both the recipient and the donor very directly.

To some extent, this general climate of support, and particularly the nurturing influence of positive reviews, differed from the atmosphere in the male-dominated avant-garde circles, where, in their early years, attack and difference seem to have been more integral to a creative exchange of thought. Michael Levenson, writing almost exclusively about male modernists in his *Genealogy of Modernism* documents this period in a way that highlights a contrast in ethos to that of these modernist women writers:

The members of the avant-garde, for their part, treated the public (and often one another) with contempt. During the first six months of 1914, the rhetorical din reached its greatest intensity. It was the period of Hulme's verbal assault on Ludovici and Fry, Pound's bitter denunciations of the reading public, the disrupting of Marinetti's lecture and, most notably, Blast itself . . . The provocation was deliberate and relentless, a desire to outrage that without question succeeded.[64]

In contrast, in the early years of the public sphere of modernist women writers, though there was an equal commitment to a generation of new ideas and creative discussion, writers tended not to use attack and hostile criticism to achieve this. Later women writers were to come closer to this model; as their sense of confidence in their own projects and that of their contemporaries became more secure, they were more able to sustain disagreement in the service of the public sphere. In this early period, however, there was still a sense of fragility about their public engagement, and therefore a perceived need to nurture each other's work rather than subject it to attack.

For these women writers the emergent sense of community also generated important collective enterprises. H.D. very soon

---

[64] Michael H. Levenson, *A Genealogy of Modernism: A Study of English Literary Doctrine 1908–1922* (Cambridge, UK: Cambridge University Press, 1984), 138.

became involved with Amy Lowell on a series of annual Imagist anthologies to succeed Pound's 1914 *Des Imagistes*. They were determined that these, unlike Pound's anthology, should be democratic forums based on the ideas of all contributors, but in taking this stance they necessarily alienated Pound. Not only would he no longer participate, H.D. suspected that he wanted actively to harm the new anthologies; she wrote to Lowell: 'Things are getting worser and worser! Our great & good friend [Pound] is taking up "Imagism" again—don't you think we'd better drop it [in the title]? . . . E.P. is making it ridiculous. . . . It is obviously E's plan to prevent our publication'.[65] Pound, furious with Lowell in particular for taking control of the anthologies, subsequently tried to limit her appearances in *Poetry* and the *Little Review* and wrote to Harriet Monroe at *Poetry* in 1915: 'If I had acceded to A.L.'s proposal to turn "Imagism" into a democratic beer-garden, I should have undone what little good I had managed to do by setting up a critical standard.'[66] In a letter to Anderson he stated of the *Little Review* that 'Lowell's talents and temperament will always be political rather than literary or artistic', and declared: 'If London and particularly Mayfair, is going to take up the magazine, we must be more careful than ever NOT to have in too much Amy and suburbs.'[67] In fact, as discussed above, Lowell had no desire to publish anywhere where Pound was influencing choices for publication.

The disagreements with Pound highlight the absolute determination of these writers to actualize their own vision of the public sphere rather than have this dictated to them. Nevertheless, in defining its own boundaries as an independent sphere of creative brilliance, innovative thought, and a broadly feminist ideology, this public sphere necessarily excluded those who did not meet its conception of itself, the less 'initiated' who were not part of its self-styled creative aristocracy, albeit one defined on lines other than those proposed by Pound. Clearly there is a contradiction here; an ideal of all inclusiveness and democracy characteristic of the public sphere was brought into play in an

[65] H.D. to Amy Lowell, [Nov. 23, 1914], typed transcript, Beinecke.

[66] Ezra Pound to Harriet Monroe, Jan. 15, 1915, quoted in Harriet Monroe, *A Poet's Life: Seventy Years in a Changing World* (New York: Macmillan, 1938), 367.

[67] Ezra Pound to Margaret Anderson, [n.d.] quoted in Anderson, *My Thirty Years' War*, 164.

arena equally committed to rigorous standards and a break from the old values much closer to those of Pound. Discussion of H.D.'s 'aloofness' is commonplace within criticism of her early work, but what needs to be recognized is that in such an attitude she was in tune with other women writers within this public sphere. Monroe, for example, felt that prize committees ought to be composed of 'exceptional high spirits in the arts' and not 'sober and earnest workers'.[68] Though she encouraged as wide a sphere of participants as possible in *Poetry*, the rationale behind this was to discover and foster those with a high level of creative brilliance, or who demonstrated a potential for creative brilliance that needed to be nurtured, and to bring these into contact with each other in energetic discussion. She certainly had no desire to encourage those inherently less able, whose work was merely capable.

Margaret Anderson's editorial policy was less tolerant; she showed no desire to encourage those showing merely 'potential', she wanted her magazine to print only the highest strata, the gifted and intuitive, and in September 1916, frustrated with the lack of such high quality contributions, left an issue almost entirely blank. Though her ideal, then, was to include as many active participants as possible, she refused to lower her standards in order to achieve this. She believed that it was pointless to try to include all people in a discursive community, since all did not have the ability to participate: 'what everybody thinks doesn't matter; what a few think matters tremendously'.[69] The following month she wrote: 'Sometimes I see peo-pul in this kind of picture: a cosmic squirming mass of black caterpillars moving first one way and then the other. . . . Once in a hundred years one of the caterpillars breaks his skin and flies away—a butterfly through the unfriendly air.'[70]

Dora Marsden was the most 'elitist' of the three editors, believing that people can never be equal as their talents are unequal: 'If one has powers in one's self everything will turn to opportunity; if one has not, the most obviously open avenues

[68] H.M., 'Editorial comment: The Tradition—"Sobriety and Earnestness"', *Poetry*, 3/4 (Jan. 1914): 142.
[69] Anderson, 'What We Are Fighting For', 3.
[70] Margaret C. Anderson, 'The Artist in Life', *The Little Review*, 2/4 (June/July 1915): 18.

will appear blocked as with impassable walls.'[71] Marsden felt that to improve educational and other opportunities for the least well off would be of no avail, since the truly gifted could overcome factors against them, and the non-gifted would not rise to the heights of the gifted however much support they were given.

H.D. very much believed in an aristocracy of the initiated few, and her work appealed primarily to this band of readers; Lowell wrote in 1917: '"H.D." is indubitably a poet for poets. It is doubtful if the great mass of poetry lovers will ever fully appreciate work of such a delicate perfection, but it is no less important for that.'[72] To read H.D., even her early work, does require a large amount of background knowledge of classics and myth, and though her work is not as 'difficult' as that of Marianne Moore or Mina Loy, it is certainly aimed at an educated and 'creative' reader, able to make the intuitive leaps that H.D. demands. Such a belief in the initiated few also comes across as an overt theme in her writing of this time; in her poem 'Cities', for example, the masses are seen as not fully human, as 'seething life', an agglomeration of people who cannot hope to interact as equals with the intuitive few, and who will necessarily fall behind.[73] The poem asserts that a new race is needed which has the creative giftedness, the space, and the leisure to appreciate beauty.

It was not only in the work of H.D. that such ideas appeared at this time; the sheer preponderance of statements within work by modernist women writers of this period concerning an idea of an intellectual aristocracy versus uninitiated 'masses' certainly adds weight to a view of these writers as a 'literary aristocracy'. In Harriet Dean's prose fiction 'Silhouettes', for example, the speaker protests: 'The little people about me fill me with disgust . . . God forbid that I am of the same breed!'[74] Again, in Amy Lowell's 'The Precinct. Rochester' the speaker condemns the masses for failing to appreciate beauty, fixated instead on bread. The speaker accuses them of ignorance, reducing them to vermin

---

[71] [Dora Marsden], 'Views and Comments', *The Egoist*, 1/14 (July 15, 1914): 263.
[72] Amy Lowell, *Tendencies in Modern American Poetry* (New York: Macmillan, 1917), 278–9.
[73] H.D., 'Cities', *The Egoist*, 3/7 (July 1, 1916): 102.
[74] Harriet Dean, 'Silhouettes', *The Little Review*, 3/4 (June–July 1916): 13.

who 'gnaw like rats'.[75] However, such attitudes to the 'masses' do not necessarily contradict the fundamental principles of the public sphere, where the exchange of ideas must be carried out between those 'qualified' to offer new ideas, in other words those as unfettered by dogma as possible, as intelligent as possible, willing to listen to new ideas, and to modify their opinions. Though such criteria will necessarily exclude a great many people this is a contingent exclusion rather than a necessary one, and rests not on class or wealth as such, but on intellectual and creative capacities, as well as education. The exclusions of this public sphere also point to the inability of any network to encompass the entire public, and the necessity therefore of an idea of various counter-publics, as discussed in Chapter 1.

The women within this public sphere did, then, tend to come from middle- or upper-middle-class backgrounds; none of the women involved were working-class, and many were financially independent. Inevitably, the issues that emerged in discussion had less relevance to women whose lives revolved around the family or around domestic duties or work, and more relevance to those leading relatively privileged lives. Even though many of the subjects that emerged in discussion were 'universal', to do with the literary text or with human psychology, even to engage with these issues implied a leisure to do so, removed from daily drudgery. The few who did have to support themselves were generally journalists, such as Dorothy Richardson and Hortense Flexner (American poet), and later Djuna Barnes and Stevie Smith. In general, these women enjoyed a level of financial independence that was unusual for women, and exercised it by taking up the freedom to travel and to write that the most privileged of their male contemporaries already enjoyed. Despite having a daughter in 1918, for example, H.D. used her own and Bryher's income to retain her freedom and independence, placing her daughter full time in a nursery. She lived much of her life in hotels where she was released from the domestic concerns that Woolf was later to write of as a serious impediment to the woman writer.[76] Again, Rebecca West was able to send her son

---

[75] Amy Lowell, 'The Precinct. Rochester', *The Egoist*, 1/4 (Feb. 16, 1914): 69.

[76] Virginia Woolf, *A Room of One's Own and Three Guineas* (London: The Hogarth Press 1929 (*A Room of One's Own*) and 1938 (*Three Guineas*); London: Penguin, 1993), 60–9 and throughout.

to boarding school from the age of three and thus escape any restrictive tie associated with mothering;[77] Elinor Wylie left her husband to elope with a married man, leaving her three-year-old son behind;[78] Mina Loy left two children behind when she left Italy for America;[79] Mary Butts left her daughter, just a few months old, and her husband, to travel to Paris with another man.[80] Though their belief in their superiority, then, was purely in their creative giftedness, it was often very much rooted in both an economic security and a freedom from domestic ties that were not available to most women, and though the *Little Review*, for example, dropped its price, it was still not going to be available (or of interest to) the great mass of women. Only a model that allows for various counter-public spheres whose interests will differ, though show some continuity, and whose ideas can compete with each other, can take account of the specific composition in terms of education and class background of these writers without having to compromise an idea of a public sphere.

Despite the privileged position of many modernist women writers the lifestyle they chose was often not one that had been traditionally led by women of the leisured classes. By dedicating their lives to their writing, and to a commitment to the writing of their contemporaries, they broke away from expectations that their lives would revolve around social engagements, entertaining, or charity work, and claimed a very different sphere of interests as their own, not just as writers, but as writers engaging in the public sphere. By entering into a creative exchange within the magazines it was possible to begin to examine the state of play of women's writing in the public sphere and to act as sounding boards for each other to test out new ideas within their work. Since the women's literary and critical communities were one and the same, a 'discussion' could take place around the literary text in which all could participate both as critic and writer. A small but growing group of writers began to assess the

[77] Victoria Glendinning, *Rebecca West* (London: Weidenfeld and Nicolson, 1987; London: Papermac, 1988), 65.

[78] Judith Farr, *The Life and Art of Elinor Wylie* (Baton Rouge: Louisiana State University Press, 1982), 24.

[79] Carolyn Burke, *Becoming Modern: The Life of Mina Loy* (Berkeley: University of California Press, 1997), 193–4.

[80] Mary Hamer, 'Mary Butts, Mothers and War', in *Women's Fiction and the Great War*, ed. Trudi Tate and Suzanne Raitt (Oxford: Oxford University Press, 1997), 219–40.

work of contemporaries appearing in the magazines, and to question fundamental principles of the written form including conventions of style, suitable subject matter, and particularly of presentations of women's experience.

It became clear to these writers that though fundamental areas of life as diverse as the human mind, religious beliefs, future security, and family identity, were open to new understandings in the early twentieth century, little of this new thought was finding its way into literary texts. A great deal of poetry in particular had got stuck in a pattern of conventional ideas expressed in hackneyed forms; the very worst of late Victorian ideas and expression had carried over into the twentieth century and become a prescriptive formula rather than a vehicle for creativity. Nineteenth-century conventions of prosody, once enabling structures for creative thought, were now stifling any expression of a twentieth-century psyche and formed a straitjacket on new developments. Agnes Lee's 'The Silent House', in the March 1913 issue of *Poetry* is typical of much poetry of the older generation:

> Corinna, come to light my heart's dim place!
> O come to me, Belovèd and Besought,
> O'er grief, o'er gladness,—even o'er death apace,—
> For I could greet your phantom, so it brought
> Love's own reality![81]

The poem centres on the devotion of a woman for her man, such that she battles her way through a storm to reach him, jeopardizing her health and life to assuage his unhappiness. Archaic forms of poetic diction—'tarry', 'hither', 'o'er' and so on—are rife, along with sentence inversions and a strict adherence to metrical convention. There are no ideas that can generate new thought, nothing challenging, contemporary, thought-provoking. Having made herself ill by battling through the storm Corinna will go out into it again to return to her old house, knowing this last endeavour will kill her; death is highly sentimentalized here— 'Tomorrow you shall see me all in white'—and means no more in the context of the poem than the last of a series of conventions fulfilled.[82]

[81] Agnes Lee, 'The Silent House', *Poetry*, 1/6 (Mar. 1913): 175.
[82] Lee, 'The Silent House', 178.

Problems of conventions grown stale were of course not only present in poetry. The realist novel still centred largely around a character's 'adventures' in the external world, with steady progression through an ordered 'plot'. Though prose fiction was not as conventionalized or locked into archaic forms as poetry, there was nevertheless a feeling of frustration that there were no new forms of prose, nothing which reflected the huge advances in understanding in all realms of life. To some extent, of course, the feelings of frustration with both poetic and prose form reflect early twentieth-century women writers' need to create a myth about—or at least exaggerate the extent of—the restriction of their immediate predecessors within unyielding and stultifying conventions, as part of what seems to have been a Bloomian 'anxiety of influence'.[83] Certainly they seem to ignore the progress in Victorian writing towards change and reflection on conventions, and the enormous amount of experimental writing undertaken by nineteenth-century women writers.[84] However, the great mass of largely trite and banal writing in the early issues of *Poetry* demonstrates that many writers were indeed caught up in restrictive conventions of prosody and thought, resulting in stale echo rather than new exploration.

Of course, this was not only a problem of women's writing; however, women's writing did find itself in some specific difficulties. Women's poetry in particular now perceived itself as having inherited an excess of sentimental emotions and 'prettiness' from its late Victorian predecessors that were felt to be incongruous with the modern woman and her ideas. As the New Woman writers had done before them, so this generation reacted against 'feminine' conventions that were perceived as limiting in both life and writing.[85] This new generation was able to build on the work of these predecessors without, in general, acknowledging the work that had already been done, and was able to go

---

[83] Harold Bloom, *The Anxiety of Influence: A Theory of Poetry* (Oxford: Oxford University Press, 1973).

[84] See Paula Bennett, 'Late Nineteenth-Century American Women's Nature Poetry and the Evolution of the Imagist Poem', *Legacy*, 9/2 (1992), 89–103 for a discussion of the kinds of experiments undertaken by nineteenth-century women writers.

[85] For writing by experimental women writers of the late nineteenth century see, for example, Elaine Showalter, ed., *Daughters of Decadence: Women Writers of the Fin de Siècle* (London: Virago, 1993).

further than ever before in challenging conventions and asserting the validity of its own experiences and modes of writing. Sentimental declarations of love or religion and conventionalized modes of 'feminine' expression now seemed increasingly trivial and vacuous; like their experimental poetic foremothers, these women had a new subjectivity to express and a dissatisfaction with the forms available for expression. Women's prose writing too had some specific problems—there was a current of feeling that the novel had been hijacked by a male tradition with a focus on external 'action' that had little connection to a woman's experience of herself and the world. The woman prose writer, like the poet, needed to find a way of bringing the form in line with the truth of a woman's experience in the twentieth century, breaking with both the perceived sentimentality of the worst of late Victorian writing and the external focus that was perceived as masculinist. In Richardson's 1919 *The Tunnel*, part of her *Pilgrimage* sequence, Miriam puts into words the uneasiness with old forms for the twentieth-century woman writer: 'Anyhow it was wonderful about English—but if books were written like that, sitting down and doing it cleverly and knowing just what you were doing, and just how somebody else had done it, there was something wrong, some mannish cleverness that was only half right.'[86]

There was no agreement about what was needed in order to bring women's writing out of its impasse, and in early issues of these magazines highly conventional ideas and texts sit alongside the more revolutionary. The publicity agents for Leona Dalrymple's unoriginal and sentimental novel *Diane of the Green Van*, for example, still felt it was a selling point that this novel was 'not a "problem" or "sex" novel' when placing an advertisement in the *Little Review*.[87] Yet readers of the *Little Review* and the other magazines were increasingly demanding precisely work that was problematic and did deal with sex. The editors of all three magazines pleaded for new ideas and in the April 1913 issue of *Poetry* Monroe stepped back and reflected on the poems that had been submitted to her magazine in the

[86] Dorothy Richardson, *The Tunnel* (Duckworth, 1919) in *Pilgrimage* vol. 2 (London: J. M. Dent & Crescent Press, 1938 (excluding *March Moonlight*); London: Virago, 1979), 131.
[87] Anon., advertisement for Leona Dalrymple, *Diane of the Green Van* in *The Little Review*, 1/1 (Mar. 1914): 64.

past year, concluding that ' . . . the greater number have been pathetically ingenuous in their intellectual attitude'.[88] Monroe felt incensed by the preponderance of formulaic thought and expression:

> Certain metric forms and rhyme tunes have been followed by so many generations of English poets that the modern world has come to think them fundamental instead of incidental . . . And these forms and tunes have been covered over with ornaments and excrescences; the Victorian tradition especially has burdened them beyond endurance, until we need to 'return to the point before occupied', to go back to first principles . . .[89]

The frustration expressed by women writers with women's writing in particular was very evident. It was often perceived as having nothing of substance beneath the ornamentation; Monroe complained of Fannie Stearns Davis's writing, for example, that it was 'all up in the air'[90] while Lowell complained of Mary Aldis's work that there was 'a wooliness, [a] vagueness of treatment'.[91] Mary Adams Stearns, reviewing Ethel Sidgwick's *A Lady of Leisure*, complained of an 'avalanche of words—words—words' that obscured what was worthwhile beneath—'It is like a continuous afternoon tea, or a lemon meringue pie with nothing but the meringue.'[92]

All three magazines were successful in attracting writers who were committed to bringing women's writing out of its impasse. Anna Wickham, for example, an Australian-born poet living in London and Paris, whose work appeared in the *Egoist*, attacked all that was most restrictive in writing, including the 'prettiness', cliché, and trite sentimentalism that many associated with women's writing. In her 1915 poem 'The Egoist' she expresses a frustration with outdated language and cliché, with learnt patterns and regular rhyme. She also expresses frustration with the conventional topics of women's writing that depict a sentimentalized view of the world. The poem ends:

---

[88] H.M., 'Editorial Comment: The New Beauty', *Poetry*, 2/1 (Apr. 1913): 22.

[89] H.M., 'Its Inner Meaning', *Poetry*, 6/6 (Sept. 1915): 304.

[90] H.M., review of *Crack o' Dawn* by Fannie Stearns Davis, *Poetry*, 6/1 (Apr. 1915): 45.

[91] Amy Lowell, review of *Flashlights* by Mary Aldis, *Poetry*, 8/6 (Sept. 1916): 320.

[92] M.A.S. (Mary Adams Stearns), 'Unfulfilled Expectations', review of *A Lady of Leisure* by Ethel Sidgwick, *The Little Review*, 1/10 (Jan. 1915): 48, 49.

It was as fit for one man's thoughts to trot in iambs, as it is for me,
Who live not in the horse-age, but in the day of aeroplanes, to
write my rhythms free.[93]

The speaker asserts her place in the twentieth century and her
wish to write in a new 'free' verse, free both in terms of an escape
from the monotony of prosodic convention and also in thought.
Wickham, like other women writers of this period, claimed the
right to make the woman's experience of her private subjectivity
into public text, a text that boldly claimed the right to express a
unique and interesting subjectivity. Padraic Colum, reviewing
the collection where 'The Egoist' appears, found such confidence
unacceptable: 'Here is a woman claiming experiences for herself,
songs for herself. The intention of the writer has put emotions
awry, and her songs are hard and twisted. The quarry is woman,
the object of her continuous contemplation is man, the pur-
suer.'[94] Colum reduces her text to a 'song', thereby bringing it
back to within the bounds of women's 'verse'; it is inconceivable
that if he were writing of, say, T. S. Eliot, that he would describe
his poetry as 'song' or complain that Eliot's conscious intentions
had upset his 'emotions'. Yvor Winters also took a dislike to
Wickham's writing: 'Mrs. Wickham's handling of sex-problems
is too obvious, coming after Lawrence, for serious consideration'.[95] Wickham was writing both against a belief that her
exploration of 'sex problems' was not comparable with that of
the 'great' male writers, and against the expectation that as a
woman her writing should be emotional and sentimental;
Colum's view that her work is 'hard and twisted' is a startling
reflection of the expectations of women's writing at this time.

The new forms of writing by women that burst into these
magazines around 1913, then, were reacting against some of the
same problems with cliché and tendency to archaism that many
of their male contemporaries were faced with, but also
specifically against a sentimentality perceived by these women
writers as a particular problem within women's writing. They

[93] Wickham, 'The Egoist', 8.
[94] Padraic Colum, 'Chap Books and Broadsheets', including review of *The
Contemplative Quarry* by Anna Wickham, *Poetry*, 6/5 (Aug. 1915): 255.
[95] Yvor Winters, 'A Woman with a Hammer', review of *The Contemplative
Quarry and the Man With a Hammer* by Anna Wickham, *Poetry*, 20/2 (May 1922):
95.

were also writing against a critical opinion held predominantly, though not exclusively, by male critics, that demanded that women writers limit themselves to 'song' and to expressing 'feminine emotions'. One of the first texts radically to challenge the poetic form in these areas was H.D.'s 'Hermes of the Ways'. H.D. had managed to strip her writing of all sentimentality, focusing on visual and sensory impression:

> The boughs of the trees
> Are twisted
> By many bafflings;
> Twisted are
> The small-leafed boughs.[96]

There is no uncontrolled or overflowing sentiment in 'Hermes of the Ways', nothing 'feminine' or 'pretty'. As Sinclair notes later of the Imagists, and of H.D. in particular: 'The Victorian poets are Protestant. For them the bread and wine are symbols of reality, the body and the blood. . . .The imagists are Catholic; they believe in Transubstantiation.'[97] In place of the symbol of deep internal processes was a more direct image that fused internal and external, and stripped this down to its bare elements. 'Hermes of the Ways' is sparse and extremely hard hitting, 'twisted' and self-conscious in exactly the way that Colum objected to in Wickham's writing. The poem is very much centred on human emotions, but is concerned to express these in a new way, divorced entirely from self-pity and trite phrases of conventionalized expression. The speaker resists the great external forces around her by subverting their aggression and turning this into the positive results of twisted boughs, ridges, and 'salt-crusted grass'. Instead of the neat 'garden' of the metrically regular and perfectly rhymed verse, this poem asserts in both its form and overt expression the need to let more powerful forces make their own individual patterns, less regular but more authentic.

Again and again in her writing H.D. attacked ornamentation and ordered forms, all outside pressures that stifle the creative life. In 'The Last Gift' she writes:

---

[96] H.D., 'Hermes of the Ways', *Poetry*, 1/4 (Jan. 1913): 120.
[97] May Sinclair, 'The Poems of H.D.', *The Fortnightly Review*, 723 (Mar. 1927): 333.

I reason:
another life holds what this lacks,
a sea, unmoving, quiet—
not forcing our strength
to rise to it, beat on beat—
a stretch of sand,
no garden beyond, strangling
with its myrrh-lilies—
a hill, not set with black violets
but stones, stones, bare rocks,
dwarf-trees, twisted, no beauty
to distract—to crowd
madness upon madness.[98]

The poem argues for the possibility of individuality against great constraining forces, using a free form to hammer away at poetic conventions of rhyme and metre as it asserts the value of 'bare rocks'; the new space is one where individuality replaces obtruding clutter. 'Beat' will be individually determined, not prescribed; the result will be a new form belonging to the 'initiates', a language 'more intense than this'. Very little of H.D.'s early work in its first published form fell victim to archaisms, but where this was the case it was rapidly altered in subsequent versions. In 'Acon', for example, the word 'pitieth' occurred in its first publication in *Poetry*,[99] was still present in the 1914 *Des Imagistes* anthology, but had been replaced with 'pities' by the publication of *Sea Garden* in 1916.[100] A similar process happened to 'Hermonax',[101] along with a shift here and elsewhere from regular capitalization of the first letter of each line to a freer use of capitalization.

May Sinclair perceived at once the value of H.D.'s project, writing:

Haven't we had enough of passion and of the sentiment that passed for passion all through the nineteenth century? . . . And isn't it almost time

---

[98] H.D., 'The Last Gift', *The Egoist*, 3/3 (Mar. 1, 1916): 35.

[99] H.D., 'Acon', *Poetry*, 3/5 (Feb. 1914): 165.

[100] H.D., 'Acon', in Pound, ed., *Des Imagistes*, 26; *Sea Garden* (1916), *Collected Poems 1912–1944*, ed. Louis L. Martz (New York: New Directions, 1983), 31–2.

[101] H.D., 'Hermonax', *Poetry*, 3/5 (Feb. 1914): 164; repr. in: *The Glebe*, 1 (1914): 28–9; *Des Imagistes*, ed. Pound, 28–9; *Heliodora and Other Poems* (London: Jonathan Cape, 1924), 87–8.

to remind us that there is a beauty of restraint and stillness and flawless clarity? The special miracle of those Victorian poets was that they contrived to drag their passion through the conventional machinery of their verse, and the heavy decorations that they hung on it.[102]

H.D.'s writing satisfied both the demands of women to 'desentimentalize' poetry, and also the demands of those of her male contemporaries in search of a new hardened and 'objective' form. Pound wrote to Monroe in 1912 of H.D.'s work: 'This is the sort of American stuff that I can show here and in Paris without its being ridiculed. Objective—no slither; direct—no excessive use of adjectives, no metaphors that won't permit examination. It's straight talk, straight as the Greek!'[103] In fact, Pound may already have misunderstood H.D.'s work, as it is far from clear that H.D. was trying to be 'objective'. Even in this early work she aimed at presenting the truth of the inner experience of both conscious and unconscious thought; the external is present in its impact on the observer, or as a correlative to her internal landscape, not in order to simply capture the 'object' itself.[104] For most of the women involved in this network, psychological truth was, and remained, the crucial factor.[105] Lowell wrote of H.D., for example, ' "H.D." 's life is that of a true artist. It is one of internal mental and emotional experiences, not of external events.'[106]

In H.D.'s 'Mid-day' we see this emphasis very clearly—the external world impacts on a psyche that is 'startled', in 'dread', 'scattered', and fears it will 'perish'; the external world is a fusion of the life of the object and the perceiving subject, described in a manner which sheds light on the psychic experience of the speaker:

---

[102] May Sinclair, 'Two Notes', *The Egoist*, 2/6 (June 1, 1915): 88.

[103] Ezra Pound to Harriet Monroe, Oct. 1912, quoted in Monroe, *A Poet's Life*, 264.

[104] In fact, of course, Pound also writes of the image as 'that which presents an intellectual and emotional complex in an instant of time'. Ezra Pound, 'A Few Don'ts By an Imagiste', *Poetry*, 1/6 (Mar. 1913): 200.

[105] Marianne Moore is an interesting case, in that her work strove always to balance the internal and external, and in avoiding the extreme of subjectivism her poetry often appears rooted in the external landscape. Moore never demonstrated the interest in psychoanalysis of many of her contemporaries, but was nevertheless as committed to internal as to external reality throughout her writing career.

[106] Lowell, *Tendencies*, 252.

> The light beats upon me.
> I am startled—
> a split leaf rustles on the paved floor—
> I am anguished—defeated.
>
> A slight wind shakes the seed-pods—
> my thoughts are spent as the black seeds.
>
> My thoughts tear me,
> I dread their fever.
> I am scattered in its whirl.
> I am scattered like the hot shrivelled seeds.[107]

The intensity here is of the internal world and its emotions, yet avoids the 'sentimental'. The internal world is valued for its own sake, despite its capacity for anguish and defeat—there is no privileging either of comfortable 'feminine' emotions and internal experiences over the unpleasant, or of the rational over the irrational, but an inclusion of disruption, of fragmentation, and incoherence. For H.D. the inner world was of interest precisely for its variety and unpredictability; she wrote to John Cournos in 1916: 'I would be lonely but for the intensity of my so called "inner life." I feel more and more how curiously practical that remark is: the kingdom lies within you'.[108]

H.D.'s focus at this time then, as for most of her experimental women contemporaries, was very much on the inner life. These writers almost universally rejected the externally oriented interest in the machine and the modern city world of the Futurist and Vorticist movements, which were often perceived as allied to 'masculine' aggression and to the forces that had led to war. During H.D.'s acting editorship of the *Egoist* John Cournos spoke out against the Poundian Vorticist project, objecting precisely to its misogynous and aggressive ethos: 'Nothing is easier to prove than that Futurism is dead—as an art. And not alone Futurism, but also Vorticism and all those "brother" arts, whose masculomaniac spokesmen spoke glibly in their green-red-and-yellow-becushioned boudoirs of the "glory of war" and "contempt for women," '.[109]

An idea of the 'glory of war'—or of war at all—was strikingly absent from much writing by women within this network during

---

[107] H.D., 'Mid-Day', *The Egoist*, 2/5 (May 1, 1915): 74.
[108] H.D. to John Cournos, [Aug. 9, 1916], Beinecke.
[109] John Cournos, 'The Death of Futurism', *The Egoist*, 4/1 (Jan. 1917): 6.

this period.[110] Where war did enter into their work it was generally perceived as a male aberration, and most of the women writers within this network who did express a view were pacifists. While the male avant-garde felt the need to position itself in relation to the war, the majority of women within this network felt no such pressure, and though it is possible to interpret much of their writing in terms of the war, analysing representations of violence or of 'outsidership', to do so is to ignore other projects that clearly took precedence. H.D. was, of course, in later work to look *back* at the war and reflect on its significant impact, as did many others.

That the war was largely ignored *at the time* within projects by these women writers is perhaps difficult to comprehend as anything other than a lamentable failure to engage with reality. Elaine Showalter sees the absence of the war in this work as a retreat, demonstrating that these women 'sought refuge from the harsh realities and vicious practices of the male world'.[111] To some extent there does seem to be an element of retreat or refusal to engage here, one which it is hard to defend and must, perhaps, be seen as a shortcoming of the work of this period. However, once it is understood that an analysis of personal motivations and psychology must inevitably precede an analysis of the external world, then their focus of this period appears to be less escapist; what takes place in their work must be seen as a facing up to fundamental issues of self and subjectivity prior to a branching out into explorations of wider issues in later years. It is possible to understand their work not purely in the negative

---

[110] Many women were of course writing of the war, but these included very few of the women who were becoming involved in this particular network. Many writers who were part of this public sphere tended to write of the war in the years immediately after it, most notably Rebecca West in *The Return of the Soldier* (Nisbet, 1918; London: Virago, 1980). An exception, of course, was May Sinclair, whose work both of this period and later is very committed to exploring the ideals of the war. Other women writers, marginal to this network, who took an active interest in the war included Gertrude Stein, Radclyffe Hall, and Vera Brittain. For studies of women's 'war writing' of this period and later, see: Tate and Raitt, eds., *Women's Fiction and the Great War*; Clare M. Tylee, *The Great War and Women's Consciousness: Images of Militarism and Womanhood in Women's Writings, 1914–64* (Basingstoke: The Macmillan Press, 1990); Dorothy Goldman, *Women Writers and the Great War* (New York: Twayne Publishers, 1995).

[111] Elaine Showalter, *A Literature of Their Own: British Women Novelists From Brontë to Lessing* (Princeton: Princeton University Press, 1977; London: Virago, 1978; rev. ed., 1982), 33.

framework of what is not included, but as a courageous facing up to a troubled inner reality. Instead of retreating into established modes of thoughts and received ideology, such as the religious framework, or the voice of the 'lady poet' whose interests are necessarily private, the work of this period looks outside of existing understandings to new ideas in psychoanalysis, ideas which threaten to upset conventional understandings of 'self' and to new developments of the literary text. The imperative within their work was to seek out a new and sophisticated understanding of woman's subjectivity as a modern subject engaged in a modern world, and to find new ways of expressing this.

For H.D., such an understanding of women's subjectivity required a situating of the female subject against a background of a male literary tradition and male-dominated history, and a seeking out of new ways of understanding and conveying the specificity of women's experiences, as opposed to those of the 'universal' subject. In 'The Tribute', for example, she explores a male-dominated tradition:

> we met
> but one god,
> one tall god with a spear-shaft,
> one bright god with a lance.[112]

The speaker finds evidence only of a phallic god, an image that evidences H.D.'s early interest in Freud; H.D. was becoming aware of Freudian ideas of the woman's feelings around 'castration' and seeking to replace these with her own understandings of gender relations and the development of self. Building on her Freudian understandings, she sought to reject the 'one god' with the phallic authority, and to find new gods, a project she shared with writers such as Dorothy Richardson and Marianne Moore. The internal landscape H.D. presents is one where sexually charged relationships, memories of the primal scene, and woman as 'castrated' can be thought about and brought into, or rejected from, the personal vision.

Such a project finds an early manifestation in her poem 'Pear Tree', where there is an attempt to explore connections between

---

[112] H.D., 'The Tribute', *The Egoist*, 3/11 (Nov. 1916): 165.

[female] fertility and conscious creativity; the speaker is in awe of a process of natural creativity that reaches beyond her own conscious 'stretching' and produces the 'ripe fruits' of the pro-creative process:

> O white pear,
> your flower-tufts
> thick on the branch
> bring summer and ripe fruits
> in their purple hearts.[113]

The fertility or creativity expressed here is one which emerges without straining, allowing the internal fertility, the purple hearts, to express itself in its natural form of blossom. H.D.'s writing of this period is teeming with sexualized images of 'petals' opening and closing revealing the purple/dark heart within yet, in the extract above, also 'white' or pure, an un-corrupted creative process.[114] Her 'Hermes of the Ways' is her most fully developed use of a highly sexualized natural world, exploring the position of the female subject within this. Female creativity is seen as stunted in the poem, the fruit that is 'too small', but the intense sexualized energy of the poem promises that this creativity is not killed, only twisted, and that this twist-ing may in itself be worthwhile.

Despite such clearly sexualized landscapes, it is notable of H.D.'s work of this period that the woman's body itself is absent. Though there are multiple images of slashing, beating, and tearing, these are invariably projected onto a natural land-scape of trees and water, not the human body. Partly this can be explained by a certain shyness or prohibition in this area by H.D. and her contemporaries, but it is also a reflection of the intensely cerebral focus of this public sphere in these years. Woman's body was presented in much of the work of this time as of far less interest than her mind, and sexuality was the focus only as regarded a woman's sexual feelings, not her corporeal experience. Whereas later these women would explore their physical sexuality in their writing, in this period, and within this network of women writers, there seems to have been a view that

[113] H.D., 'Pear Tree', *Collected Poems*, 39; first published in *Others—A Magazine of New Verse*, 3 (Sept. 1916): 57.

[114] See, for example, H.D., 'Evening', *Collected Poems*, 18–19; first published in *Others—A Magazine of New Verse*, 3 (Sept. 1916): 57.

a serious challenge to perceptions of woman as sexual object demanded a renouncing of expressions of her physical sexuality (though not her sexual feelings or the construction of her subjectivity through sexual experiences). Lowell's work, like H.D.'s, focused in these years on the specificity of psychic experience, conveyed in sparse images of external events impacting on an intensely aware subject. Lowell set out to make her work the very antithesis of the 'wooliness' she had complained of in Mary Aldis's work; her 'Middle Age', for example, uses only nineteen words to explore the effect of ageing on the emotional life:

> Like black ice
> Scrolled over with unintelligible patterns by an ignorant
>   skater,
> Is the dulled surface of my heart.[115]

Like H.D., Lowell sought to take the inner recesses of the psyche and give them a form that would best objectify them. This was perhaps most successfully achieved in her work 'Breakfast Table', a section of the longer 'Spring Day':

Wheels of white glitter in the silver coffee-pot, hot and spinning like Catherine Wheels, they whirl, and twirl—and my eyes begin to smart, the little white dazzling wheels prick them like darts. Placid and peaceful the rolls of bread spread themselves in the sun to bask. A stack of butter-pats, pyramidal, shout orange through the white, scream, flutter, call: 'Yellow! Yellow! Yellow!' Coffee steam rises in a stream, clouds the silver tea-service with mist, and twists up into the sunlight, revolved, involuted, suspiring higher and higher, fluting in a thin spiral up the high blue sky.[116]

'Spring Day', one of the first instances of Lowell's distinctive 'polyphonic prose' pieces, moves through the ordinary events of a day from 'Bath',[117] through 'Breakfast Table', 'Walk', 'Midday and Afternoon' to 'Night and Sleep'. The impression is of a world experienced at a high level of intensity, an alert speaker noticing pattern in the world around her. This text is not a

---

[115] Amy Lowell, 'Middle Age', *The Egoist*, 2/7 (July 1, 1915): 113.

[116] Amy Lowell, 'Spring Day', *The Egoist*, 2/5 (May 1, 1915): 76.

[117] Lowell received ridicule and hostility for describing the experience of taking a bath when she read 'Bath' at a Poetry Society meeting. See Jean Starr Untermeyer, *Private Collection* (New York: Alfred A. Knopf, 1965), 75.

rendering of the 'objectivity' of spring, but of an experience of a particular day as lived by a particular person, exploring the psychic reality of the inner landscape. The basking bread rolls take on the contentment of the speaker; the steam curls upwards as the possibilities of the day are open and undefined, limitless. The whiteness reflects the speaker's perception of the newness of the day.

Despite very different approaches, then, (the 'Imagist' poem versus 'polyphonic prose'), Lowell's work shows a similarity of direction to that of H.D., in terms of an intense focus on the external world that is also a deep examination of an internal landscape. Bryher writes: '"Spring Day" . . . is April come to literature again . . . in the union of colour with sound and the feeling of Spring, vivid with an intense, though merely suggested individuality, set before the vision, not flatly, but round and luminous, fluid with light.'[118] H.D. recognized at once the similarities between Lowell's work and her own, and wrote to her to express her admiration at Lowell's writing: 'I think your prose-poems very beautiful! . . . I wish I had one tenth of your outputt [*sic*]. Mine seems to be a most tenuous shoot of this Imagist Tree of Life! However I <u>care</u>—as you know—most awfully—and I can fight for the things that we all care for'.[119] Though H.D. and others showed an interest in Lowell's work both in private letters and within the three little magazines that formed the core of this public sphere (Lowell's work was reviewed in the *Egoist*, *Poetry*, and the *Little Review*), in the wider critical community Lowell's work was scarcely noticed. John Gould Fletcher writes: 'A new poetic form, equal if not superior in value to vers libre, has made its appearance in English. The discoverer is a woman. Had it been a man, we should probably all have heard by now of the richness of the find.'[120] Already we can see the splitting off, to some extent, of a community of women writers from male-dominated avant-garde projects, due to a divergence of interests.

---

[118] W. Bryher, *Amy Lowell: A Critical Appreciation* (London: Eyre and Spottis-woode, 1918), 33.

[119] H.D. to Amy Lowell, [Nov. 23, 1914], typed transcript, Beinecke.

[120] John Gould Fletcher, 'Miss Lowell's Discovery: Polyphonic Prose', *Poetry*, 6/1 (Apr. 1915): 32. It is worth noting here the class-specific references in 'Spring Day' to the 'silver coffee pot' and 'stack' of butter-pats that locate Lowell's familiarity with an upper-class background; it is perhaps not difficult to see why work with such a focus might be passed over at a time of mass loss of life.

Like H.D. too, Lowell sought to examine woman's position in a literary tradition dominated by men, and to seek to find representations of woman's subjectivity as both a private and a public being. Her texts are highly concerned with the inter-section of public and private; to become a public voice was something she valued highly, and in her writing we find multiple images of the woman's frustration with her confinement in a pri-vate space, or her lack of opportunity. In 'Miscast: I' she writes:

> I have whetted my brain until it is like a Damascus
>   blade,
> So keen that it nicks off the floating fringes of
>   passers-by,
> So sharp that the air would turn its edge
> Were it to be twisted in flight.
>
> .   .   .   .
>
> But of what use is all this to me!
> I, who am set to crack stones
> In a country lane![121]

The speaker is 'miscast'—she has the potential for a much wider engagement with the world, a more public and more skilled involvement, but finds her skills confined to uses that are more pedestrian and less subject to the public gaze. Again, in 'Miscast: II' the speaker is confined, this time in a 'dark closet' with 'broken crockery', a highly troubled domestic environment.[122] Lowell was trying here, as H.D. was, to 'place' the woman's internal reality, to release it from its past confinements, and carve for it a new space. With freedom in terms of a break from conventional written forms and stylistic devices, came freedom of thought, and vice versa, as well as escape from the confines of the private. As Bryher notes of Lowell's work: 'Of course it is more than form alone, still it is curious to notice in the following volume, how with the discovery of "unrhymed cadences" came also the discovery of life; it is only with the casting aside of trad-itional form, that the poet leaps from wistfulness and twilight, triumphantly to morning.'[123]

Lowell's work also shows a strong similarity to that of H.D. in her use of sexual landscapes to ground female sexuality; her

[121] Amy Lowell, 'Miscast: I', *The Egoist*, 1/15 (Aug. 1, 1914): 298.
[122] Amy Lowell, 'Miscast: II', *The Egoist*, 1/15 (Aug. 1, 1914): 298.
[123] Bryher, *Amy Lowell*, 13.

1913 'In A Garden', published in both the *New Freewoman* and the *Little Review*, is a poem of a highly sexualized landscape with strong overtones of female–female love. The poem describes a fountain in a garden, with water flowing from the mouths of 'stone men' into 'granite-lipped basins'. Yet in these basins and stone tunnels, life flourishes in the form of damp ferns and irises. The air throbs with the potency of sexuality, there are sounds of a 'deep, cool murmur'; the final image, of the desire to see the lover in the swimming-pool, white flesh reflecting moonlight, keeps the (female) body as the pinnacle of sexual desire, highlighted by the (traditionally female gendered) moon:

> I wanted to see you in the swimming-pool,
> White and shining in the silver-flecked water.
> While the moon rode over the garden,
> High in the arch of night . . .[124]

Yet a full expression of physical sexuality is of course still absent in Lowell's work, as from that of her contemporaries; apart from the single image of the 'white' body in the water, the poem avoids the human body and embodied expressions of human sexuality. As in the work of H.D., sexual feelings are transposed onto the natural world, and thereby given a public space, at the same time that the placement of these onto the natural landscape mutes and distances them. For the women writers involved in this network, this period must be regarded to a large extent as one of 'testing the water' both in terms of stylistic/formal experimentation and in terms of the issues which were allowed to be explored within their writing.

In contrast, in Greenwich Village towards the end of this period, several writers were already experimenting with much more open portrayals of the physical and sexual relationship (as well as much more violent assaults on language and form). In this early period Mina Loy in particular was attacking the sentimental head on, rewriting sexuality as physical and erotic and rewriting maternity as involving pain and blood. Like H.D., she was beginning to be interested in psychoanalytic understandings, and to use these in her work; in 'Parturition', for example, disturbing images rise into the speaker's mind from the sub-

---

[124] Amy Lowell, 'In a Garden', *The New Freewoman*, 1/6 (Sept. 1, 1913): 114; also published in *The Little Review*, 1/5 (July 1914): 38–9.

conscious revealing the new mother's deep feelings about her maternity:

> Rises from the sub-conscious
> Impression of small animal carcass
> Covered with blue-bottles
> —Epicurean—
> And through the insects
> Waves that same undulation of living
> Death
> Life
> I am knowing
> All about
> Unfolding.[125]

Loy attacked multiple taboos, including expectations of 'poetic language' and particularly suitable language for the 'lady poet'. In her 'Song to Joannes' we find various bodily fluids such as 'saliva' and 'spermatozoa', the sexual experience as 'erotic' involving 'suspect places' and the 'seismic orgasm'; nothing is sacred here, even 'Bird-like abortions | With human throats' appear.[126] Relationships are problematized, and a true union of two people seen as impossible, separated always by irreconcilable differences.

However, though her work was making radical challenges to women's writing and to the written form, Loy was not yet part of the network of exchange under consideration here, her work appearing largely in local Greenwich Village publications. There was not yet contact with the other writers discussed in this chapter, who were already building up connections with each other and working together on various projects. In these early years many of the crucial networks between these writers were not yet in place, or were only tentatively being tested. Individual contacts were able to form, however, that would just a few years later slot into the wider public sphere of modernist women writers and allow for a truly international and diverse community to engage in an exchange of ideas.

[125] Mina Loy, 'Parturition', *The Lost Lunar Baedeker*, ed. Roger L. Conover (Manchester: Carcanet Press, 1997), 7; first published in *The Trend* 8/1 (Oct. 1914): 93–4.
[126] Mina Loy, 'Songs to Joannes', *The Lost Lunar Baedeker*, 53–68; first published as 'Love Songs' in *Others—A Magazine of New Verse*, 1/1 (July 1915): 6–8 and in full in *Others—A Magazine of New Verse* 3/6 (Apr. 1917): 3–20.

Within the network of women publishing in the same magazines as H.D. and already part of this emergent public sphere, one other poet was helping to pioneer a break from convention that was to liberate a whole wave of women poets—Marianne Moore. Like Lowell and H.D., she had no patience with the superfluous, and was notoriously to spend much of her writing career honing down existing works to their bare bones. In this period she too was concerned with representing the individuality of experience without sentimental excesses. In 'To a Steam Roller' she defends individuality against impersonality, refusing a levelling down to generalizations. However, unlike Lowell or H.D., in pursuit of this she invented her own 'convention', her own metrical and phonic regularity, thereby giving her own 'free' vision its specificity; in 'To a Steam Roller' she demonstrates the pattern she follows in much of her writing, the *vers libre* first stanza and then the characteristic echoing of this form in the subsequent stanzas:

> The illustration
> Is nothing to you without the application.
> You lack half wit. You crush all the particles down
> Into close conformity, and then walk back and
> forth on them.
>
> Sparkling chips of rock
> Are crushed down to the level of the parent block.
> Were not 'impersonal judgment in æsthetic
> Matters, a metaphysical impossibility', you
>
> Might fairly achieve
> It. As for butterflies, I can hardly conceive
> Of one's attending upon you, but to question
> The congruence of the complement [*sic*] is vain, if it
> exists.[127]

The poem is like the 'butterfly' not the machine, it 'attends' rather than imposes rational ideals. It is both an argument and a visual image, both ordered and yet allowing for the presence of the unpredictable, the movement of the butterfly. The rigid stanza form with a, a, b rhyme and five, twelve, and twelve syllables, and final line or lines with a total of fifteen syllables, contrasts to the individual and idiosyncratic movement of the

---

[127] Marianne Moore, 'To a Steam Roller', *The Egoist*, 2/10 (Oct. 1, 1915): 158.

butterfly which refuses ordering and control. By defining her own form rather than accepting an existing convention, the personal form is achieved, without crushing the particles down to a prescribed or traditional form. Moore's poetry is very insistent on the individual, the personal truth rather than abstraction or the purely rational, even to the point where this might confuse or alienate the reader. H.D. was aware of the puzzlement of readers confronted by Moore's challenge to poetic form, but clearly recognized its value and the alliance of Moore's projects with her own. H.D. saw Moore as a fellow defender of language against erosion into cliché and banality and felt that 'we must strengthen each other in this one absolute bond—our devotion to the beautiful English language.'[128] Like H.D. then, Moore's crusade in these early years was not against any external situation or political issue, but was focused on achieving individuality through a close attention to the possibilities of language.

The fundamental impetus within the poetry by modernist women writers in these early years then, as carried out by H.D., Lowell, and Moore, was to challenge expectations of women's writing as sentimental and 'feminine', to find new and individual directions for their work, and rigorously to examine the internal landscape and attempt a fresh and more honest representation of this psychic reality. Of these challenges, it was the formal challenges, and particularly experiments in *vers libre*, that sparked the most heated resistance and the most interesting discussion. In the November 1914 issue of the *Little Review* Tietjens writes in 'The Spiritual Dangers of Writing Vers Libre' that while risks to any poet include sentimentality, over-intellectualizing, 'determined modernity', a harking back to the past and 'cosmicality', the poet using *vers libre* is especially prone: 'Anything that comes to mind can be said at once, and with a little instinct for rhythm, is said. The result of this mental laziness is that the ideas expressed are often obvious.'[129] In fact, the opposite seems to have been true—by breaking with conventional form, conventionalized thought was also abandoned. However, what Tietjens correctly recognized was that once formal constraints were lifted then other limits also disappeared, putting in danger the whole

[128] H.D., 'Marianne Moore', *The Egoist*, 3/8 (Aug. 1916): 119.
[129] Eunice Tietjens, 'The Spiritual Dangers of Writing Vers Libre', *The Little Review*, 1/8 (Nov. 1914): 25–6.

edifice of critical norms. There was an anxiety that *vers libre* would provide a natural outlet for unimaginative writing, for prose disguised as poetry, an issue which will be further explored in Chapter 3. As a result, *Poetry* felt called on to defend the new wave of *vers libre* writing appearing in its pages; Alice Corbin Henderson writes: 'To say that poets write the new free verse out of sheer indolence, to escape the restrictions imposed on them by metrical rhymed verse, is nonsense. . . . it seems easier to disguise lack of thought and feeling when a conventional metrical pattern and a rhyme scheme are adopted'.[130] Henderson recognized that the newer form was connected with the emergence of a long-awaited new thought, and that both must be fought for against the hostility of traditionalists. She also recognized that by using the new forms writers were entering a space unmasked by the conventions that could stand in place of interesting ideas, and were laying their ideas bare to potential attack.

In prose too, many of these women sought to find new ways to present the specificity of (female) psychic experience, very clearly both challenging ideas of the 'universal' human subject, as well as ways in which women's 'essential' natures had been understood. Dorothy Richardson's *Pilgrimage* charts the very ordinary life of a working woman, without obvious plot or structured development. Miriam, the central character, lives life with the sensuous observations of the Imagist poet, and the novel shows the attention to detail and refusal to allow in emotionalism or sentimentality of the Imagist work:

The sound of the waves was muffled. They were beating and washing outside in the sunlight. The gaslit interior was a pier pavilion. It was like the inside of a bathing-machine, gloomy, cool, sodden with sea-damp, a happy caravan. Outside was the blaze of the open day, pale and blinding. When they went out into it it would be a bright unlimited jewel, getting brighter and brighter, all its colours fresher and deeper until it turned to clear deep live opal and softened down and down to darkness dotted with little pin-like jewellings of light along the esplanade; the dark luminous waves washing against the black beach until dawn. . . . The curtain was drawing away from a painted spring scene . . . the fresh green of trees feathered up into a blue sky.[131]

---

[130] A.C.H., 'Lazy Criticism', *Poetry*, 9/3 (Dec. 1916): 148.
[131] Dorothy Richardson, *Honeycomb* (Duckworth, 1917) in *Pilgrimage* vol. 1 (London: J. M. Dent & Cresset Press, 1938, excluding *March Moonlight*), 480.

Of course the precision and tight focus of the typical Imagist poem is the antithesis of the lengthy *Pilgrimage* project, however the use of the highly specific and detailed visual image in place of descriptions of emotion, do make the two projects analogous; here, as in the work of the poets already discussed, Richardson manages to convey Miriam's subjectivity by describing the world around her. In making this assertion, this study departs from conventional understandings of Imagism derived from Pound's 'Don'ts' and attempts to reinterpret Imagist projects according to ways in which these women were themselves understanding their writing. It is impossible, perhaps, to make the usual clear-cut division between Imagism and Impressionism given that much 'Imagist' writing by these women was attuned to the world of internal reality and emotions; this was an Imagism that sought to convey the precise and immediate sensory experience and its emotional and idiosyncratic resonances in a new way, whether this was the prototypical highly condensed form, or a much longer narrative.

There appears, then, to be a continuum from Imagist verse, through polyphonic prose, and into Richardson's prose. As Sinclair observed in an article appearing simultaneously in the *Egoist* and *Little Review*: 'It is as if no other writers had ever used their senses so purely and with so intense a joy in their use.'[132] There is little 'action', only the personal experience, and the language attempts to be as faithful as possible to the sensory impression. All observations are presented in such a way that they resemble as closely as possible the ways in which thoughts come into consciousness, making this one of the first 'stream of consciousness' novels, a term first used by May Sinclair.[133] Sinclair writes: 'In this series there is no drama, no situation, no set scene. Nothing happens. It is just life going on and on. It is Miriam Henderson's stream of consciousness going on and on. And in neither is there any grossly discernible beginning or middle or end.' The accumulation of impressions, not any authorial commentary, conveys to us Miriam's psyche, her 'contemplated reality'. This, Richardson felt, was closer to the truth

---

[132] Sinclair, 'The Novels of Dorothy Richardson', 58.
[133] Jean Radford, 'Introduction', in *Mary Olivier: A Life* by May Sinclair (London: Macmillan, 1919; London: Virago, 1980), [ix].

of experience, an idea she shared with Sinclair who writes: 'The first-hand, intimate and intense reality of the happening is in Miriam's mind, and by presenting it thus and not otherwise Miss Richardson seizes reality alive.'[134] Richardson wanted, as H.D., Lowell, and Moore did, not only to 'make it new', but to make 'it'—language and thought—tell the authentic 'being' of the experiencing subject, divorced from all distractions, whether conventions of form or subject-matter—that might distort it.

However, unlike H.D., Lowell, or Moore, Richardson explicitly stated her intention to try to capture the specifically female psyche. She felt that the well punctuated and tight sentence could not do this, that it did not reflect the patterns of thought that she knew to be true of her own experience. She believed that her experience was neither that of the 'lady' whose mind is supposedly occupied with moral and religious sentiment, nor did it resemble her understanding of a man's experience (a more objective relation to external reality that could be represented via ordered linguistic structures). Richardson writes years later of her project in *Pilgrimage* as against a male tradition:

Since all these novelists happened to be men, the present writer, proposing at this moment to write a novel and looking round for a contemporary pattern, was faced with the choice between following one of her regiments and attempting to produce a feminine equivalent of the current masculine realism. . . . Aware, as she wrote, of the gradual falling away of the preoccupations that for a while had dictated the briskly moving script, and of the substitution, for these inspiring preoccupations, of a stranger in the form of contemplated reality having for the first time in her experience its own say, and apparently justifying those who acclaim writing as the surest means of discovering the truth about one's own thoughts and beliefs . . .[135]

In both attempting to portray the specifically female experience, and in attempting to portray the truth of the internal experience at all, without the ordering intervention of 'plot' and 'character', Richardson inevitably risked antagonizing many who did not believe in an essentially female psyche or did not see the necessity of attempts to portray it. Alice Smith notes that 'Male critics are wont to note with pained surprise that she cannot use the word

---

[134] Sinclair, 'The Novels of Dorothy Richardson', 58, 59.
[135] Dorothy Richardson, 'Foreword' (1938), *Pilgrimage* vol. 1, 9–10.

<u>man</u> without getting cross'[136] while Sinclair writes that she has heard readers complain of *Pilgrimage* that it has 'no art and no method and no form, and that it is this formlessness that annoys them'.[137] This line of discussion, still in its infancy, was to become heated and energetic with later volumes of *Pilgrimage* and with the publication of Sinclair's *Mary Olivier*, as discussed in Chapter 3.

Sinclair's projects were themselves similar to Richardson's, and she suffered similar criticisms; Richard Aldington, reviewing her novel *Combined Maze*, writes:

Miss Sinclair treats her subject from within; I believe this is an ancient allegation, but it is quite true. There is nothing artistically wrong about it; if your mind is emotional and not scientific it is absurd to try and write scientifically. . . . It seems to me that people like Miss Sinclair always lend their own sensitive emotions to their characters, and make a realism which is quite unreal.[138]

What Aldington seems to miss here is that while treatment 'from within' was nothing new, Sinclair's handling of it was. Like the other writers discussed in this chapter, Sinclair uses concrete images to evoke subjective mood, and allows the psyche of the character to emerge without intrusive authorial comment. Sinclair's characters are as much motivated by their unconscious as conscious desires, and the characters' infant experiences are given the prominence that they have in Freudian theory. In her writing of this period we see the very beginnings of new departures within the novelistic form, replacing externally determined structure and plot with one rooted in internal reality.

Such changes as Sinclair and Richardson were making to prose form, and H.D., Lowell, and Moore to poetic form, were rapidly adopted by other women writers within this network. There was an eagerness to participate, to contribute new texts to the exchange of ideas taking place through literary works and related criticism and theoretical statements. By choosing to develop experiments by these first pioneers a new wave of women writers expressed their fundamental agreement with the

---

[136] Alice A. Smith, 'Some English Women Novelists', *The North American Review*, 213/793 (Dec. 1921): 802.
[137] Sinclair, 'The Novels of Dorothy Richardson', 58.
[138] Richard Aldington, 'Books and Papers', *The Egoist*, 1/3 (Feb. 2, 1914): 49.

importance of these projects, and in turn contributed fresh 'ideas' that were accepted or rejected as new ways of developing the literary text. Often these changes were theorized, but not necessarily; a 'dialogue' of direct influence or refusal of influence was beginning to take place, whereby the writers of the new texts implicitly or explicitly entered into dialogues with their predecessors. Ideas could be taken on board and developed in a new wave of texts, or subtly modified to generate new questions and issues. In this way the text itself could become a contribution to an exchange of ideas—could be an 'utterance' in the public sphere, alongside the more overt critical and theoretical discussion that formed around the texts. This idea will be returned to in greater detail later in this book.

Though the flood of new writers influenced by the early pioneers was largely yet to come, even within the period 1913–17 there are several significant instances of women who had been writing in more conventional ways beginning to show the influence of experiments undertaken by the writers discussed above. Clara Shanafelt, for example, developed her poetry from a highly sentimental and mediocre verse into a much more skilful use of *vers libre* that reveals her opening up to more radical influence. Her 1913 'Caprice' does not stand out from the mass of rather banal work in the early issues of *Poetry*:

> Who will be naming the wind
> That lifts me and leaves me;
> Swelleth my budding flame,
> Foully bereaves me?
> From the land whose forgotten name
> Man shall not find,
> Blowest thou, wind?[139]

By January 1915 Shanafelt renounced her adherence to conventional forms:

> I have written stalely, echoing others,
> But all this is not myself,
> This imitative chatter
> Of a debutante in a drawing-room
> Aware of her mother's ear.[140]

---

[139] Clara Shanafelt, 'Caprice', *Poetry*, 3/1 (Oct. 1913): 16.
[140] Clara Shanafelt, 'Ego', *The Egoist*, 2/1 (Jan. 1915): 11.

Her 1916 poem 'July Morning' is a short, detailed observation, a single image of wind and blossoms, far removed from her work of a few years before:

> The wet pavement is crusted with gold
> Blossoms of the linden-tree;
> A cold wind like water
> Darting here and there
> Unbinds the heavy fragrance of the linden-blossoms;
> The languid scent droops about me—
> A sense of being dragged heavily.[141]

Though this poem cannot be regarded as in any way 'avant-garde', nevertheless it is able to develop the visual image in a far more sensitive and individualized vision than that of a few years earlier, skilfully combining the speaker's psychic experience with her external surroundings. There is a sense that each word has been carefully chosen to be the 'thing itself', and archaisms have been replaced by a more contemporary diction.

Again, we can contrast the early work of Grace Hazard Conkling to that of just a few years later; Conkling's 1913 poem ' "The Little Rose is Dust, My Dear" ' is typical of the highly conventionalized and sentimental writing of the time:

> The little rose is dust, my dear;
>   The elfin wind is gone
> That sang a song of silver words
>   And cooled our hearts with dawn.
>
> And what is left to hope, my dear,
>   Or what is left to say?
> The rose, the little wind and you
>   Have gone so far away.[142]

By 1917 Conkling's poem 'Spring Day' demonstrates the influence of writers such as H.D. and Lowell in using sensory stimulus to evoke deep internal experiences, conveyed in her own semi-regular, yet no longer regimented, verse:

> The pomegranate tree at the foot of the garden
> Stands close to the river.
> Its blossoms stain the air:

---

[141] Clara Shanafelt, 'July Morning', *The Egoist*, 3/2 (Feb. 1, 1916): 30.
[142] Grace Hazard Conkling, 'The Little Rose is Dust, My Dear', *Poetry*, 7/2 (Nov. 1915): 71.

They shake against the white water,
Wavering on the fluent brightness
Like the vermilion found with quicksilver.[143]

Though 'vermilion' and 'quicksilver' are rather conventional poetic terms, the verse itself has rejected the simple emotionalism of her earlier work, replacing the glib sing-song voice with the detailed examination of landscape. Both Conkling and Shanafelt, then, were able to break out of a conventional and sentimental mould, and make attempts at a new poetic form which sought a more honest and thorough representation of the internal and external world.

As the period progressed there were many more instances of moves away from older conventions and a willingness to reinvent the written form. Adelaide Crapsey, for example, invented her own poetic form, the 'Cinquain' with lines of two, four, six, eight, and two syllables, a unique discipline within which her writing developed along broadly Imagist lines.[144] Like the Imagists, her poetry sought the utmost concision and a rejection of the sentimental, and like them she sought a new form for this, one that could develop her own individuality rather than conforming to existing prescriptions. Like H.D., her work used external natural landscape to convey an internal experience, and like H.D. she was not afraid to break with conventions of 'sense'—the 'sound' is 'dry', the leaves have agency, the ghosts create a sound of footfall. Though the experiments of these early years were relatively conservative, and though many conventions of diction and subject matter remained in place, the work of these early years was important in that it began to make inroads on formal and thematic conventions, to be followed in later years with much more radical avant-garde and experimental texts.

What we can trace over this period, then, are the very beginnings of a renaissance in women's prose and poetry. Many of the women writers within this emergent network were focusing on their own experience of internal reality, and were seeking for new ways of representing this subjectivity. For some—Dorothy Richardson in particular—this needed to be a representation of

---

[143] Grace Hazard Conkling, 'Spring Day', *Poetry*, 10/1 (Apr. 1917): 20.

[144] See, for example, Adelaide Crapsey, 'November Night', in *Others—An Anthology of the New Verse*, ed. Kreymborg, 24.

a specifically female internal identity, reinstating this against the background of a literary and philosophical tradition where the 'universal' experience was perceived not to include women's experiences. More generally, it was crucial to portray the self as actually experienced, not as mediated by outworn convention. Marguerite Swawite writes:

> To-day I am woman,
> Less—yet a little more;
> For I am learning to sing
> Not his, not another's, but mine own song.[145]

In particular, the focus had shifted from the 'sentimental' to what were experienced as much deeper explorations of internal reality. Florence Kiper Frank predicts (correctly) in 1916: 'It will take perhaps another five years for the discoveries of psycho-analysis to penetrate the popular consciousness.'[146] However, we can already see a deepening awareness of the interaction of conscious and unconscious and of internal processes that reflect the growing awareness of psychoanalytic understandings that will be seen much more clearly after 1918.

By 1917, then, the ground had been laid for the significant developments in women's writing that were to follow. A new public sphere had begun to open up, involving women in Britain and America, who were actively involved in exchanging and generating new ideas and in bringing women's writing into the twentieth century. Monroe's comment about Amy Lowell might as easily apply to any one of the women writers engaged in this newly formed network: 'She lives in her own time, not in the Victorian or the Elizabethan; and knows what is going on in her art, not only in New York and London, but in Paris.'[147] These writers, newly emerged in a wide open public arena, were beginning to exchange ideas about *vers libre* forms, Imagism, women's subjectivity, and the novelistic form that in turn brought in more writers and more ideas. Isobel Armstrong's assertion that 'despite the gifts of individual poets such as Charlotte Mew, a major renaissance of women's poetry took

---

[145] Marguerite Swawite, 'I Am Woman', *The Little Review*, 1/10 (Jan. 1915): 40.

[146] Florence Kiper Frank, 'Psychoanalysis: Some Random Thoughts', *The Little Review*, 3/4 (June–July 1916): 17.

[147] H.M., '*Sword Blades and Poppy Seed*', review of *Sword Blades and Poppy Seed* by Amy Lowell, *Poetry*, 5/3 (Dec. 1914): 137.

place only after the Second World war'[148] already appears to be misguided.

After 1918 the public sphere was to expand rapidly, and to open itself up to new influences, as the base that had been established in these early years widened and was consolidated. New writers were to be drawn in, including the Greenwich Village writer Mina Loy, whose influence would help to move the public sphere out of its early cerebral nature into a more physically engaged expression. The period 1913–17 marks the setting in place of some of the apparatuses of public debate, and the establishment of some of the key participants. Crucially, during this period, as will be demonstrated in Chapter 3, their work was being read by a new generation of writers who would be subject to its influence and would themselves become active participants in this public sphere in the years 1918–24.

[148] Isobel Armstrong, *Victorian Poetry: Poetry, Poetics and Politics* (London: Routledge, 1993), 483.

3

Expansion and Consolidation—New
Experiments in the Public Sphere
(1918–24)

A psychological state that a scientist might take a volume to
describe is crystallized into a couple of pages.

W. Bryher[1]

Between 1918 and 1924 the public sphere of modernist women
writers underwent expansion, diversification, and consolidation.
Whereas in its early years a few pioneers—largely H.D., Moore,
Lowell, Sinclair, and Richardson—had attacked thematic and
stylistic conventions adhered to by the majority of their contemporaries, they were now joined by many more women
writers, together forming a diverse and broadly experimental
group. Their work spread over a much more extensive publishing base of magazines, representing different emphases in literary experimentation and editorial policy. In turn this more
diverse arena brought them into contact with original and challenging ideas, helping to fuel a more confident exchange of ideas
that in turn generated new literary experimentation. This public
sphere was increasingly aware of itself as a communicative body,
understanding its own boundaries and theorizing its own existence.

An initial important development to note is that the publishing base of the public sphere of modernist women writers underwent significant changes in this period. Two of the initial three
magazines that had formed the core of this public sphere
between 1913 and 1917 were now no longer able to offer the
same accessible yet experimental space. One of these, the *Egoist*,

[1] W. Bryher, 'Spear-Shaft and Cyclamen Flower', review of *Hymen* by H.D.,
Poetry, 19/6 (Mar. 1922): 336.

stopped publication in 1919 in order to concentrate instead on the Egoist Press, publishing texts including H.D.'s *Hymen* and Moore's *Poems*, as well as Wyndham Lewis's *Tarr*. Though it was of importance, then, to a handful of established writers, it no longer offered a more open and inclusive space to a larger number of known and unknown writers, and was therefore of less importance in terms of the operation of this public sphere. The publishing base in America also suffered a loss, as *Poetry* became increasingly conservative, with Monroe either refusing to accept the most experimental work, or, worse, making substantial alterations. Her criticism reveals her dislike of the new wave of experimental writers and her preference for more traditional forms. She described Mina Loy's 'Parturition', for example, as 'descriptive, explanatory, philosophic—in short, prose, which no amount of radical empiricism in the sound and exclamatory arrangement of words and lines, can transform, with prestidigitatorial magic, into the stuff of poetry'.[2] In contrast she gave lavish praise to more traditional (and 'feminine') writers such as Edna St Vincent Millay whose poems 'present an utterly feminine personality of singular charm'[3] and the poets Alice Meynell and Josephine Preston Peabody: 'Both were literary artists of delicate quality and fine achievement who practiced reserve and restraint'.[4] *Poetry* did, however, include both literary and theoretical texts with which Monroe was not in total agreement and printed more experimental work by writers including H.D., Amy Lowell, Bryher (English poet and novelist) and Kay Boyle (experimental American poet), as well as criticism by Marya Zaturenska and Evelyn Scott (American novelist and critic).

Of the three little magazines that had formed the original foundation of this public sphere, only the *Little Review* retained its position at the forefront of experimental women's writing. However, until Pound's resignation as foreign correspondent in May 1919, his editorial choices continued to dominate the magazine, to the detriment of women's writing and at the cost of alienating many readers. 'M.S.F.' wrote in the 'Reader Critic'

---

[2] H.M., 'Guide to the Moon', review of *Lunar Baedecker* [*sic*], by Mina Loy, *Poetry*, 23/2 (Nov. 1923): 103.
[3] H.M., 'Edna St. Vincent Millay', *Poetry*, 24/5 (Aug. 1924): 266.
[4] H.M., 'Of Two Poets', *Poetry*, 21/5 (Feb. 1923): 262.

section: 'As you ask me, I will tell you what I think of *The Little Review*. The first two years I received it, it was a constant source of joy to me; but for the last year and a half it has been filled with pointless eccentricities and gargoyles,—with once in a while a very beautiful thing in it.'[5]

The assistant editor, Jane Heap, having earlier supported Pound's efforts, now described him as 'foreign to taste, foreign to courtesy, foreign to our standards of Art'.[6] She objected to Pound's role as the leader of a 'movement' demanding conformity by his followers: 'Pound to me has appeared always as some Pied Piper, luring his swarm of literary rodents out of their conventional stables to their doom.'[7] *The Little Review* was rejecting, then, the dominance over the tone of the magazine that Pound's single-mindedness was having. Several readers of the *Little Review* saw Pound's involvement as a power game, the antithesis of democracy and free exchange. Lola Ridge, for example, an Australian-born experimental poet in New York, part of the *Others* group, wrote in to the *Little Review*: 'You can't let any one rock the *Little Review*. And E.P. has for some time needed just such a cool and unperturbed hand to press him back into his seat.'[8] This was also H.D.'s view; until Pound's resignation she felt alienated from the kinds of 'power' being exercised and celebrated in the magazine: 'That rag is a puzzle & E.P. as always. E. wrote me for poems but I have put him off. The L.R. leaves us quite faint with its cynicism'.[9] Sinclair was one of the few women writers who supported Pound's efforts: 'He may have been guilty of a few blunders, a few indiscretions and imperfections, but he has rendered services to modern international art that in any society less feral than our own would have earned him the gratitude of his contemporaries.'[10] Sinclair was certainly right in noting the quality of the work Pound brought into the magazine and his tireless efforts on its behalf, but seems oblivious to the detrimental effect he was having on

[5] M.S.F., 'Criticism', *The Little Review* [4]/11 (Mar. 1918): 59.
[6] jh [Jane Heap], 'The Episode Continued', *The Little Review*, 5/6 (Oct. 1918): 35.
[7] jh, 'Pounding Ezra', *The Little Review*, 5/6 (Oct. 1918): 38.
[8] Lola Ridge to jh, *The Little Review*, 5/9 (Jan. 1919): 63.
[9] H.D. to Amy Lowell, [Sept. 1918], typed transcript, Beinecke.
[10] May Sinclair, 'The Reputation of Ezra Pound', *The North American Review*, 211/774 (May 1920): 659.

women's writing. However, from 1919, though Pound maintained connections with the journal, there was a move back into the control of Margaret Anderson and Jane Heap, together producing some of the most dynamic issues in the *Little Review*'s history.[11] H.D. returned to the magazine with the 1923 publication of her 'At Croton', while Richardson (1919), Barnes (1919), and Loy (1920) appeared for the first time.

Other magazines too were now playing an important role in fostering the public sphere of modernist women writers, but were not edited by women or expressing any explicit commitment to women's writing; this public sphere had become sure enough of itself and its projects not to require the nurturing within broadly feminist publications that it had received in its infancy. One of this new platform of magazines was the London-based *Adelphi*, edited by John Middleton Murry, which encouraged heated critical debate in its pages and included H.D., Katherine Mansfield, and Richardson. Murry's aims echo the earlier views of Monroe and Anderson in a refusal of commercialism and belief in 'life': 'THE ADELPHI is nothing if it is not an act. It is not a business proposition, or a literary enterprise, or a nice little book in a pretty yellow cover; it is primarily and essentially an assertion of a faith that may be held in a thousand different ways, of a faith that life is important, and that more life should be man's chief endeavour'.[12]

Another London magazine, *The [Monthly] Chapbook*, edited by Harold Monro, was also important to modernist women writers; it attempted to give space to writers from diverse literary currents, including the British/British-based H.D., Iris Barry, Edith Sitwell, Charlotte Mew, Frances Cornford, and Anna Wickham, and the American writers Edna St. Vincent Millay, Marianne Moore, and Babette Deutsch. Monro aimed at, and succeeded in, bringing together 'a critical survey of contemporary literature, and numerous examples of the creative work of the present period'.[13]

On the other side of the Atlantic the *Dial*, edited by Scofield Thayer (and later by Moore) in New York, was an important site for the more experimental women's writing. The *Dial* had

[11] Jane Heap took over sole editorship from 1922.
[12] John Middleton Murry, 'The Cause of it All', *The Adelphi*, 1/1 (June 1923): 8.
[13] Anon., *The Chapbook*, 1/1 (July 1919): unnumbered, inside front cover.

a subscription list of up to sixteen thousand,[14] and published predominantly American writers including H.D., Marianne Moore, Amy Lowell, and Babette Deutsch. Also in New York, *Rhythmus*, edited by Oscar Williams, was interested in experimental poetry; Frederick Hoffman et al write: 'Its appearance is, in fact, a bit "precious"; editorial sympathies, though never dogmatically announced, seem to be with whatever experimental writing is available.'[15] Women appearing here included H.D. and Sitwell (both in England), Lowell, Teasdale, Wylie, and Millay (all based in America). The *North American Review*, a long-established mainstream publication, offered a base for established writers including H.D., Sinclair, Lowell, and Flexner and newer writers including Bryher and Margaret Widdemer. Other important magazines of the period in terms of this public sphere of women's writing included *Contact* (edited by William Carlos Williams and Robert McAlmon in New York, financially assisted by Bryher) and *The Double Dealer* (New Orleans).

The body of reviews and criticism by these women cut across the magazines, demonstrating an awareness of individual magazines as part of a wider base; it is clear that these writers were reading a wide range of these magazines and were committed to reading each other's work in diverse publications, discussing it, and assimilating it into this public sphere. There was a continued influx of new writers bringing fresh ideas, such as Kay Boyle, first published in *Poetry* in this period, and Laura Riding, first published in *The Fugitive* in 1923, her work also now appearing in *Poetry*. Even in the most male-dominated magazines such as *The Nation* (later *The Nation and the Athenaeum*), *Sphere* (London magazine edited by C. K. Shorter), *Transatlantic Review* (Paris magazine edited by Ford Madox Ford), and *Contact* (edited by William Carlos Williams), we nevertheless find an extension of this female-centred public sphere. H.D., for example, published in all of these magazines, joined by Richardson and Charlotte Mew in the *Sphere*, Barnes and Loy in *The Transatlantic Review*, and Millay in the *Nation*; though

---

[14] Roger L. Conover notes that the *Dial* sold out of the sixteen thousand copies of the *Waste Land* issue (*The Dial*, 73 (Nov. 1922)). 'Editorial Guidelines and Considerations', in *The Lost Lunar Baedeker* [Poems of Mina Loy], ed. Roger L. Conover, 198.

[15] Hoffman et al, *The Little Magazine*, 271.

these magazines were not at the heart of this public sphere, nevertheless they facilitated the continued exchange of ideas across a much wider base. This move to involvement in a more competitive male-dominated arena parallels, of course, the move by women into previously male-dominated careers, and their entry into mainstream politics via their newly won right to vote, granted in 1918 in Britain and 1920 in the USA.

Within this wider base, discussion became more heated, reflecting the increased confidence of individuals; this network was now able to accommodate constructive disagreement oriented towards new thought, and contributors felt empowered to challenge both each other and editorial policy. As in the ideal Habermasian model, contributors felt themselves to be equals in a conversation taking place through the magazines, and resisted any limitations placed on their utterances that might restrict a free flow of ideas. Evelyn Scott wrote to the *Little Review*, for example, to complain about the assistant editor, Jane Heap: 'Has "jh" any particular objection to the introduction of a fresh view-point so that she requires all opinion to be delivered from the same angle of her preconception?' Scott objected to any power differential between editor and contributor: ' "jh" is in a position of vantage as she can exercise the editorial prerogative of the last word. She can refuse to publish my retort, but once admitting me to her pages she can not, I should think, rule out my statements simply because they do not meet with her approval.'[16] Scott's objection demonstrates the supreme value she attached to the 'ideal speech situation'[17] characteristic of the public sphere, and it is indicative of the importance she and others attached to the central qualities of the public sphere— equal and open access, equal opportunities for speech, equal positions of authority, equal value granted to all participants— that she makes this challenge. The *Little Review*'s editors believed in the ideal speech situation, but in practice sometimes found it difficult to maintain. In the September–December 1920 issue, for example, Anderson expressed her annoyance with Else von Freytag-Loringhoven[18] who had refused alterations to her

---

[16] Evelyn Scott, 'The Last Word', *The Little Review*, 6/10 (Mar. 1920): 45, 47.

[17] See, for example, Seyla Benhabib, 'Models of Public Space', in *Habermas and the Public Sphere*, ed. Calhoun, 89.

[18] Else Baroness von Freytag-Loringhoven was a very eccentric writer living in

work: 'The policy of the LITTLE REVIEW has always been: a free stage for the artist. There are moments when I believe this to be an uninteresting policy.'[19] On the one hand this incident points towards a possible usurpation of too much authority by the editors, losing sight of the more democratic forum they had hoped to create. However, what it also points towards is the ego-centricism of some of the writers involved. Though the structures of this public sphere were oriented towards democracy and equality of opportunity, some individual writers were far more self-focused, believing in their own 'genius' above collective interest.

Outside the magazines, the public sphere extended itself into other forums, such as Lola Ridge's discussion meetings which included Boyle, Moore, Babette Deutsch (prominent American critic and theorist, also a poet), and Elinor Wylie (American poet, niece of the poet Helen Hoyt),[20] and the *Little Review*'s informal discussion groups held in its Chicago offices and in Anderson's house. Anderson writes of these meetings, paradigmatic of the operation of the public sphere: 'The younger poets came for talk. We had long discussions on the making of poetry—stamping it indelibly with the element of one's self, measuring the area of one's personal existence, searching the specific gravity of emotions'.[21] Discussion ranged over a wide spectrum of aesthetic and philosophic issues that in turn could feed back into writing within the *Little Review* and elsewhere.

The links forged in the magazines were also developed through personal contact and correspondence; H.D.'s correspondents of this period included Lowell, Ridge, Bryher,[22] Sinclair, Richardson, and the young English novelist [Margaret]

Greenwich Village at this time and a German national. She was highly involved in the Dada movement, both as a model and as an artist and poet, writing in her native German and in English. Her name appeared inconsistently as either 'Else' (the German spelling) or 'Elsa' (the American version). In general, she used 'Else' while critical discussion preferred 'Elsa'. Freytag-Loringhoven was notable for her eccentric way of dressing, for consistently getting into trouble with the police and for her modelling work.

[19] M.C.A., announcement in *The Little Review*, 7/3 (Sept.–Dec. 1920): 59.
[20] Sandra Whipple Spanier, *Kay Boyle: Artist and Activist* (Carbondale: Southern Illinois University Press, 1986), 11.
[21] Anderson, *My Thirty Years' War*, 153.
[22] Bryher was H.D.'s partner at this time, and close friend for life; she forms the model for Althea in *Paint It Today* and Beryl in *Asphodel*.

Storm Jameson, offering and receiving criticism as well as support for each other's work. Cyrena Pondrom writes of the H.D./Moore correspondence:

These letters include detailed praise for each other's work and reflect continual efforts to foster mutual self-confidence and to secure publication for each other's books. They demonstrate one way in which a supportive community of female writers can function. The letters contain confirming evidence of mutual influence and the exchange of imagery and theme. . . . And most important they reveal congruencies in aesthetic theory and constructs of the relationship of the self to the other that set the two apart from most male modernists.[23]

This type of relationship in fact existed between many of these writers, it was not an isolated phenomenon of the H.D./Moore correspondence. This now established network used close links to promote each other's work and to assist in publication; so, for example, Moore and Lowell used their influence with editors to help H.D. get her work published, while in 1921 H.D. and Bryher undertook to get Moore's *Poems* published. There are also numerous instances of dedication of work to each other and inter-textual reference. So we find Eunice Tietjens's poems titled 'To Sara Teasdale' and 'To Amy Lowell who visits me in a hospital',[24] Emmy Veronica Sanders's poem 'Adelaide Crapsey',[25] Richardson's dedication of *The Trap* to Bryher[26] and Sara Teasdale's dedication of *Flame and Shadow* 'to E[unice Tietjens]'.[27] H.D.'s *Hymen* carries a dedication to Bryher and to Perdita, her daughter, a more personal acknowledgement of their supportive and life-affirming presence in her life.[28] Of course such close relationships in terms of influence and mutual support might seem indicative of the formation of a coterie, as has been noted, for example, of the Auden generation, rather

[23] Cyrena N. Pondrom, 'Marianne Moore and H.D.: Female Community and Poetic Achievement', in *Marianne Moore: Woman and Poet*, ed. Patricia C. Willis (Orono, Maine: The National Poetry Foundation, 1990), 372.

[24] Eunice Tietjens, *Body and Raiment* (New York: Alfred A. Knopf, 1919), 58, 59.

[25] Emmy Veronica Sanders, 'Adelaide Crapsey', *Poetry*, 17/5 (Feb. 1921): 249.

[26] Dorothy Richardson, *The Trap* (Duckworth, 1925) in *Pilgrimage* vol. 3 (London: J. M. Dent & Cresset Press, 1938 (excluding *March Moonlight*); London: Virago, 1979), 398.

[27] Sara Teasdale, *Flame and Shadow* (London: Jonathan Cape, 1924), [5].

[28] H.D., *Hymen* (London: The Egoist Press, 1921), [2].

than of the more open public sphere.[29] Certainly there were by now smaller groupings of writers whose relationship to each other was particularly close and who tended to support each other's interests, as in the H.D.–Moore–Bryher friendship. However, such close ties did not prevent these writers being fully involved in a wider public sphere, participating in more open and inclusive discussions and welcoming the contributions of new writers. There was not the closure to outside influence of a coterie, nor the narrowing of vision.

Over this period we find far more explicit discussion than in earlier years of the role of the public sphere. In H.D.'s work, for example, the value to be gained from an exchange of ideas is a dominant theme: 'Two or three people gathered together in the name of truth, beauty, over-mind consciousness could bring the whole force of this [electric-thought] power back into the world',[30] clearly an appropriation of the Biblical: 'For where two or three are gathered together in my name, there I am in the midst of them';[31] instead of God the Father/Son there is a creative community seeking its own truth. H.D. felt hopeful that her work would influence others, would spark off their creativity: 'My sign-posts are not yours, but if I blaze my own trail, it may help to give you confidence and urge you to get out of the murky, dead, old, thousand-times explored old world, the dead world of overworked emotions and thoughts.'[32]

Nevertheless, there continued to be, as in the years 1913–17, a gap between idealizations of a supportive discursive community and the actuality, and also between principles of democratic exchange and the sense of inherent superiority expressed by several writers. The feeling of membership in an 'aristocracy of the spirit'[33] that had emerged in the earlier period was now entrenched, and this view permeated H.D.'s work; she writes in her theoretical work *Notes on Thought and Vision* (*Notes*) (written in 1919): 'Today there are many wand-bearers but

---

[29] See Samuel Hynes, *The Auden Generation: Literature and Politics in England in the 1930s* (London: The Bodley Head, 1976), 390; Valentine Cunningham, *British Writers of the Thirties* (Oxford: Oxford University Press, 1989), 146–50.

[30] H.D., *Notes on Thought and Vision and The Wise Sappho* (San Francisco: City Lights Books, 1982), 27.

[31] Matthew 18: 21.

[32] H.D., *Notes*, 24.

[33] H.D., *Asphodel* (Durham: Duke University Press, 1992), 28.

few inspired.'[34] In her literary work of this period, as in that of many of her contemporaries, the masses are seen as uncritical, brutal, even actively hostile; in *Asphodel* (written 1921–22), for example: 'They would always trap them [the initiates], bash their heads like broken flowers from their stalks, break them for seeing things, having "visions" '.[35] Again and again in the work of this period we find a celebration of the 'initiate' and denigration of the unthinking or uninitiated 'masses'.[36] There was by this period a much more stark separation between a women's literary elite and the 'mass' of women writers, theorists, and critics who were perceived as having failed to break out from restrictions and conventions.

A gulf had opened up, then, between traditionalists and 'modernists'. For the latter, in poetry the innovative *vers libre* had now become the norm, with older forms of prosodic convention perceived as the preserve only of the rank and file. In Bryher's novel *Two Selves* the schoolgirl Nancy, very closely modelled on a Bryher of a few years earlier, thinks: 'Vers Libre. She must throw her old note books away. It was a hard discipline. Without rhyme one had to create. Create an experience.'[37] Nancy recognizes that the new forms demanded something behind the ornament, that once this is stripped away the depth (or shallowness) of thought becomes clear. Within this public sphere we see a definite awareness of the radical changes that had taken place in poetry, and of its debt to the earlier pioneers, especially to H.D., Moore, and Lowell. Jessica Nelson North writes: 'Among other teachings, the feeling for the sanctity of words was instilled into the younger poets by the first exponents of vers libre, and a complete verbal democracy has been the result.'[38]

Bryher's work of this period clearly demonstrates her indebtedness to H.D., Lowell, and Moore, all of whom she acknowledged as influences. In 1940 she writes of Moore's poetry:

---

[34] H.D., *Notes*, 31.

[35] H.D., *Asphodel*, 9.

[36] See Emmy Veronica Sanders, 'Hill Speech', *Poetry*, 20/6 (Sept. 1922): 305; Mina Loy, 'The Anglo-Mongrels and the Rose', [Part Two], *Contact Collection of Contemporary Writers* [eds. William Carlos Williams and Robert McAlmon] (Dijon: Maurice Darantière, 1925), 148.

[37] Bryher, *Two Selves* (Paris: Contact Publishing Co., [1923]), 10.

[38] Jessica Nelson North, 'The Late Rebellion', *Poetry*, 22/3 (June 1923): 154.

I had to be shown Marianne Moore but once I discovered
         'wade
                  through black jade
                  of the crow-blue mussel shells'
I was her prisoner for life.[39]

Bryher demonstrated a similar attention to the specific and idiosyncratic in her own work, honing down her writing to capture
the essence of the experience. She was just one of many in a new
generation whose values and poetic style had been greatly
influenced by the experimentation that had taken place between
1913 and 1918, and who was now seeking to develop their projects in her own writing. Values of tightness and a clearing away
of superfluity were clearly present in her 1918 review of Lowell's
work: 'There is not a single useless word. The whole atmosphere
is etched by a single line at the beginning and merges into an
emotion, stripped to its beating elements, into a dream rhythmic
with colour.'[40] Bryher had been studying Lowell's work, and
when she sent H.D. a fan letter she included this work on
Lowell; by so doing she sought to demonstrate to H.D. that she
was a serious member of the literary community, and asked for
friendship as a literary colleague who was part of a new wave of
experimentation and interest in *vers libre*.[41] It was H.D.'s
influence that had already had most impact on Bryher, who
writes: 'There will always be one book among all others that
makes us aware of ourselves; for me, it is Sea Garden by H.D.',[42]
and several of Bryher's works include fragments of H.D. in
homage.[43] The resemblance of some of Bryher's work to H.D.'s
at this time is striking, and itself forms a tribute to H.D.;
Bryher's 'From Helix' (1922) is a poem portraying in crisp detail
the wreathing of violets around the head of a loved one by the
goddess Athene, with 'owl-white leaves'; the speaker feels
tenderness towards this woman, whose 'soft breasts' are 'roses
Aphrodite loosens from her heart'. The female body is here
something to be lovingly and slowly caressed and admired, the

[39] Bryher, 'My Introduction to America', *Life and Letters To-Day*, 26/37 (Sept.
1940): 237.   [40] Bryher, *Amy Lowell*, 16.
[41] See Hanscombe and Smyers, *Writing for their Lives*, 33.
[42] Bryher, *The Heart to Artemis: A Writer's Memoirs* (London: Collins, 1963),
187.
[43] See, for example, W. Bryher, *Development* (London: Constable, 1920), 87–8.

poem includes only the simplest details of actions to convey the slow progress of the eyes over the body of a woman likened to a goddess.[44] Again, there is no extraneous detail, no 'feelings' as such, these are inferred directly from the loving care of the description of the body.

Other poets participating in a new generation of broadly Imagist verse included Evelyn Scott, Laura Sherry, and Marion Strobel.[45] While in general the male 'Imagists' had either never positively committed to Imagism per se (D. H. Lawrence, James Joyce) or had moved on to other projects (Pound, Wyndham Lewis) without being succeeded by a second generation, for these women Imagism opened up more long-term possibilities. In part this was because they felt less need to identify with the 'latest project'; throughout the period covered by this book there are very few instances of these women writers aligning themselves with any 'movement'. Additionally, they tended to remain committed to Imagism since, as was discussed in Chapter 2, its rejection of the extraneous and sentimental connected to specific needs of women writers to break from perceptions about their poetic foremothers. Henderson writes in 1918, a year after Imagism is generally agreed to have ended:[46] 'Nowadays everyone is writing imagist vers libre, particularly those who at the beginning made the most outcry against it.'[47] 'Imagism' had not, then, ended with Pound's departure, but continued to form a basis for new writing.[48]

Of course the discarding of existing poetic conventions by

[44] Bryher, 'From Helix', *Arrow Music* [London: J. & E. Bumpus, 1922], 11.

[45] See, for example, Evelyn Scott, 'Rainy Season', *Poetry*, 15/2 (Nov. 1919): 71; Laura Sherry, 'Light Magic', *Poetry*, 20/6 (Sept. 1922): 297–8; Marion Strobel, 'Encounter', *Poetry*, 21/6 (Mar. 1923): 292.

[46] See, for example, Natan Zach, 'Imagism and Vorticism', in *Modernism: A Guide to European Literature 1890–1930* eds. Malcolm Bradbury and James McFarlane (London: Penguin, 1961, repr. 1991), 240, who dates Imagism 1909–17, as does Gary Day, 'The Poets: Georgians, Imagists and Others', in *Literature and Culture in Modern Britain. Vol. 1: 1900–1929*, ed. Clive Bloom (London: Longman, 1993), 45; see also Chris Baldick, *The Concise Oxford Dictionary of Literary Terms* (Oxford: Oxford University Press, 1990), 107, who dates Imagism 1912–17.

[47] A.C.H., 'Imagism: Secular and Esoteric', review of *Some Imagist Poets*, 1917, *Poetry*, 11/6 (Mar. 1918): 339.

[48] C. K. Stead's account of the end of Imagism is typical of accounts that connect the movement to Pound's career: 'Imagism exhausted itself in a shorter time, and diminished to insignificance when Pound and Eliot decided that vers libre had gone far enough.' C. K. Stead, *The New Poetic* (London: Hutchinson University Library, 1964), 111.

these women also opened the way for some poor derivative writing; as Lowell points out: 'the man who would never have had the force, nor the industry, nor the originality to write interesting poetry in quatrains, is just as uninteresting, as unoriginal, as lazy, in *vers libre*'.[49] There were two risks in the new *vers libre*; firstly, as Jessica Nelson North notes, that the honed-down poem could become an aesthetic shorthand, indecipherable to many readers.[50] At the other extreme, the risk was that weaker poets might feel that any loose description arranged appropriately on the page could constitute 'poetry'. Henderson parodies this:

And then there is the very simple statement, reiterated, upon which much free verse builds itself in what we may call the Primer Style of Vers Libre:

> I am sitting in my room.
> I am looking out of the window,
> At the leaves.
> The brown leaves,
> They fall,
> They flutter,
> They drop.
>
> Do you see the leaves fall?
>
> It is night.
> The wind is blowing.
> Oh, how it blows!
>
> Do you hear it blow?[51]

Bryher too writes of the 'unlearned horde who translated "vers libre" to mean an idle jargon of barren words and unrhythmic thought'.[52] The new wave of *vers libre* then, both opened a new way forward and was felt to carry with it a risk of contamination by weaker derivative writing. These two possibilities created a great deal of critical discussion and continued attempts, invariably unsuccessful, to more fully define the boundaries of *vers libre* and Imagism.[53]

[49] Amy Lowell, 'Jean Untermeyer's Book', *Poetry*, 14/1 (Apr. 1919): 48.
[50] North, 'The Late Rebellion', 155.
[51] A.C.H., 'Mannerisms of Free Verse', *Poetry*, 14/2 (May 1919): 97.
[52] Bryher, *Amy Lowell*, 7.
[53] See, for example, Babette Deutsch, 'Freedom and the Grace of God', *The Dial*, 67 (Nov. 15, 1919): 441–2.

As the new wave of second generation Imagists emerged, so did the work of the early poetic experimentalists move forwards, developing the single-image work to more complex texts where multiple images or extended reflections on the single image allowed for a greater emotional and intellectual complexity. Sinclair writes of H.D.'s latest poems: 'Comparing them with her earlier work, even admitting that they have lost something of its sharp simplicity, one sees that she has gained immeasurably in depth and range.'[54] Again, Bryher writes: '. . . "Hymen" is a long flight beyond the poet's earlier "Sea Garden" both in depth of thought and originality of vision'.[55] H.D.'s 'Hymen' typified her newer work, extending over thirteen pages, with alternation between prose sections and poetry. The chorus is split into strophe and antistrophe; the reader must be aware of the different speakers and their voices, must draw context from the prose descriptions of movement. The poem invokes Hera, Hymen, Hermes, Tanagra, and Artemis, and the reader is challenged to understand 'the chryselephantine Hermes' and 'the Chelidonia'. The change in H.D.'s work from the clear single image to more complex and compound images, baffled some of her critics. An anonymous reviewer of *Hymen* writes of H.D.'s newer poems: 'the difficulty of extracting any meaning from many of them is not relieved by any special beauty of utterance'.[56] This critic, as others, found the new work obscure, a charge that annoyed May Sinclair who wrote back: 'Whereas unclarified thought means shallow thinking, emotion at a certain depth *is* obscure.'[57]

H.D.'s poetry of this period is positioned halfway between traditional forms and the more avant-garde. *Paint It Today* opens with a statement that captures H.D.'s own position: 'Do not paint it of yesterday's rapt and rigid formula not of yesterday's day-after-tomorrow's criss-cross—jagged, geometric, prismatic. Do not paint yesterday's day-after-tomorrow destructiveness nor yesterday's fair convention. But how and as you will—*paint it today*.'[58] Do not, in other words, abandon

[54] May Sinclair, 'The Poems of H.D.', *The Dial*, 72/2 (Feb. 1922): 204.
[55] Winifred Bryher, 'Thought and Vision', review of *Hymen* by H.D., *The Bookman* [New York], 56/2 (Oct. 1922): 226.
[56] Anon., review of *Hymen* by H.D., *The Times Literary Supplement*, 1032 (Oct. 27, 1921): 702.
[57] Sinclair, 'The Poems of H.D.', 203.
[58] H.D., *Paint It Today* (New York: New York University Press, 1992), 3.

referential meaning altogether in a Steinian cubist form, nor retreat back to older forms, but find a path in between. H.D. demonstrated a wariness that she shared with many other women writers—including Bryher, Lowell, Katherine Mansfield, West, and others—about fully embracing avant-garde attacks on the referential. It was important to her that her texts shared in a communicative framework, potentially able to offer new insight to others, and therefore had a certain level of accessibility; yet it is impossible to see her work as anything other than 'experimental' in testing the limits of referential meaning and prose/poetry structures; in addition, much of her work would only have been intelligible to the well educated reader familiar with Classical history and its use in a long tradition of literary texts.

The work of Marianne Moore in this period went further than that of H.D. in risking lack of comprehension by a great many readers; by now her lifelong obsession with honing her poetry down to its bare elements, eliminating all 'superfluous' elements that might aid intelligibility, was well under way. Moore's work verged on the avant-garde; in her earlier work she had already demonstrated a willingness to question structures and syntax in radical new ways, and now, in part no doubt due to the influence of those around her in Greenwich Village, including Loy and Else von Freytag-Loringhoven, her work became increasingly experimental. In 'Poetry' Moore writes:

> One must make a distinction
> however: when dragged into prominence by half poets, the
>   result is not
>   poetry,
> nor till the autocrats among us can be
> 'literalists of
> the imagination'—above
>   insolence and triviality and can present
> for inspection, 'imaginary gardens with real toads in them', shall
>   we have
>   it.[59]

This poem both formally enacts and thematically discusses a more vivid poetic form, the Imagist principle of the 'thing itself'

---

[59] Marianne Moore, 'Poetry', *Poems* (London: The Egoist Press, 1921), 22.

taken to an extreme, attempting to turn words into the 'real', not representations of the real. The task is of course impossible, but the striving for the 'real' is characteristic of women's writing of the period, and forms the basis of the avant-garde challenge to poetic 'ornament' that distances the reader from the 'real toads'.

Toads are, of course, generally considered ugly, they make no concessions to 'conventions' of 'nice' appearance or behaviour, just as this poem makes no concession to clearing up difficulty and ambiguity, leaping out unexpectedly at the unwary reader. Moore, though she never embraced the interest in the seamy and squalid of many Greenwich Village writers, was nevertheless, like H.D., absolutely rejecting the 'pretty' or 'sentimental' in her writing, allowing in ideas and images that disrupted expectations of women's writing. Monroe recognized this motivation in Moore's work, but objected to it: 'Miss Moore is in terror of her Pegasus; she knows of what sentimental excesses that unruly steed is capable, and so her ironic mind harnesses down his wings and her iron hand holds a stiff rein.'[60]

Inevitably Moore, like H.D., was criticized for obscurity; Marion Strobel objects: 'we would rather not follow the contortions of Miss Moore's well-developed mind—she makes us so conscious of her knowledge! And because we are conscious that she has brains, that she is exceedingly well-informed, we are the more irritated that she has not learned to write with simplicity.'[61] In the same symposium Andelson complains that 'where Emily Dickinson's not infrequent obscurities arise out of an authentic mysticism, Moore's are more likely the result of a relentless discipline in the subtler "ologies" and "osophies"'.[62] Moore's work is far more openly 'difficult' than that of H.D., and Andelson is right in noting Moore's increased difficulty, indicative of a growing chasm between ordinary reader and experimental text. Yet Moore valued clarity, and viewed her writing as seeking the most direct communication possible, without compromising the integrity of the 'experience'/poetic form. Her writing bars access to those unable to follow the convolutions of her mind, but once

---

[60] H.M., 'A Symposium on Marianne Moore', review of *Poems* by Marianne Moore, *Poetry*, 19/4 (Jan. 1922): 213.
[61] Marion Strobel, quoted in ibid. 210.
[62] Pearl Andelson quoted in ibid.

inside her work the reader finds that Moore makes every effort to include the reader in the experience of a place or object.

The 'difficulty' of Moore's language, as that of H.D. at times, raises questions about its compatibility with an ideal of rational exchange in the public sphere, where the imperative is to use the most direct communication possible, to conform with H. P. Grice's conversational maxims as discussed in Chapter 1, whereby the speaker attempts the maximum possible clarity and truthfulness of utterance.[63] Grice writes: 'We might then formulate a rough general principle which participants will be expected (ceteris paribus) to observe, namely: Make your conversational contribution such as is required, at the stage at which it occurs, by the accepted purpose or direction of the talk exchange in which you are engaged.'[64] Such a principle seems fundamental to the public sphere, where the desire of participants to make themselves understood is surely a basic requirement, and would seem to be flouted by the more avant-garde and experimental writers of this period. In fact, however, Moore's work, as that of her experimental contemporaries, facilitated the operation of this public sphere in three ways. Firstly, it formed a basis for discussion around the possibilities of language and the literary text, generating critical discussion paradigmatic of the rational discourse of the public sphere. The deviance from accepted norms of clarity of utterance in itself formed a basis for new (rational) ideas about language, such that even the most extreme avant-garde work was able to engender a critical dialogue that had a profound impact on thought. Secondly, it must be remembered in the case of Moore in particular that her difficulty stemmed not from a desire to be obscure, but from a desire to be exact. She resented deliberate obscurity, but also any slackness in language. Her work, as Margaret Holley points out, was 'modernist in style rather than in spirit',[65] and must be seen as always attempting rather than refusing communication. To this extent it does seek the maximum clarity possible for that particular idea or

---

[63] Grice, *Studies in the Way of Words*, 26–30; Grice argues that in playing the conversational game participants agree to try to uphold principles of the maximum 'quality' (maximum truth), 'quantity' (no unnecessary detail, nor too little), 'relation' (relevance) and 'manner' (no more obscurity than is necessary) (pp. 26–7). To uphold these is to uphold the 'Co-operative Principle' (p. 30).

[64] Ibid. 26.

[65] Holley, *The Poetry of Marianne Moore*, 19–20.

experience, and the text would be doing violence to the principle of 'truthfulness' if it attempted to simplify this for the sake of wider comprehension. Finally, it needs to be understood that even the most avant-garde work, far from the 'rational' as such, was able to participate in a network of influence, as between H.D.'s and Moore's work, or between Moore and Bryher. An exchange of ideas between interested individuals could be maintained in this way, through the experimental text, without this process necessarily manifesting itself as critical ('rational') discussion. The 'rationality' so fundamental to the public sphere existed here not in the utterance itself, but in the reader's reflections on the utterance and modification of its ideas in new pieces of writing. For several reasons, then, the avant-garde form was not necessarily in conflict with the imperatives of a public sphere rooted in rational discourse, even though its forms would seem to be the very antithesis of the imperative for rational discourse.

Mina Loy was one of the most avant-garde writers to participate in the public sphere at this time, and her work therefore points to some of the problems of applying a model of rational exchange in this way. Her work had shifted from appearing primarily in local Greenwich Village/New York publications (*The Trend*, *Camera Work*, *Rogue*) to appearing in the *Little Review*, *Dial*, and *Contact*. Loy attacked any vestige of the 'comfortable' reading experience, making her readers work hard to [re]create meaning. Her work typified the work of Greenwich Village in its refusal of sentimentality and ornament and interest in the bodily and sexual, but also drew on her Futurist roots as well as demonstrating a Steinian influence. Although Stein was not central to an exchange of ideas within this public sphere,[66] nevertheless, as Bryher later points out: 'Her attack on language was necessary and helped us all, even if we did not follow her.'[67] Loy

---

[66] Stein very explicitly distanced herself from her female contemporaries; most of her close relationships and friendships were with men, and she perceived herself as an isolated genius rather than part of a network through which ideas could be generated. Furthermore, though she published in some of the same magazines as the women writers in this public sphere, her work did not engage with that of her contemporaries, nor did she participate in a network of reviews and criticism. Finally, she seems to have cared little what others felt of her work. For these reasons I do not consider her to be part of this network of women writers.

[67] Bryher, *The Heart to Artemis*, 215.

praised Stein for seeking the 'radium of the word'[68] or 'gorgeous reticence',[69] the 'truth' stripped of all waste.

These were very much the values that Loy adopted and brought into this public sphere as ideas for discussion, reflection, and influence; in her autobiographical poem 'Anglo-Mongrels and the Rose' she uses no punctuation other than dashes, and she plays with the shape and sound of words in unusual juxtapositions, foregrounding the poem's linguistic (constructed) nature:

> An insect   from an herb
> errs on the man-mountain
> imparts   its infinitesimal tactile stimulus
> to the epiderm   to the spirit
> of Exodus
> stirring   the anaesthetised load
> of racial instinct frustrated . . . [70]

The representation of the insect on the man's skin calls attention to itself as representation; instead of trying to create 'natural' rhyme, Loy brings together, for example, 'herb' and 'err' as consecutive words, and then 'epiderm', drawing attention to this poem as linguistic artifice. The 'rationality' within her work lies, then, not in its overt form, but in the ideas it raises about language and the connections between signifier and signified. In addition, just as the writer Freytag-Loringhoven wore her coal scuttles for hats, thereby implicitly commenting on the artifice of finery and humanity's lack of any essential elevation, so Loy challenged the elevation of the literary representation by presenting a more seamy reality. Loy was in part reacting against Futurism's ethic of control and human power, reconnecting the human to the uncontrollable, the path of the insect across the human skin. That Loy's work was at least partly intelligible as a 'conversational utterance' in these sorts of ways is clear from the amount of discussion that was generated around her work, but also by her role as a pioneer behind whom many more would follow.

Increasingly Loy's avant-gardism became a gender issue for

[68] Mina Loy, 'Gertrude Stein', *Transatlantic Review*, 2 (1924): 305, quoted in Virginia M. Kouidis, *Mina Loy: American Modernist Poet* (Baton Rouge and London: Louisiana State University Press, 1980), 89.

[69] Mina Loy, 'Brancusi's Golden Bird', *The Dial*, 73/5 (Nov. 1922): 508.

[70] Loy, 'Anglo-Mongrels and the Rose', 12.

her; after negative criticism from John Rodker of the *Others* group, including specific comments about her own work, she noted that Rodker did not treat male and female avant-garde poets equally in his discussion, giving the men full consideration while most of the women 'must content themselves with exclamation marks'.[71] Rodker seems to have perceived their work as unworthy of the more detailed criticism he gave to their male contemporaries; these avant-garde women were dismissed with statements such as 'Lola Ridge ! !'; 'M. A. Seiffert and Evelyn Scott ! ! !'[72] Loy was astutely aware of such inequalities, which relegated the work of herself and others to the irrational utterance that could only be greeted with the irrational response, while male contemporaries received a much more full and rational assessment of their work. To continue to use avant-garde forms and to continue to bring her work into the public sphere was then, for Loy and for others, a statement of her ability to participate as a public subject in the public arena, and a refusal to be pushed back into her 'place' in the private sphere by reactions such as Rodker's discussed above. Loy's fearlessness and her willingness to stand up for women's contributions to the avant-garde, formed a strong pattern which others were able to follow; though she was a new influence within this network her work immediately had a profound effect on the work of her contemporaries and on critical discussion.

Women's prose writing of this period also demonstrated both the influence of early experimenters, particularly Richardson, as well as the impact of new writers and new thought. Richardson's *Pilgrimage* now fuelled similar experiments by May Sinclair, H.D., and Bryher, all three of whom had been reading *Pilgrimage* as it developed. Bryher met Richardson in 1923, having written to her to tell her how much her work had meant: 'I tried to tell her what *Backwater* had meant to me during the darkest days of the war, "I could grow again, I could grow"'.[73] What Bryher had gained from *Pilgrimage* was an alternative way of conceiving of the novel, a new 'woman's sentence' and

---

[71] Mina Loy, 'John Rodker's Frog', *The Little Review*, 7/3 (Sept.–Dec. 1920) [no issue no.]: 57.

[72] John Rodker, 'The 'Others' Anthology', *The Little Review*, 7/3 (Sept.–Dec. 1920): 56.

[73] Bryher, *The Heart to Artemis*, 240.

form. *Pilgrimage* inspired a new wave of texts that attempted to capture the ordinary flux of life as experienced by a central female character.

Pilgrimage itself was increasingly 'difficult' for the ordinary reader, leading to criticism, as the more experimental poetry was doing, concerning its obscurity. Alice Smith complained: 'Miss Sinclair maintains that Miss Richardson has simply imposed on herself the conditions that life imposes on us all. . . . The reader, whose mind staggers on the brink of delirium, after a frenzied pursuit of ten minutes' worth of Miriam's consciousness, would fain retort that it is the author's job, and not the reader's, to make Miriam's experience coherent.'[74] Smith is complaining about being invited into a participatory process of meaning formation, whereby the 'rational utterance' of the text is not predetermined by the author, but is worked out in a critical interaction of the reader with the text, and of the reader with other readers.

Another objection made about *Pilgrimage* was that it failed in its own objective, to present something altogether radical and new; several critics and readers were at a loss to see what this was, and felt that the changed perspective did not result in 'truth' but banality. Virginia Woolf was one such reader, who felt: 'Having sacrificed not merely "hims and hers," but so many seductive graces of wit and style for the prospect of some new revelation or greater intensity, we still find ourselves distressingly near the surface. Things look much the same as ever.'[75] The problem she noticed was that a new approach to perspective in the novel—the character's flow of ideas rather than the author's more obvious summary or appraisal of them—did not necessarily make these ideas more interesting. She felt, and she was not alone, that many of Miriam's ideas were so commonplace as to make the reading experience profoundly unstimulating. Sinclair's *Mary Olivier*, very much influenced by *Pilgrimage*, was subject to the same opprobrium. Critics began to observe with disquiet that since every person had a history of personal observations of an everyday world, including formative childhood experiences, then in theory almost anyone could set these

[74] Smith, 'Some English Women Novelists', 803.
[75] [Virginia Woolf], 'The Tunnel', review of *The Tunnel* by Dorothy Richardson, *The Times Literary Supplement*, 891 (Feb. 13, 1919), 81.

out on paper in something resembling *Pilgrimage* or *Mary Olivier.*[76] In fact, it was precisely because these texts raised these difficult issues that they were of such importance. They forced readers and critics to ask questions concerning the nature of 'literature', the boundaries of the purely personal, and the border between autobiography and fiction. Both these novels threatened the whole edifice of 'literature', making writers question and justify their own projects and differences. Woolf certainly felt her own work to be under threat by *Pilgrimage*—'If she's good then I'm not.'[77] Again, Katherine Mansfield felt *Mary Olivier* to be implicitly saying 'If I am to be taken in and welcomed, then the whole rest of the family [of literature] must be thrown out of the window.'[78] *Pilgrimage* and *Mary Olivier* were vital, then, not as templates for all future novels, but as catalysts for discussion of fundamental importance to the literary sphere. By their difference from more conventional novels, both texts stimulated a much needed assessment around the possibilities of this form and its limitations, and both texts were highly influential in a new wave of prose writing which felt liberated to break out of the bounds of 'plot' and authorial control.

H.D. was reading both Richardson[79] and Sinclair at this time,[80] a reading which had direct results on her own first attempts at novel-length prose writing. In *Paint It Today* Midget realizes that her own story is 'a very long story or it is a very short story, depending on how you look at it. I could more or less tell it in a paragraph. I could spend my life on ten long volumes and just begin to get the skeleton framework of it'.[81] Like Richardson, H.D. found existing narrative structures limiting, and the texts of *Paint It Today* and *Asphodel* very much echo Richardson and Sinclair's experiments, interlacing interior narrative, direct authorial control, first and third person narra-

---

[76] See, for example, Katherine Mansfield, 'The New Infancy', review of *Mary Olivier: A Life* by May Sinclair, in Katherine Mansfield, *Novels and Novelists* (London: Constable, 1930; Boston: Beacon Press, 1959), 41.

[77] Virginia Woolf, diary entry Nov. 11, 1919, *The Diary of Virginia Woolf*, 1, ed. Anne Olivier Bell (London: The Hogarth Press, 1977), 315.

[78] Mansfield, 'The New Infancy', 40–1.

[79] See, for example, H.D. to Bryher, Aug. 23 [1924], Beinecke.

[80] See, for example, H.D. to Bryher, Sept. 18, [1924], Beinecke.

[81] H.D., *Paint It Today*, 27.

tive, and direct outpourings from Midget's mind. *Asphodel*, like *Pilgrimage*, is also aware of its own failure to capture the full reality of lived experience: 'O ho, ho. That is no sound for laughter. But how write laughter?' Hermione, the central character in *Asphodel*, has the mind of a writer, with a distaste for stale language and cliché. War jargon and slang fill her with disgust, she cannot assimilate discussion of 'Fritz' or the 'Hun', or later 'unfaithful' into her world understanding: 'Unfaithful wife, returned officer husband, lover, baby . . . words out of the Daily Mail meaning nothing.'[82] She knows that reality is more individual than existing language can deal with, and that a new language is needed to take account of that individuality.

Asphodel had in common with many other texts by modernist women writers of this period a project to discover and represent the individual psychic reality. For H.D. and her contemporaries this continued to take clear precedence over the external political and economic world. As in the earlier years the war, if present at all, generally only existed as a background to psychic event, as for example in H.D.'s 'After Troy' where it is not the Trojan war, but a realization of the superiority and integrity of the enemy that had been fought against and lost to, that is the focus of the poem. The weapons of the poem are all internal— 'hate' and 'passion'—and the 'victory' comes from 'wit of thought' rather than military power.[83] In *Asphodel*, Hermione finds she 'can't any more believe in the reality of war-fare', it has far less meaning for her than her internal landscape.[84]

Though male contemporaries also focused at this time on the processes of the mind, on psychic crisis, and internal loss of meaning, this personal focus is more often linked to the state of 'civilization' or shared neurosis, contrasting with the more exclusively personal focus of women writers at this time. Though T. S. Eliot's *The Waste Land*[85] for example, focuses on loss of value and a feeling of disorientation, these are the losses of Western humanity, not of an individual perceiving psyche. Again, in D. H. Lawrence's *Women in Love* (1920), individual

[82] H.D., *Asphodel*, 25, 199.
[83] H.D., 'After Troy', *Transatlantic Review*, 1/2 (Feb. 1924): 5.
[84] H.D., *Asphodel*, 151.
[85] T. S. Eliot, *The Waste Land, Collected Poems 1909–1962* (London: Faber and Faber, 1963; new edn., 1974), 61–86.

relationships are constantly invoked against a wider background of human civilization. When, for example, Mrs Crich proposes that Birkin be Gerald's friend, Birkin's mind immediately turns to the global rather than the specific in a way that typifies Lawrence (rather than simply Birkin): 'Is every man's life subject to pure accident, is it only the race, the genus, the species, that has a universal reference? Or is this not true, is there no such thing as pure accident? Has everything that happens a universal significance? Has it? Birkin, pondering as he stood there, had forgotten Mrs Crich, as she had forgotten him.'[86] *Women in Love* then, relates the external and abstract back to the personal, and the personal to the abstract and external. In contrast, prose and poetry by most women writers of this network at this time more often begins and ends with the personal, not relating it directly either to wider social issues or to abstract generalizations; there is very little philosophizing about 'civilization', class relations, or the state of society, but much reflection on the personal psyche and its intimate connections to friends or family.

The central characters in women's writing of this period are, almost without exception, women, and the external world that they inhabit is generally the family sphere or a world of close relationships, not the more 'public' (in conventional understanding) worlds of work and industry. When the wider world of work is present, it is generally subsidiary to the inner emotional life. Though in Richardson's *Pilgrimage*, for example, Miriam goes out to work, we learn very little of the work of a dental surgery and very much about Miriam's relationships with others who work there and the wanderings of her mind as she sits at her desk. Miriam knows that 'no doubt those people did best who thought of nothing during hours but the work' but also that 'There was something wrong in them'.[87] Even though Miriam has 'escaped' to London, with its much wider scope for her inter-action in a more public world than the work of a governess or school-teacher had allowed her, the world she inhabits is dominated by her internal reflections rather than her public engagements. Even though it is possible to recreate London by reading these novels, this is very much Miriam's London, coloured by

[86] D. H. Lawrence, *Women in Love* (New York, 1920; Ware: Wordsworth Editions, 1992), 27.
[87] Richardson, *The Tunnel*, 65.

her intense reflections on place and object that turn these into parts of her internal landscape. For Miriam the internal landscape with its pressures on women and restrictions on her life must be negotiated before she can fully inhabit the external landscape. It is not that she privileges the private world, but that she recognizes that her struggles in that arena must be resolved before she can also become a 'public' subject. Throughout the *Pilgrimage* sequence, then, external 'public' structures, such as the Lycurgan discussion group and the world of work cannot be fully inhabited.

One of the key arenas in which these women writers placed their characters in order to resolve issues of 'private' influences on subject formation was the world of the family; this, of course, was the arena within which women's lives had conventionally been restricted and the arena in which the 'self' as 'private' or 'public' is brought into being, and therefore a crucial location for explorations of the public and private self, and the relationship between internal and external reality.[88] In Bryher's *Two Selves* Nancy is 'tied up' by her socialization process within the family: 'But there was no freedom. Only an invisible but actual clutch of circumstance that wove grey chains back and forth across her limbs and mind a chain . . . no being a cabin boy, no miracle of release happening, no great book, no liberty, no friends, no hope.'[89] Again and again in women's writing of this period, as in Loy's 'The Anglo-Mongrels and the Rose'[90] and Sinclair's *Mary Olivier*, we find images of the daughter bound up in the family's expectations of her. Mary feels of her family's attempts to model her as a good girl: 'Wool, spun out, wound round you, woven in a net. You were tangled and strangled in a net of unclean wool. They caught you in it when you were a baby a month old. Mamma, Papa and Uncle Victor. You would have to cut and tug and kick and fight your way out. They were caught in it themselves, they couldn't get out.'[91] Mary fights these pressures, but is

[88] Of course the family is also very important in texts such as Joyce's *A Portrait of the Artist as a Young Man* (first published in *The Egoist*, 1914–15; London: Penguin, 1992). However, for modernist women writers this is by far the dominant constrictive force on the self. Discussions of the impact of church and education are far less frequent, and discussions of class relations, race, industrialism and so on are negligible.   [89] Bryher, *Two Selves*, 95.

[90] Loy, 'The Anglo-Mongrels and the Rose' [Part Two], 155.

[91] Sinclair, *Mary Olivier*, 113.

never able to fully escape her mother's influence. Katherine Mansfield observed with irritation: 'In the beginning Mary is two, but at the end she is still two';[92] the interest in the novel is not on Mary's adult self, but the ways in which the child self is perpetuated. What Mary learns as a child is her own inability as a girl to compete with her brother, Mark, for her mother's love; the sexualized child-mother and mother-child bonds are at the heart of a novel that explores how these condition adult existence. The family is presented not as a safe space for growth and development, but as a threat to this; instead of being woman's natural 'sphere' it becomes the place she is tied to but desires to escape.

Explorations of family influence such as in H.D.'s *Asphodel* and *Paint It Today*, Bryher's *Two Selves* and Sinclair's *Mary Olivier* and *Harriet Freen*, were of course rooted in the deepened interest by modernist women writers in psychoanalysis. Sinclair, who was reading Freud's *The Interpretation of Dreams* and Jung's *Psychology of the Unconscious* and *Analytical Psychology* at this time, accepted and worked with the Freudian and Jungian beliefs that childhood experience and particularly family relationships are crucial in the development of the self. She writes in one of several theoretical discussions of this material: 'A large portion of Professor Jung's book is given up to the myth of the return to the mother for rebirth, and to the conflict with the mother. That conflict begins in childhood and is waged most fiercely on the threshold of adolescence. It must be fought to a finish, and the child must win it or remain for ever immature.'[93] These ideas are pervasive across many texts by H.D., Bryher, Richardson, Loy, and others in this period and fuelled heated debate. On the one side were those attempting to integrate such material into their work, and on the other side those resolutely denying the importance of early childhood sexual experience and sexualized family dynamics. Amy Lowell, for example, writes: 'To suppose that all life under the surface consists of violent sexual desires crushed out or sublimated, that all personal relation is a war of sexual antagonisms is to see life

---

[92] Mansfield, 'The New Infancy', 43.
[93] May Sinclair, 'Symbolism and Sublimation: II', *The Medical Press and Circular*, 102/4,032 (Aug. 9, 1916): 144.

through a perfectly distorted medium.'[94] In taking such a stance Lowell implicitly allied herself with an older generation, distancing herself from the majority of her contemporaries who were embracing psychoanalytic thought.

Many readers, critics, and writers objected not to the psychoanalytic perspective itself, but to a perceived swamping of texts with untransmuted psychoanalytic theory. Jane Heap, for example, objected that 'the line-up of her characters in "Mary Olivier" reads like the list for a clinic. Pathological predestination bears small relation to creative inevitability';[95] Edna Kenton, also in a review of *Mary Olivier*, complained: 'the translation, not to say transmutation of subconscious motivation into dramatic action demands more "treating" than the novelist in general has ever felt called on to give.'[96] In fact, what is remarkable about *Mary Olivier* is the extent to which this material is integrated, one of the first attempts to very deliberately explore psychoanalytic theorizations of sexual family dynamics within the novel.[97] It was, however, the startling newness of these ideas, derived from contemporary psychoanalytic material, which drew attention to them and problematized the reading experience for the reader encountering them for the first time. Inevitably such a reader would find that engagement with these issues dominated his or her experience of the text, and it was perhaps not until many years later, when these ideas had become more common currency, that texts such as *Mary Olivier* could be enjoyed as novels, rather than dissected for their psychoanalytic import. In these early years the key role of these texts was in bringing more readers into contact with psychoanalytic thought than would otherwise have been exposed to such ideas. In engaging with these ideas writers were reflecting on issues with 'universal' human applicability, rather than simply of interest within this network. The later widespread adoption of

[94] Amy Lowell to Helen Bullis Kizer, Oct. 23, 1917, quoted in S. Foster Damon, *Amy Lowell: A Chronicle* (Boston: Houghton Mifflin, 1935), 431.

[95] jh, 'Eat 'em Alive!' review of *Mary Olivier* by May Sinclair, *The Little Review*, 6/8 (Dec. 1919): 30–1; see also Babette Deutsch, 'Freedom and the Grace of God', *The Dial*, 67 [no issue no.] (Nov. 15, 1919): 441.

[96] Edna Kenton, 'May Sinclair's "Mary Olivier"', review of *Mary Olivier* by May Sinclair, *The Little Review*, 6/8 (Dec. 1919): 30.

[97] Clearly D. H. Lawrence's *Sons and Lovers* (London: Heinemann, 1913; Heinemann Educational Books, 1963) was an important precursor.

many of these ideas within work of the 1930s is testimony to the work that these early texts undertook in enabling readers to come into contact with, and critically reflect upon, new ideas in psychoanalytic theory.

H.D.'s work of this period also opened up new ideas in psychoanalysis to a literary readership, though in general it was along Jungian rather than strictly Freudian lines that her work developed. Although there is no evidence that H.D. had read Jung at this time, her theoretical *Notes* is particularly close to Jungian thought. She describes a person as composed of 'body, mind, over-mind'; the over-mind is akin to the Jungian collective unconscious, above rather than below consciousness, a heightened transcendent state of being, structured around 'eternal, changeless ideas', 'dramas already conceived'. H.D. asserts of a connection between people beyond their conscious minds: 'The minds of men differ but the over-minds are alike.'[98] This is very close to Jung's 1916 assertion: 'We know that, although individuals are widely separated by the differences in the contents of their consciousness, they are closely alike in their unconscious psychology.'[99] H.D. explored these ideas across both her theoretical and her literary work; in *Notes*: 'These [over-mind] feelings extend out and about us; as the long, floating tentacles of a jelly-fish reach out and about him.'[100] Again, in her novel *Asphodel*, Hermione is affected by 'jelly-fish' transcendence:

The body within her was a mysterious globe of softly glowing pollen-light. It would give light in the darkness, she was certain, it would give light in the darkness, would, she was certain, glow pollen-wise in the darkness if the rest of her should be darkness, mysterious glow-worm within her would give light, show her the straight path . . . and many there be that go in thereat.[101]

Jungian understanding is evident in many texts by women writers of this time to an extent that it does not seem to be in the work of male contemporaries. In particular there is a shared interest in the collective unconscious. Eunice Tietjens writes:

---

[98] H.D., *Notes*, 17, 23, 40.
[99] C. G. Jung, *Psychology of the Unconscious* (New York: Moffat, Yard, 1916; London: Kegan Paul, Trench, Trubner, 1918), 198. Translation of *Wandlungen und Symbole der Libido. Beiträge zur Entwicklungsgeschichte des Denkens* (Leipzig and Vienna: Franz Deuticke, 1912).   [100] H.D., *Notes*, 19.
[101] H.D., *Asphodel*, 162–3.

> Something stirs and struggles in me,
> Something out of reach
> Of surface thoughts, a slow and formless thing—
> Not I, but a dim memory
> Born of the dead behind me. In my blood
> The blind race turns, groping and faltering.

Within the speaker's psyche are all the struggles of humanity; in her mind she finds a 'Hunger for violence' and 'dark memory', 'horrid sounds' and 'Blood-crazed' dead. The collectively repressed threatens to break into her conscious mind, however, the speaker is saved from the 'primal fear' by its sublimation into legitimized and formalized 'Bacchanalian revels', a human construct of legitimated wildness where the barbarism of the collective unconscious can find a harmless release.[102] Tietjens was just one of the many women writers using these ideas, and for whom it is now very difficult to determine the extent of familiarity with primary theoretical psychoanalytic material. The 'Hunger for violence' only touched on here would become central in explorations of the psyche in the 1930s and early 1940s, as discussed in Chapter 5.

There is a sense in the material of this time of writers actively engaged in charting new territory, in exploring areas of the mind that were concurrently being explored by psychoanalysis. There are multiple images of peering into dark corners and opening up unopened spaces and an interest in the hidden depths of the psyche, such as in Emmy Veronica Sanders's poem 'Driftwood' where in the mind's 'dim-lit shore' drift 'Strange things' that lack a name or a 'home'. These are things 'On the edge of the mind', creating a disturbance in consciousness. There is a sense of unpredictability here and elsewhere, an idea that the knowledge that had allowed these images to be described and catalogued at all is as yet incomplete and untested, that these writers were therefore part of, rather than passive reflectors of, new discoveries about the human mind.[103] Again and again in numerous texts there is an anxiety that in the night-spaces all that is feared and unknown will surface and take control. Consistently there is a portrayal of something creeping, lurking, unable to be defined. Dorothy Easton's narrator in 'Moments' writes: 'Sad, white-

---

[102] Tietjens, 'Fire', *Poetry*, 19/5 (Feb. 1922): 262, 263, 264.
[103] Emmy Veronica Sanders, 'Driftwood', *Poetry*, 17/5 (Feb. 1921): 251–2.

faced things come to live in me—they are heavy, like weight of crushed rain in November cloud . . . when I grasp them to ask are they real, they writhe with unutterable anguish and fade.'[104] Helen West Heller's speaker in her prose-poem, 'Alone in the House', fears that at night: 'Through locked doors at height of storm THE INSIDIOUS THING | will come.'[105] These writers would have been familiar with the Freudian view that 'the content of anxiety dreams is of a sexual nature, the libido belonging to which content has been transformed into fear'.[106] Yet there are few attempts to pin down the 'thing' in theoretical terms; instead there is an enjoyment in allowing into literary texts aspects of the psyche that were beginning to be understood through the new psychoanalytic discoveries, and a belief that the reader will be familiar with these sources and make their own 'readings' of this material.

H.D.'s writing of this period is very much engaged in such examinations of the dark side of the psyche; in *Asphodel*: 'The mist was full of shapes and odd looming creatures and you never knew in the darkness (day dark or night dark) what might or mightn't loom up at you.' The foggy city here is an objective correlative for a disturbed unconscious where what is repressed reaches out and grabs the subject, day or night. Hermione 'knew in the dark sub-consciousness an abyss of unimaginable terror, the pain, the disappointment, the utter horror of the last thing'.[107] Her quest to know herself is relentless, confronting aspects of herself that are uncomfortable to recognize. She comes up against her own sadism through her relationship to Shirley, recognizing her complicity in engaging in talk about Shirley that was 'cruel' and 'petty' and that gives her a 'shiver of apprehension'. Later, when Shirley dies, Hermione experiences this as murder: 'It was Hermione who had killed her.' In understanding this, she recognizes the part of her that would sadistically attack others. She must also come to terms with her own self-absorption, her 'white spider' self that wraps her up in a 'mesh

---

[104] Dorothy Easton, 'Moments', in *The Golden Bird and Other Stories* (London: Heinemann, 1920), 222.

[105] Helen West Heller, 'Alone in the House', *The Little Review*, 6/3 (July 1919): 63.

[106] Sigmund Freud, *The Interpretation of Dreams*, trans. A. A. Brill (London: Allen & Unwin, 1913), 136–7. Trans. of *Die Traumdeutung*, Vienna, 1990.

[107] H.D., *Asphodel*, 139, 154.

of self'.[108] Hermione's ruthless self-analysis is part of a wave of deep excavations of the psyche in the work of other modernist women writers.

A great many of these writers did have a detailed theoretical understanding of latest developments in psychoanalytic theory. H.D., for example, read original sources[109] and attended lectures, and was to have several periods of psychoanalysis including two, in the 1930s, as Freud's 'pupil'. Both H.D. and Bryher had analysis with Havelock Ellis in 1919;[110] Mina Loy met Freud in Vienna, studied his work,[111] drew his portrait, consulted a Freudian psychiatrist (Roberto Assagioli) in 1913, and was part of a group where psychoanalysis was a central topic of discussion;[112] Dorothy Richardson was acquainted with Barbara Low;[113] Djuna Barnes expressed a profound interest in Freud; Rebecca West and Louise Bogan were both deeply interested in Jung and Freud; Edith Sitwell was later to read Jung's *Psychology of the Unconscious*;[114] Elizabeth Bishop was to have

---

[108] H.D., *Asphodel*, 100, 103, 104.

[109] One of H.D.'s books in Bryher's library was Freud's *The Interpretation of Dreams* (Virginia Smyers, 'H.D.'s Books in the Bryher Library', *H.D. Newsletter*, 1/2 (Winter 1987): 20); the catalogue of H.D.'s library at the Beinecke Library includes *The Life and Work of Sigmund Freud*, 3 vols, by Ernest Jones (London: The Hogarth Press, 1953–7), and H.D. and Bryher between them were to come to own both the complete works of Freud in German and at least a substantial collection of his works in English (see Bryher to H.D., April 12, 1935, Beinecke.) It has not been possible to establish for certain that they owned those of Freud's volumes already in print at this time, however their level of familiarity with his work would seem to indicate that they did.

[110] Havelock Ellis was of course a surprising choice of analyst for H.D. and Bryher, given some of his views on women (as dependent, less capable of abstract thought, less artistic, and in particular women's poetry—'Strong poetic art, which involves at once both a high degree of audacity and brooding deliberation, is very rare in women.' Havelock Ellis, *Man and Woman: A Study of Human Secondary Sexual Characters* (London: Walter Scott, 1894), 322. Ellis also had strong views on homosexuality as an aberration found most often amongst the 'savage' and 'uncultured man', and feminism as potentially leading to 'sexual inversion' by promoting 'hereditary neurosis'. Havelock Ellis, *Studies in the Psychology of Sex* (London: The University Press, 1897), 9, 100 and throughout. However, he did take an active interest in literature, publishing for example 'A Note on Conrad', *Contact Collection*, 53–6.

[111] Kouidis, *Mina Loy*, 17.

[112] Burke, *Becoming Modern*, 146, 214.

[113] Dorothy Richardson to Bryher, [Fall 1923], in *Windows on Modernism: Selected Letters of Dorothy Richardson*, ed. Gloria G. Fromm (Athens: The University of Georgia Press, 1995), 85.

[114] Edith Sitwell, 'Of the Clowns and Fools of Shakespeare', *Life and Letters To-Day*, 57/124 (May 1948): 108.

psychoanalysis.[115] There was scarcely a writer within this network unaffected (now or in later years) by an interest in psychoanalysis. H.D.'s own interest in psychoanalysis then, needs to be contextualized within the widespread interest of her contemporaries, and it is because her work tends to be interpreted against personal biographical information that this has been so neglected. In part the failure to contextualize H.D.'s interest is also due to the personal nature of psychoanalysis, seemingly the antithesis of an analysis of collective trends and interests. However, if we begin to locate H.D. in the context of other uses of psychoanalysis by modernist women writers, we can understand the kinds of background discussions that sustained her own interest and the ways in which she worked towards a development of her own unique version of psychoanalysis. H.D. appears to be less introspective, and her texts less solipsistic, if it is understood that psychoanalysis was a *de rigueur* topic of discussion at this time.

The widespread adoption of psychoanalytic thought does raise some difficult questions when considering these writers as part of a public sphere. It must be asked how it is possible to reconcile texts that demonstrate such an interest in the unconscious into a model of the public sphere rooted in rational exchange. In answering this it should be remembered that the critical discussion generated around a text is one of the crucial mechanisms for an exchange of ideas within this public sphere. It is therefore this critical discussion that needs to be demonstrated to have met certain standards of clarity and rationality if this cultural formation of women writers is to be understood as having possessed the essential dynamics of a public sphere; clearly these texts did generate such rational and informed discussion. In addition, texts such as *Mary Olivier, Harriet Freen*, and *Asphodel* are in no way attempts to allow an 'outpouring' of the author's unconscious, but are very deliberate and conscious applications of theoretical ideas to a novel; they offer interpretation of theoretical material which is then offered for discussion in the public sphere, they are a 'rational utterance' which may be met with rational critical discussion. They enabled writers and readers who personally had no contact with theoretical psycho-

[115] Victoria Harrison, *Elizabeth Bishop's Poetics of Intimacy* (Cambridge, UK: Cambridge University Press, 1993), 117.

analytic texts nevertheless to be subject to its influence, and subsequently to adopt these ideas in their own work. In this way these texts contributed to a dissemination of theoretical understandings that facilitated an exchange of new ideas in the public sphere. Furthermore, the presentation by Freud in particular of psychoanalytic ideas as 'science' tended to give psychoanalysis a rational underpinning in contrast to the purely 'spiritual' or 'mystical'. Finally, many of these writers backed up their literary explorations of the unconscious and psychoanalytic thought with theoretical work, such as H.D.'s 1919 *Notes*; this demonstrates H.D.'s engagement with underlying concepts behind the more esoteric explorations of psychoanalysis in her literary material, and constitutes an attempt to give a rational account of irrational thought processes.

It is more problematic, however, to understand the role played by another group of texts, those which presented themselves as, or appeared to be, direct outpourings from the unconscious. Readers of the *Little Review* were confronted with difficult questions following the publication of Freytag-Loringhoven's work 'Mineself—Minesoul—and—mine—Cast-iron Lover' ('Mineself'), a nine-page poem of seemingly incoherent psychotic outburst:

ANIMAL—mine body—CAST IRON ANIMAL?
CHISELLED animal—mine soul aloof— — — those hands
LIVE—never came to life— — — are afraid—never were BORN![116]

This poem generated heated discussion as to the extent to which it was either a successful sublimation of a disturbed unconscious or simply its discharge. Lola Ridge wrote to the *Little Review*: 'Are you hypnotized, or what, that you open the Little Review with such a retching assault upon Art . . . ?'[117] to which Heap replied: 'No one has yet done much about the Art of Madness.'[118] Heap perceived in Freytag-Loringhoven's work a clear element of conscious control and creative artifice: 'In the case of Freytag-Loringhoven I am not talking of mania and disease . . . hers is a willed state.'[119] Evelyn Scott agreed that this might have

[116] Freytag-Loringhoven, 'Cast-iron Lover', 7.
[117] Lola Ridge, 'Concerning Else von Freytag-Loringhoven', *The Little Review*, 6/6 (Oct. 1919): 56.   [118] jh, reply to Lola Ridge, ibid.
[119] jh, reply to Evelyn Scott, 'The Art of Madness', *The Little Review*, 6/8 (Dec. 1919): 49.

been Freytag-Loringhoven's intention, but felt that this had been swamped by a discharge of psychotic unconscious material: 'The artist often courts the speech of the madman because he desires the emotion he has ensnared to escape the petrification of intellectualism, but there is a point at which the will weakens beneath the onrush of forces it has itself loosed.'[120]

After much exchange between Scott and Heap, Freytag-Loringhoven wrote in to defend her work, insisting on it as a creative sublimation in the tradition of the carnival: 'in the nations of high culture [madness] was a public custom, as it still is—for instance in the mardi gras—or "Fasching"—and in old Greece in the feast of Dionysus'. She argued for art as a constructive sublimation of otherwise destructive repression: 'Is it not wonderful to be able to control that then, that emotion which otherwise would throttle you?'[121] Instead of understanding her work as Freudian symptom, she took the Jungian view of art as creative application of the unconscious, the 'higher' interpretation rather than the 'lower'. However, only a few years later the balance tipped, and Freytag-Loringhoven wrote of unconscious forces in her art taking control over consciousness: '[My art] is traitor—it turns dust within my hands! I am indifferent to it—I despise it—I am afraid of it! I am somnambule—shaken to awakeness before abyss of absolute icy nonsense. . . . Shall I leap it—tumble into it?'[122]

These alternative positions, the Freudian symptom[123] versus Jungian creative sublimation,[124] and the issue of whether there

---

[120] Evelyn Scott, 'The Art of Madness': I, *The Little Review*, 6/9 (Jan. 1920): 26.

[121] Else von Freytag-Loringhoven, 'The Art of Madness': III, *The Little Review*, 6/9 (Jan. 1920): 29, 28.

[122] Elsa Baroness von Freytag-Loringhoven, 'Selections from the Letters of Elsa Baroness von Freytag-Loringhoven', ed. Djuna Barnes, *transition*, 11 (Feb. 1928): 23.

[123] Sigmund Freud, 'The Paths to the Formation of Symptoms', *Introductory Lectures on Psycho-Analysis*, trans. and ed. James Strachey ([1916–17]; London: Allen & Unwin, 1922; New York: W. W. Norton, 1966), 467–8. Translation of *Vorlesungen zur Einführung die Psychoanalyse* (Leipzig and Vienna: Heller, 1917).

[124] See, for example, C. G. Jung, *Collected Papers on Analytical Psychology*, trans. Constance E. Long (London: Baillière, Tindall & Cox, 1916; 2nd edn., 1917), 397; see also C. G. Jung, 'The Psychology of Dementia Praecox' in *The Psychogenesis of Mental Disease*, trans. R. F. C. Hull, *The Collected Works of C. G. Jung* vol. 3 (London: Routledge & Kegan Paul, 1960), 50. Trans. of *Über die Psychologie der Dementia Praecox: Ein Versuch* (Halle a. s., 1907). In later works Jung spells out more clearly the differences between his own views and those of Freud in this regard.

could be a productive and creative channelling of the unconscious into works of art or whether any 'release' of the unconscious remained at the level of neurotic symptom, surfaced again and again in discussions of literary texts. Babette Deutsch agreed with Freud that: 'All art is to a degree pathological. It is a means of throwing off waste emotion.'[125] Not surprisingly this view was not widely embraced, and there were attempts to find other ways of understanding the creativity that did not conceive of it as a 'symptom'. Sinclair felt that more attention needed to be paid to the artist's conscious handling of the unconscious material: 'When you come to art and religion you feel that what you may call their sublimative value will depend not only on the amount of libido actively and voluntarily "carried over", but on the extent to which the higher psychic channels are involved. It is not enough to transfer; you must transform.'[126]

Jung's views were much more sympathetic to such a creative transformation than those of Freud, allowing the work of art to be conceived of as the coming together of the unconscious with the conscious artistic process. However, even this compromise was anathema to some; Amy Lowell, for example, felt that to grant the unconscious even this level of influence was to fail to give due recognition to the work of the artist:

Art is not, as so many believe, primarily an outlet for personal emotions. On the contrary, it is the creating of something apart from the artist which, when created, should have a separate existence and justify itself by its power of reproducing an emotion or a thought in the mind of the reader. The amateur writes poetry under great stress of emotion to free himself of an oppressive state of mind. The professional poet . . . writes . . . with the object of making a beautiful poem, not with the object of relieving himself from any particular state of mind.[127]

Such a view is of course close to the ideas of T. E. Hulme (1909)[128] or T. S. Eliot (1921), who conceive of the work of art as 'dry' object, separate from the personality of the artist and his

---

[125] Babette Deutsch, 'The Romance of the Realists', *The Dial*, 66 (May 31, 1919): 560.

[126] May Sinclair, 'Symbolism and Sublimation: II', 143.

[127] Amy Lowell to 'a young lady whose sister was developing a neurosis in the attempt to become a poet', n.d., quoted in Damon, *Amy Lowell*, 650–1.

[128] See, for example, T. E. Hulme, 'Searchers after Reality: Haldane', in *New Age*, 5 (Aug. 19, 1909): 315–16, repr. *Further Speculations*, ed. Samuel Hynes (Minneapolis: University of Minnesota Press, 1955), 10.

or her direct emotional experience.[129] Such a perspective was anathema to the majority of women writers and critics within this network whose literary and critical work in general took a far more personal approach, linking personal (conscious and unconscious) experience and personality, including dream, to the production of their texts.

In addition to exploring new areas of the unconscious mind in these years, a great many of the women writers within this network also turned to the physical and sexual dimensions of the self, the self as body rather than detached mind, bringing psychoanalytic theories of mind into contact with the female experience of her body. Alicia Ostriker's assertion that these writers (H.D., Lowell, Moore, Stein, and Loy specifically) were cerebral, detached from all representations of bodily experience, is not supported by an examination of their writing of this period.[130] While the years 1913–17 in women's writing were markedly cerebral, almost eliminating the female body from texts and discussion, in this period the emphasis is much closer to a Jungian rejection of Cartesian Dualism in favour of the unified mind and body. H.D.'s work was central in this development; she speculates in *Notes*: 'Should we be able to think with the womb and feel with the brain?' This idea indicates H.D.'s interest in specifically female creativity and thought, and the linking of her body to her creative processes, moving away from a false 'universality'. She argues that the mind needs to be aware of its bodily rooting in order to function to its full potential, and that an overbalance of either body or mind is disastrous. H.D. describes a state of transcendence in *Notes* that involves the mind reaching into the body, so that the whole being is animated: 'I should say—to continue this jelly-fish metaphor—that long feelers reached down and through the body, that these stood in the same relation to the nervous system as the overmind to the brain or intellect.'[131] The mind in its transcendent state must have a physical dimension, must produce bodily 'feeling' that parallels the mind's feeling.

---

[129] T. S. Eliot, 'Tradition and the Individual Talent' [1921], *Selected Essays* (London: Faber and Faber, 1932; 3rd enlarged edn., 1951), 20.

[130] Alicia Suskin Ostriker, *Stealing the Language: The Emergence of Women's Poetry in America* (Boston: Beacon Press, 1986), 52–3.

[131] H.D., *Notes*, 20, 19.

Again and again H.D.'s literary work of this period is insistent
that a focus on the mind alone is inadequate, that there needs
also to be an acknowledgement of the body. In 'Demeter', for
example, the 'grapple of mind to reach | the tense thought' is
frustrated because it does not take account of the physical body:

> Useless to me who plant
> wide feet on a mighty plinth,
> useless to me who sit,
> wide of shoulder, great of thigh,
> heavy in gold, to press
> gold back against solid back
> of the marble seat: . . .[132]

Having emphasized her physicality Demeter urges the seeker of
wisdom, who finds him or herself 'drawn out from yourself', in
a transcendental state of knowledge, not to forget that she herself is the 'greatest and least', the origin,[133] in Jungian terms the
'symbol of the mother's womb'.[134] Through a recognition of
body then, Demeter points the way to deeper psychic processes
and experiences; the mind begins in the mother's body, source of
all thought. Mental and physical combine in the figure of
Demeter who represents both the ultimate body, and ultimate
mind, the source of thought as well as of babies. This concept
connects to H.D.'s later, also highly Jungian, interest in alchemy,
the mental-physical process that produces new substance and
psychic revelation.

In H.D.'s work there is often an uneasy tension between body
and mind, as the two elements seek to have their own needs met;
so in 'Hippolytus Temporizes' Hippolytus hesitates between
worship of the goddess Artemis, and the tangible physical being
of Phaedra, finding his thoughts turning to the physical woman
rather than the ethereal goddess.[135] Again, in the Sapphic
'Fragment Thirty-Six' the speaker hesitates between satisfying
her desire to wake her lover, her physical desire, or to letting the
lover sleep and enjoying instead the state of mind she is in, the
night sounds of her lover's breathing. The mental conflict is itself

---

[132] H.D., *Hymen*, 15.
[133] Ibid. 16.
[134] Jung, *Psychology of the Unconscious*, 263.
[135] H.D., 'Hippolytus Temporizes', *The Bookman*, 56 (Oct. 1921): 123.

given a physical embodiment, as the mind struggles with two potential sources of satisfaction, physical and mental:

> As two white wrestlers,
> Standing for a match,
> Ready to turn and clutch,
> Yet never shake
> Muscle or nerve or tendon;
> So my mind waits . . .[136]

This mind-body tension was part of the climate of thought among modernist women writers as the cerebral/spiritual was brought into contact with the bodily/physical/sexual.

In Freytag-Loringhoven's 'Mineself' there is again a struggle between the needs of body and mind, the two entering into dialogue with each other about their differing needs and desires. The soul feels that the lover possesses a 'soulless beauty', focusing on the pure and spiritual aspect of the loved one, but the body expresses its physical desire for the lover as vital and powerful:

> Ha—mine soul—I say 'alas' and I say 'alas' and 'alas' and
> 'alas'! because I am thine BODY! and this is mine flaming desire to-day: that he shall step into THEE through ME as it was in olden times and that we will
> play again that old WONDERFUL play of the
> 'TWOTOGETHER'! . . .

The body argues for its needs—'I Suffer! I MUST TOUCH! HERE MINE EYES—HERE MINE HANDS!'[137] The soul accuses the body of being an animal, simply following brute instinct; the body feels the soul to be cold and remote, and so the tension of mind–body is played out. Of course part of the tension of this poem is inherent in Freytag-Loringhoven's choice of the Dadaist form; her involvement in the New York Dada group is evident in the style of much of her writing, the random processes of the mind and disjointed thought. However, what she herself adds to this is an injection of very personal, including female sexuality; as Robert Reiss writes: 'Thus, while her work is the unalloyed embodiment of Dada, it transcends Dada and thereby offers itself as a pivotal passage of transition between

---

[136] H.D., 'Fragment XXXVI', *Poetry*, 19/1 (Oct. 1921): 27.
[137] Freytag-Loringhoven, 'Cast-iron Lover', 3, 4, 5.

Dada and Surrealism. . . . Freytag-Loringhoven contributes her remarkably feminine Dada to the canon, foretelling the inevitable reintroduction of deep emotionality into art.'[138] Freytag-Loringhoven was a pioneer ahead of a wave of women writers attacking the separation of mental from physical, and specifically the woman's body from the mental, that would open up new directions in later Surrealist explorations by women writers.

For now there was more straightforwardly a feeling of a collective enjoyment of the release of the physical into the writing of this period. The woman's body was allowed into these texts as a physical entity, cutting out the distancing or deification that had been part of Victorian and earlier modernist women writers' portrayals of a woman's body; Mina Loy writes of a woman giving birth, for example:

> Her face
> screwed   to the mimic-salacious
> grotesquerie of a pain
> larger than her intellect
> ———— They pull
> A clotty bulk of bifurcate fat
> out of her loins . . . . [139]

Instead of raising the moment of birth to the purely spiritual level on which it had often been represented, Loy allows the painful physical reality to be present; Loy admired Joyce for this same quality, the physical embodiment, the 'word made flesh'.[140]

Such an embracing of the physical applied also to the physical-sexual, with modernist women's writing perceiving itself to be far more open than any previous women's writing about the physical dimensions of sexuality. Dora Russell sets out the position: 'To me the important task of modern feminism is to accept and proclaim sex; to bury for ever the lie that has too long corrupted our society—the lie that the body is a hindrance to the mind, and sex a necessary evil to be endured for the perpetuation of our race.'[141] She continues: 'To enjoy [sex] and admit we

---

[138] Robert Reiss, '"My Baroness": Elsa von Freytag-Loringhoven', *Dada/Surrealism*, 14 (1985): 89.

[139] Mina Loy, 'Anglo-Mongrels and the Rose: Continued', *The Little Review* (no issue no.) (Autumn and Winter 1923–24): 49.

[140] Mina Loy, 'Joyce's Ulysses', *The Lost Lunar Baedeker*, 88.

[141] Dora Russell, *Hypatia: Or Woman and Knowledge* (London: Kegan Paul, Trubner, [1925]), 24–5.

enjoy, without terror or regret, is an achievement in honesty.'[142] These women were rejecting the strong current within suffragism that had argued for women's 'purity' against men who were 'base' and sexual. Rebecca West satirizes such views in her 1922 novel *The Judge*; in the view of Ellen, a young suffragette: '"There's something awful like an animal about a man", she thought, and shivered.'; 'under decent life there was an oozy mud and she had somehow wallowed in it'.[143] Such views were now relegated to an older age of feminism, replaced by women's assertion of their rights as sexual subjects.[144] In the Eleusinian mysteries that H.D. discusses in *Notes* (and that Jung discusses in his 1916 *Psychology of the Unconscious*[145]), the first stage that the would-be initiate must pass through is sexual: 'The first step in the Eleusinian mysteries had to do with sex. There were images set up in a great room, coloured marbles and brown pottery, painted with red and vermilion and coloured earthen work or clay images. The candidates for admission to the mysteries would be shown through the room by a priest or would walk through at random, as the crowd walks through the pornographic chamber at the museum at Naples.'[146] To be fully spiritual, H.D. argued, you must first be fully sexual; her writing is full of physical images of sexuality, far removed from the sexual 'landscapes' of plants and flowers that distanced the reader from a more direct sexual experience in her earlier work.

The reception of H.D.'s poem 'Hymen' is interesting in this regard in that critics universally failed to note the transition to a presentation of the sexual, and interpreted 'Hymen' purely in terms of the Ancient Greek god of marriage, failing to see its clear referent of the membrane over the vagina. The anonymous reviewer for the *Times Literary Supplement* in 1924, for example, argued that her work exhibited a 'glacial purity',[147] while in the *Boston Evening Transcript* the reviewer saw her work as 'intrinsically a little cold'.[148] 'Hymen' is, in fact, physically

[142] Russell, *Hypatia*, 33.

[143] Rebecca West, *The Judge* (Hutchinson, 1922; London: Virago, 1980), 28, 135.

[144] Marianne Moore is clearly an exception here.

[145] Jung, *Psychology of the Unconscious*, 378 and throughout.

[146] H.D., *Notes*, 29.

[147] Anon., 'Another Athens', including review of *Heliodora* by H.D., *The Times Literary Supplement*, 1172 (July 3, 1924): 416.

[148] Anon., 'Poems by H.D.', review of *Heliodora and Other Poems* by H.D., *The Boston Evening Transcript* (Aug. 16, 1924): 3.

grounded in a loss of virginity, seen here as a serious privation for which the bride must be prepared; initially the 'curtain hangs motionless in rich, full folds'. Then:

> (Ah, stern the petals drawing back;
> Ah rare, ah virginal her breath!)
>
> . . . . . .
>
> One moment, then the plunderer slips
> Between the purple flower-lips.

After this 'The purple curtain hangs black and heavy.'[149] H.D.'s critics failed to note the very clearly evoked moment of sexual penetration, and thereby missed an important development within H.D.'s work of this period. The poem equates an assimilation into the role of wife with a violent sexual initiation that has nothing to offer the woman.

H.D.'s unpublished prose fiction of the period is still more physically and sexually grounded; in both *Paint It Today* and *Asphodel* she explores lesbian relationships. *Paint It Today* contrasts Midget's destructive, suffocating, intensely intellectual relationship with Josepha to a later relationship with Althea, where both spiritual union and pleasure in each other's body is possible: 'All the power of the wood seemed to circle between those two alert and vivid bodies, like two shafts attracting the two opposite currents of the electric forces of the forest.'[150] Cheryl Walker's assertion that H.D.'s work, along with that of Amy Lowell, Sara Teasdale, and Elinor Wylie, suffered from 'problems of alienation from [the] flesh'[151] is incongruous in this context, as is Shari Benstock's assertion that 'lesbianism was not a subject immediately related to [H.D.'s] work'.[152] *Paint It Today* depicts the utopian union of spiritual and physical, not shying away from portraying the physical dimension of sexuality.

A refusal to allow woman's sexuality its physical expression is widely shown in women's texts of this time to be debilitating. In Sinclair's *Mary Olivier*, for example, Aunt Charlotte 'goes mad' because she is denied the sexual experiences she longs for, her

---

[149] H.D., 'Hymen', *Poetry*, 15/3 (Dec. 1919): 118, 127, 129.

[150] H.D., *Paint It Today*, 84.

[151] Cheryl Walker, *Masks Outrageous and Austere: Culture, Psyche, and Persona in Modern Women Poets* (Bloomington, Ind.: Indiana University Press, 1991), 138.

[152] Benstock, *Women of the Left Bank*, 175.

repressed desires surfacing as neurotic and eventually psychotic symptoms. Even as a child Mary unconsciously realizes the importance of a physical sexuality, and that it has been denied to Aunt Charlotte: 'That night she dreamed that she saw Aunt Charlotte standing at the foot of the kitchen stairs taking off her clothes and wrapping them in white paper; first, her black lace shawl; then her chemise. She stood up without anything on. Her body was polished and shining like an enormous white china doll.'[153] Mary herself grows up to find physical relationships problematic because of family prohibitions. The text is clear that the inhibitions Mary has inherited are detrimental to her well-being, and that a stifling of physical/sexual creativity will precipitate a stifling of other forms of creativity.

In discussing the intensely personal focus of these texts and the interest in the body and the mind–body duality, what also becomes notable is an apparent conflict between the kinds of supportive community and relationships underlying this public sphere as discussed in the first half of this chapter, and the very self-absorbed texts that actually emerged through these networks. In fact, however, it was the desire to introspect and to explore the psyche that formed the common interest between these writers, their shared concern out of which conversation was able to develop. Instead of looking deeply into the self in isolation, what we find here is a desire to take on board the ideas of others, both the work of other women writers and of the psychoanalysts. In addition, the commonality of interest in, for example, psychoses, sexuality, dream, the unconscious, and other areas, demonstrates that what was taking place was more than a period of purely personal reflection; the new ideas that emerged in the public sphere of modernist women writers at this time, the radical explorations and applications of psychoanalysis in particular, are a result of a community of women coming together out of a shared interest rather than the product of individual thought. Nevertheless, it was only because these writers felt such issues to be of a personal concern, that the level of interest was as high as it was, and the level of exchange and interaction so high. They were not discussing topics of a merely abstract interest, but ones that deeply affected their lives and

---

[153] Sinclair, *Mary Olivier*, 37.

identities, and the disagreements between writers over specific subjects are a reflection of the depth of feeling and the amount of energy invested.

During this period, then, the conversation between these writers developed from a cautious investigation of possible areas of mutual interest to a flourishing arena of dynamic debate. As different contributors brought their own areas of expertise or knowledge into the public sphere, ideas could be generated within the public sphere that drew on many different backgrounds and did not originate with any one individual. The diversity of the base of little magazines that supported this public sphere was particularly beneficial in allowing for a disparate range of opinions to enter the arena, and for allowing discussion to flourish not only within, but also between, the little magazines.

If H.D.'s work of this period is to be understood, it must be against a background of such discussion. Not only was this a productive period in terms of her literary career, but it was also so for many of her contemporaries. Her ideas did not emerge from a process of introspection alone, but from shared analysis of issues that were of interest to a public sphere of women writers involving hundreds of women writers across the Anglo–American divide. H.D.'s work both became an important 'conversational' contribution, and reflected the process of the exchange of ideas in which she was immersed. The most significant developments in her texts seem to have been an increased interest in psychoanalysis within her work and a rigorous analysis of subjectivity and the unconscious, as well as an increased attention to the mind as rooted in physical and sexual body; all these issues were ones that arose in discussion with her contemporaries. In addition, as will become clear in Chapter 5, these were interests that were to underlie much of her powerful writing of later years.

4
Incubation (1925–31)

It is almost just to say that at the present moment there
is no poetry but rather an embarrassing pause after an
arduous and erudite stock-taking.

Laura Riding[1]

By 1925 there was a sense of a pause in the public exchange of
ideas in this public sphere, replaced by a period of more private
reflection and exploration. Though much work of individual
merit was being written in this period, there was a loss of a sense
of collective endeavour and sharing of ideas. For many of the
writers under discussion there was a feeling that it was
insufficient to continue writing in ways that had now become
established, and insufficient to continue probing issues that had
now entered general consciousness. Many of these writers
turned inwards in this period to draw on their own resources
rather than turning to the public sphere to engage in an exchange
of ideas. It is significant that H.D.'s most successful work of this
period, *Her*, remained unpublished for many years; it was part
of her private space of thought and reflection rather than of a
public exchange.

Many of the women writers who had been part of the first
wave of experimentation in *Poetry*, the *Little Review*, and the
Egoist were now either retiring from the public arena, or were
pausing to take stock of their achievements and find new ways
forward. Loy and Moore, for example, were simply not contributing any new ideas to the public sphere;[2] Amy Lowell died
in 1925 and Freytag-Loringhoven in 1927. As yet very few

[1] Laura Riding, 'The New Barbarism, and Gertrude Stein', *transition* 3 (June
1927): 160.
[2] The reasons why Loy stopped writing at this time are unclear; according to
Carolyn Burke, 'By 1925 . . . Mina's own sources of poetic inspiration had run dry.'
Burke, *Becoming Modern*, 338. Marianne Moore was concentrating on her editorship of *The Dial*.

younger writers were part of H.D.'s network, and so there were few new ideas coming into this literary arena. For those outside of this network—notably Woolf, Gertrude Stein, Kay Boyle (not yet part of the network around H.D.), Colette, Edith Wharton, Jean Rhys—this was, of course, a highly productive period. Even within this network, some work of significant interest emerged, such as H.D.'s *Her*; however, what is significant for this study is the temporary loss of a creative network which allowed for innovation out of a meeting of minds rather than individual endeavour. One of the few issues of shared concern was, ironically, the loss of direction that was being suffered by this literary community.

For many of these writers there was a feeling that the world itself had lost direction and no longer had any recognizable landmarks. Dorothy Richardson felt:

Everyman lives in a world grown transparent and uncertain. Behind this experience of the rapidity and unpredictability of change in the detail of his immediate surroundings is a varying measure of vicarious experience of the rapidity and unpredictability of change all over the world, and a dim sense that nobody knows with any certainty of which his world is a part.[3]

In Chicago Monroe expressed very similar sentiments: 'What are we? Where are we? Whither are we going? These questions, by no means new, seem more poignant today, and their answers more uncertain, than for many centuries. All is drift and flux in new immensities, and the little landmarks, the familiar harbors, no longer invite us.'[4] Clearly in the literary arena in general there was no mass uncertainty; however, for those writers whose work has been traced in earlier chapters, who had been caught up in a collective creative energy so powerful that it had created a sense of belonging to a dynamic new community and a sense above all of optimism and vitality, to lose direction and be forced to slow down and take stock seems to have been experienced as a crippling loss.

Part of the problem lay in the loss of the publishing base that had been necessary for this public sphere to exist. The writers concerned had relied on the little magazines to enable their work

[3] Dorothy Richardson, 'Continuous Performance: This Spoon-fed Generation?' *Close Up*, 8/4 (December 1931): 306.
[4] H.M., 'Christmas Again', *Poetry*, 37/3 (Dec. 1930): 151.

to be published, to enable a reviewing of each other's work, to enable discussion through letters and to foster a creative and innovative community with shared concerns; as many of these magazines gradually ceased publication, the life-blood of this network was severely affected. *Contact* stopped publishing in June 1923, *Rhythmus* in June 1924, the *Transatlantic Review* in December 1924, the *Chapbook* in 1925, *The Double Dealer* in May 1926, *The Measure* in June 1926, and *This Quarter* in 1929. The whole basis of this public sphere was disintegrating; there was nowhere for new ideas to be debated, for new writers to join into existing 'conversations' and for existing writers to take on board the ideas of the newcomers.

As a result of such changes H.D.'s relatively wide readership and involvement in a literary community were adversely affected. Unlike her earlier work, the majority of the poems in *Red Roses For Bronze* did not appear previously in little magazines, and as a result these poems reached a far smaller audience.[5] The twenty-seven poems of *Sea Garden* had between them made thirty-seven appearances in print (generally in little magazines) between 1913 and 1916 when *Sea Garden* was published. In contrast, the twenty-three poems of *Red Roses For Bronze* had between them only made nine appearances in print prior to the publication of the collection. Furthermore, the poems in *Red Roses For Bronze* were never to receive the wide audience of *Sea Garden*; between the 1916 publication of *Sea Garden* and 1969, the poems in this collection made a total of 102 further appearances, the majority in little magazines, whereas between the 1931 publication of *Red Roses For Bronze* and 1969, only a single poem—'Let Zeus Record'—was ever republished in any form.[6] Again, between 1913 and 1917 H.D.'s poems appeared in magazines on thirty-nine occasions, compared to just nineteen between 1924 and 1931. Despite H.D.'s established name and greater number of contacts as compared to earlier years, then, her work was actually less widely available.

There was some bemusement about where the 'literary renaissance' had gone. The *Little Review* ended in 1929 not with a

[5] H.D., *Red Roses For Bronze* (London: Chatto & Windus, 1931).
[6] These figures were determined using Jackson R. Bryer and Pamela Roblyer, 'H.D.: A Preliminary Checklist', *Contemporary Literature*, 10/3 (Autumn 1969): 632–75.

sense of a job well done but with the comment in an article by Heap entitled 'Lost: A Renaissance': 'Self-expression is not enough; experiment is not enough; the recording of special moments or cases is not enough. All the arts have broken faith or lost connection with their origin and function. They have ceased to be concerned with the legitimate and permanent material of art.'[7] In *Poetry* Monroe, who had always exuded optimism, now expressed dissatisfaction and some measure of defeat. She was disappointed in the reading public and felt that not enough libraries had subscribed to *Poetry*: 'We thought that the women's clubs would be interested, but now we know that as a stimulus to our circulation they are almost undiscoverable.'[8] Monroe observed that this sense of defeat was shared across the board by literary magazines: 'Editorial writers of the *Nation*, the *Saturday Review* and other papers have been asking each other and the public whether poetry has 'retired' since its brave dash into the lime-light—no, the sunlight—which dazzled us all during the ten or twelve years after 1912.'[9]

Between those magazines that had formed the basis of this public sphere in earlier years, an earlier sense of shared projects was now lost, turned into hostilities and bitterness; even the once broadly supportive relationship between *Poetry* and the *Little Review* was affected. Monroe writes of Anderson's auto-biographical *My Thirty Years' War*: 'it is egocentric to the nth degree . . . this rushing disposition to "hog it all"—rather surprised me, for POETRY antedated The Little Review by a year and a half . . . and was plainly the primary inspiration for Margaret's great magazine idea'.[10] Monroe now felt it necessary to assert *Poetry*'s supremacy rather than its participation in a collective enterprise. The editors of the *Little Review* seem to have felt the same need—Jane Heap wrote a 'wreath': 'TO . . . POETRY, a Magazine of Verse. Sound, sane, safe, and subsidized. More prosaic than poetic'.[11] Kay Boyle, whose work had appeared in *Poetry* in December 1922 when she was little

---

[7] jh, 'Lost: A Renaissance', *The Little Review*, [12] (May 1929): 6.

[8] H.M., 'Another Birthday', *Poetry*, 27/1 (Oct. 1925): 33.

[9] H.M., 'The Procession Moves', *Poetry*, 30/5 (Sept. 1927): 270.

[10] H.M., 'Personality Rampart', review of *My Thirty Years War* by Margaret Anderson, *Poetry*, 37/2 (Nov. 1930): 96.

[11] jh., 'Wreaths', *The Little Review*, [12] (May 1929): 60.

known, now placed Monroe on her 'Unrecommended List'[12] in *This Quarter*, while the editors of *This Quarter* described her as the 'kind of critic that ought to *shut up*'.[13]

In poetry, the *vers libre* form that had in earlier years sparked an excited discussion within this public sphere, was now perceived as static and stagnant, with little more revolutionary value than the sonnet. Yet the same stale debates about *vers libre* carried on in the magazines, with critical discussion apparently locked in a time warp.[14] The mass of Imagist writing being published echoed rather than developed earlier experiments. Dudley Fitts complains of Evelyn Scott's[15] poetry: 'Miss Scott's book is a typical example of the competent, frankly imitative verse, deriving from the symbolists through Imagism, that is characteristic of our more conservative "advanced" periodicals.'[16] It is symptomatic of the deadlock in which writing was caught up that in 1930 another Imagist anthology appeared, thirteen years after its day; the volume had 'no propagandist intentions', was 'not fighting for anything'. The anthology brought out the Imagists again 'not as a challenge' but only 'for parade', imbued with an air of nostalgic reverie for a time now lost.[17] Monroe writes: 'Reading these 1930 poems by those 1913 imagists, I cannot but feel that the War, or something else, has come between them and the muse.'[18]

In 1925 H.D. produced her *Collected Poems*, perhaps an indication that she felt one stage in her life as a writer to be over.[19] Though she continued to write, her poetry of this period lacks

[12] Spanier, *Kay Boyle*, 31.

[13] Anon., '"This Quarter" Gets Reviewed', *This Quarter*, 2 (1925): 305, quoted in Spanier, *Kay Boyle*, 30.

[14] See, for example, [Harriet Monroe], 'News Notes', *Poetry*, 28/1 (Apr. 1926): 58; Eugene Jolas, 'Enter the Imagination', *transition*, 7 (Oct. 1927): 157.

[15] Evelyn Scott (1863–1946) was a poet and novelist living in New York, who published in magazines including *Poetry*, *Chapbook*, *The Little Review* and *Rhythmus*.

[16] Dudley Fitts, 'The Verse of Evelyn Scott', review of *The Winter Alone* by Evelyn Scott, *Poetry*, 36/6 (Sept. 1930): 338.

[17] Glenn Hughes, 'Foreword', *Imagist Anthology 1930* (London: Chatto & Windus, 1930), p. xviii.

[18] H.M., 'Imagism Today and Yesterday', *Poetry*, 36/4 (July 1930): 217.

[19] Gary Burnett in *H.D. between Image and Epic: The Mysteries of Her Poetics* (Ann Arbor: UMI Research Press, 1990), 91 makes the point that producing her *Collected Poems* might be interpreted by others as H.D. having completed her most productive years.

a clear sense of development or energy, and failed to inspire critics. In her collection *Red Roses For Bronze* it is evident that she is seeking new directions, that she is trying to break from the Imagist pattern, and yet the results are thin. 'In the Rain' is typical of this collection, spread over ten pages, lacking the tightness of earlier work and with an insistent and somewhat forced rhyme:

> a snare is Love,
> a shame,
> who are maimed with Love,
> totter and falter and stare,
> lost in a world
> defamed . . . [20]

Monroe comments accurately on this poem that: 'H.D. meanders along with In the Rain in most unimagistic fashion.'[21] Her work of this period does seem to be struggling to shake off the Imagist label without having achieved any new sense of purpose. Eda Lou Walton notes, accurately, of H.D.'s recent writing: 'The poems incline to be vague; the emotions are overstressed; the imagery lacks variety.'[22]

The poems in *Red Roses For Bronze* certainly have a hesitancy and uncertainty that neither her earlier nor her later work has. They are spaces of exploration and gestation rather than definite expression. While such experiments had pay-off for her in some of her later work, and in her novel *Her*, this is a difficult and not entirely satisfying collection for the reader, who needs to see it as a working notebook rather than a polished collection. In a sense these poems granted H.D. a freedom to think again about the possibilities of language, distancing herself from the 'image' and exploring ways of conveying human experience in all its meandering, overlapping and at times frustratingly circular nature. In place of perfect image, the classical sculpture, she wanted to try to conjure up a living experience, the 'red rose' rather than the bronze. Throughout *Red Roses For Bronze* H.D. experiments with repetition and the non-linear. At times the effect of this on the reader is exasperation, as her work can feel

---

[20] H.D., 'In the Rain', *Red Roses For Bronze*, 17.
[21] H.M., 'Imagism Today and Yesterday', 217.
[22] Eda Lou Walton, 'The Poetic Method of H.D.', *The Nation*, 134 (Mar. 2, 1932): 264.

unduly repetitive and monotonous. For example, she makes use of the exclamation 'O', such as 'O strange, dark Morpheus',[23] on sixty-two separate occasions. There is, however, a clear sense of H.D.'s endeavour to take her writing to a new level and express human consciousness in a new way. For H.D. there was a fascination with the layering of text and the repetition of elements as a musician repeats musical notes and phrases, to produce a cumulative effect that requires hard work and perseverance on the part of the reader. H.D. certainly did not see this work as in any sense finished, rather she found it frustrating, writing to Brigit Patmore that she felt 'disgust' with her latest writing.[24] Nevertheless, when placed in the context of her life's work this period must be seen as granting a fascinating insight into how H.D. spanned the gulf between the Imagist poetry of her early years and the more narrative, extended, and exploratory poems of the 1930s.

Several studies of H.D.'s work of this period note a decline in intensity and a lack of final and polished expression, attributing this largely to difficulties in H.D.'s personal life.[25] Certainly H.D.'s personal life was difficult at this time, including an abortion in 1928 and her divorce from Aldington. However, comparable difficulties in earlier years, such as her stillbirth in 1915, her breakdown in 1918, and the loss of her brother in the war, did not trigger the 'artistic paralysis' that critics such as Donna Krolik Hollenberg ascribe to H.D.'s personal struggles.[26] In any case, H.D. was far from alone in such a faltering in her public expression. Surveying American poetry as a whole Monroe observed: 'One finds little of that stern compression which has been our discipline during most of the present century'.[27] Laura Riding noted the lack of new experiment and energy in poetry: 'It is almost just to say that at the present moment there is no poetry but rather an embarrassing pause

[23] H.D., 'Choros Sequence from *Morpheus*', *Red Roses For Bronze*, 66.

[24] See Brigit Patmore to H.D., Sept. 10, 1925, Beinecke, where Patmore makes a reference to this.

[25] See, for example, Susan Stanford Friedman, *Penelope's Web: Gender, Modernity, H.D.'s Fiction* (Cambridge, UK: Cambridge University Press, 1990), 218; Dianne Chisholm, *H.D.'s Freudian Poetics* (Ithaca: Cornell University Press, 1992), 68.

[26] Donna Krolik Hollenberg, *H.D.: The Poetics of Childbirth and Creativity* (Boston: Northeastern University Press, 1991), 97.

[27] H.M., 'Pan-American Concord', *Poetry*, 26/3 (June 1925): 155.

after an arduous and erudite stock-taking.'[28] In fact, beneath the surface where this was indeed true, this pause seems in retrospect to have been highly productive, allowing writers to move away from tired currents of thought and allow new developments in politics, in media, and in psychoanalysis to impact on their work.

In women's prose writing too there was some measure of uncertainty about public expression. H.D.'s *Palimpsest*, while probably her most successful work of this period, demonstrates a hesitancy, and Alyse Gregory[29] writes of it: 'In the matter of rhetoric one suspects that inattention betrays almost always a lack of intensity, and one feels that although H.D. has emotional power and authentic inspiration, her passion, when it does lapse, becomes by turns turgid, arid, or irritatingly mannered.'[30] Partly, of course, this can be explained by *Palimpsest*'s subject matter, the constricting and stagnant lives of the three female protagonists. In addition, here as elsewhere H.D. was captivated by the effects of repetition, and deliberately used this to produce the layers of the palimpsest. Whereas H.D. had earlier 'underused' language in her absolutely sparse Imagistic verse, now she was experimenting with overstatement and almost excessive descriptive language. In the first section, 'Hipparchia', set in Ancient Rome, the description of Hipparchia's return to her former lover, with his letter pleading for her return under her clothes, is typical in its overstatement: 'The letter-script burned like a Tyrian flower, the dark heart of a Tyrian wind-flower, (no crystal and ice petal but authentic blossom) blood and heart-beat and black heart of disaster, battle and the wavering line of chariots, life, life the invincible.'[31] H.D. herself lacked confidence in *Palimpsest*, writing to Harold Collins: 'I don't think for one moment that you will like it. . . . I am tempted always to be sterile, to stand off and stop writing.'[32] Yet she did not stop, and the experiments she undertook in *Palimpsest* would come to fruition in later work such as *Kora and Ka* and *Nights*. Though

---

[28] Riding, 'New Barbarism', 160.

[29] Alyse Gregory, 1884–1967, was a critic and novelist particularly interested in women's issues and exploration of the psyche.

[30] Alyse Gregory, 'A Poet's Novel', review of *Palimpsest* by H.D., *The Dial*, 82/5 (May 1927): 418.

[31] H.D., *Palimpsest* (Paris: Contact Editions, 1926), 80.

[32] H.D. to Harold Collins, Mar. 4, [1925], Beinecke.

Palimpsest seems to have had minimal impact in terms of H.D.'s engagement in the public sphere, forming instead a much more private space for working through ideas, for today's reader *Palimpsest* forms a fascinating insight into H.D.'s development as a writer. As Susan Friedman writes, this is 'essentially the story of H.D.'s exile and search for healing in the 1920s'.[33] It typifies H.D.'s work of this period in its much more private nature, its engagement with issues that affected her on a personal level rather than emerging from discussion in a more public arena.

In the same way, in H.D.'s novel *Her*, which remained unpublished in this period, there is a stretching of language and use of repetition rather than concision. Critics were in general hostile to H.D.'s prose writing of this period, as they were to her poetry, again largely on the grounds of its circularity and over intensity. An anonymous reviewer for the *Spectator* writes of *Hedylus*,[34] for example: 'the colours and shapes are so closely confounded that one gets the impression of splintered mosaic'.[35] Again, an anonymous reviewer in the *Dial* writes of a sense of 'adjectives and italics and "manner," which one cannot think of as characteristic of H.D.'[36] What is important in *Her* is that it is through creating patterns and through examining stagnancy and repetition that Her seeks new direction. Though she cannot find absolute release within the novel, she does find an alternative to linearity in a layering of meaning on meaning that allows her to excavate down the layers and find new ways of thinking. Susan Stanford Friedman points out: 'Hermione's feet are a mute form of speech as they act out the repetitive, rhythmic, visual discourse of her consciousness, in which, to use Kristeva's terminology, the Semiotic register overwhelms the Symbolic modality of language.'[37] *Her* is a novel of pre-communication, of an excavation of meanings that precedes the ordered Symbolic, a private laboratory space for H.D. to play with alternative methods of representation that defy linear narrative. Donna Krolik Hollenberg writes:

[33] Friedman, *Penelope's Web*, 239.
[34] H.D., *Hedylus* (Oxford: Basil Blackwell, 1928).
[35] Anon., 'HEDYLUS. By H.D.', *The Spectator*, 5, 254 (Mar. 9, 1929): 396–7.
[36] Anon., review of *Hedylus* by H.D., *The Dial*, 86/3 (Mar. 1929): 264.
[37] Friedman, *Penelope's Web*, 112. For a detailed analysis of *Her*, this is an excellent place to start.

Hermione's gestation of an autonomous self is successful in the end . . .
In a finale that bridges the psychic chasm between procreativity and
creativity, her breakdown becomes a breakthrough. Approximately
nine months after the novel's beginning, she traces a fresh path across
the virginal snow in the neighboring Farrand forest, 'sure of finding
something growing'.[38]

This statement sums up far more than *Her*'s search; it is indicative of the state of the writing in this public sphere in this period
that though nothing definite yet emerges there is a planting of
seeds and a sureness that something will grow out of apparent
sterility.

Richardson was also finding that *Pilgrimage* had become a site
of troubled exploration. At times this frustrated her. She wrote
to Bryher of poor sales of the *Oberland* section: 'I can no longer
count my books as any sort of asset. Now that there are so many
young people on the same tack it doesn't really matter.'[39] She felt
that the public had stopped believing in the project of *Pilgrimage*
and though the project continued much as before it was without
the feeling of a crusade or certainty of new ground, and without
a feeling of a reading public alongside her. In her writing she felt
that there was a thinness that had not been there before, that it
lacked depth and continuity: 'The lay-out is too awful &
the book fills me with despair by reason of its "thinness" and
brevity; the shadow of a book it is, the result of momentum of the
unconscious, got going a thousand times in these four years, & a
thousand times broken off with devastating results to both
author & work.'[40] What is significant here is less any real collapse of the *Pilgrimage* project than Richardson's feelings about
it, her lack of belief in her own sense of direction and purpose.

Sinclair's work seems to have suffered a more profound loss of
direction, her work of this period comparing very poorly to
earlier writing; without the precise direction of *Mary Olivier* her
novel *Far End* (1926) flounders in stereotypes, and is sickly
sweet, and highly predictable. At the start of the novel two
couples, one married (Hilda and Christopher), one shortly to be

[38] Hollenberg, *Poetics*, 50, quoting H.D., *HERmione* (New York: New
Directions, 1972), 225.
[39] Dorothy Richardson to Bryher, [Spring 1929], in *Windows on Modernism*, ed.
Fromm, 167.
[40] Dorothy Richardson to Bryher, Sept. 1931, in ibid. 219.

married (Cecily and Maurice), share a time of blissful happiness together in the years immediately preceding the First World War. The characters are cardboard cut-outs, the narratorial voice gushes with sentimentality: 'And Hilda and Christopher were happy. They were happier because Cecily was there. Her happiness reflected theirs and gave it back to them doubled. And, because she loved them she set them in a happy light and kept them there, and they saw themselves and each other as they were in Cecily's eyes, beautiful.'[41] It is hard to believe that such sentiment, particularly coming from Sinclair, is not ironical. The plot line is just as weak; Maurice predicts that something 'unpleasant' will happen to spoil the peace, and predictably it does. He goes missing in the war and Cecily, remaining at home, thinks she hears him calling to her; she runs out, followed by Christopher and Hilda: 'They found a white heap flung across the threshold where Cecily had fallen dead. She lay on her side, with her arms stretched out in front of her, as if she had held them so for an embrace before she fell.'[42] Sinclair's work of this period shows none of the sophisticated psychoanalytic understanding of *Mary Olivier*, descending instead into mediocre and sentimental generalizations and banal conventions. Nevertheless, it does represent a refusal by Sinclair to let her earlier work become a template for her later work, and an endeavour to constantly reinvent the process of writing. She had not found a formula with which to work, but was seeking out new ways of representing the human experience.

For both British and American women, this period also posed specific difficulties concerning the feminist ethos behind much of the work of earlier years. By 1925 women writers found themselves in the position of being an older generation of feminists, whose collective identity was under threat by a younger generation whose values were very different and who to a large extent took past feminist gains for granted. In H.D.'s 'Murex' Raymonde feels herself to be one of this older generation, and feels derision for the standardization she perceives in a new wave of women, yet she also wishes to hand over responsibility for literary experimentation to this younger generation: 'I don't want to think in metres. I'm tired of being a sort of lightning-rod

---

[41] May Sinclair, *Far End* (London: Hutchinson [1926]), 40.
[42] Ibid. 86.

for all the metres. Let someone with Joan of Arc hair, let Martin be a lightning rod—'.[43] Raymonde is aware of being part of an older group of women who have lost direction and certainty, as opposed to a younger generation who have a certainty that appears to her to be superficial. For the older generation there was a significant period of women's speech in the public sphere behind them, paradoxically now undermining the protest at women's 'silencing' that had generated powerful writing, both literary and critical, in earlier years. Issues that had given women's writing its identity, such as its challenge to sentimentality, its broadly feminist outlook, its attack on taboos about expressions of women's sexuality, were now to some extent passé within this public sphere, because already brought to the attention of the literary public. Of course there were crusades left to fight, both within and outside of this public sphere; the trial of the 'obscenity' of Radclyffe Hall's 1928 *The Well of Loneliness*[44] proved, for example, that lesbianism, openly expressed, was still unacceptable; however the great tide of protest in women's writing had now largely been appeased. Though this was 'success', it was accompanied by feelings of anti-climax and a fragmentation of interests.

There was some awareness that the kinds of feminist protest being presented in the period were outmoded, but no obvious new direction.[45] Dora Russell's (1894–1986) feminist text *Hypatia: or, Woman and Knowledge* was reviewed as: '[a] violent flogging of dead horses. Most of the information she imparts is stale; most of the reforms for which she agitates are already accomplished facts, and most of her assumptions about the moral and ethical habits of her fellow-beings are gratuitous to the verge of impertinence'.[46] For the younger generation Laura Riding (1901–91) correctly observed: 'For the most part the feminist still has the mentality of the recipient in sex demanding

---

[43] H.D., *Palimpsest*, 206.

[44] Radclyffe Hall, *The Well of Loneliness* (London: Jonathan Cape, 1928; London: Virago, 1982).

[45] Several texts by writers of the older generation tended to retreat to a reiteration of outworn polemical rhetoric. Bryher's *Civilians*, for example, draws on unconvincing stereotypes of brutal behaviour by men and women who are victims of an androcentric society. Bryher, *Civilians* (Territet: Pool, 1927).

[46] Anon., review of *Hypatia: or, Woman and Knowledge* by Dora Russell, *The Adelphi*, 3/2 (July 1925): 151.

compensation for the indignity of her position'.[47] Riding was part of a post-war generation of women who had not had to fight for the vote and who had found opportunities of work and education far more open to them, and as such she objected to the attitude of earlier feminists, including feminist poets and novelists, that the 'war' must be fought as strenuously as it always had been. For the older generation, Rebecca West (1892–1983) writes: 'I am an old-fashioned feminist. I believe in the sex war. . . .When those of our army whose voices are inclined to coo tell us that the day of sex-antagonism is over and that henceforth we have only to advance hand in hand with the male I do not believe it.'[48] The older generation needed to find ways of taking on board the energy and optimism of a younger generation without losing sight of all that had been gained and without abandoning fundamental values.

There were two magazines that provided clues to the new ways forward and provided sites of relief from the generally troubled state of the women's literary arena. Firstly, the film magazine *Close Up*, funded by Bryher and edited by Kenneth Macpherson, and secondly Eugene Jolas's Paris-based experimental little magazine *transition*. Together these were perhaps the only little magazines in this period able to foster the conditions necessary for new developments in the 1930s.[49] In *Close Up* the world of cinema sparked the kinds of animated discussion that had been lost around the literary text. H.D. writes of cinema: 'There is one beauty, it is the beauty of belief, of faith, of hope. And if that beauty is allied to sheer grit and technical efficiency, you get a new sort of art creation.'[50] *Close Up* allowed these writers—H.D., Richardson, Bryher, and others—to continue to find new ways to express a disaffection with the sentimental and hackneyed and to seek out radical new forms.[51]

In *Close Up* specialists and non-specialists in film—poets,

[47] Laura Riding, 'The Damsel Thing', *Anarchism is not Enough* (London: Jonathan Cape, 1928), 192.

[48] Rebecca West, quoted in Martin Pugh, *Women and the Women's Movement in Britain 1914–1959* (Basingstoke: Macmillan, 1992), 72.

[49] *transition* only had a small circulation of around one thousand. See Hoffman et al, *The Little Magazine*, 175.

[50] H.D., 'Borderline', page proofs with corrections by H.D., 1930, 15, Beinecke.

[51] Male contributors involved included Oswald Blakeston, Robert Herring, and the Soviet film director Sergei Mikhailovich Eisenstein.

prose writers, psychoanalysts, educationalists—came together around an issue of mutual concern in a way paradigmatic of the ideal public sphere. Moore described the project: 'To burst into feeling so to speak, and praise an art through a medium other than its own, without having mastered the terms of the auxiliary art is surely an experiment; but zeal, liberty, and beauty are allied phenomena'.[52] *Close Up* was open to all new ideas, not affiliated to any 'group'; Macpherson writes: 'It did not take long to prove that Close Up found "isms" as old-fashioned, dull and pompous as any progressive body must do'.[53] The discussion within its pages therefore had about it a refreshing sense of new territory covered, and allowed poets and novelists to find an open and inviting space for new thought not present in the literary sphere. As Havelock Ellis expressed it: 'It is only by experimentation and discussion in this way that progress is possible.'[54] H.D. felt that 'The cinema has become to us what the church was to our ancestors . . . we were redeemed by light literally.'[55] Similarly, Richardson writes: 'Never before was [there] such all-embracing hospitality save in an ever-open church';[56] she envisaged a more united world community as a result:

. . . must we not, to-day, emerge from our small individual existences and from narcissistic contemplation thereof? Learn that we are infinitesimal parts of a vast whole? Labour and collaborate to find salvation for a world now paying the prices of various kinds of self-seeking? And, for the re-education of humanity, is any single instrument more powerful than the film . . . ?[57]

Interestingly then, the world of the cinema, an instrument of popular or 'mass' culture, opened up, for a brief period in its earliest years, genuine open and creative discussion. In his account of the invasion of 'popular' culture since the middle of the nineteenth century, Habermas and others cite the role of the mass media, particularly television and cinema, as negative, as

[52] [Marianne Moore], 'Comment', *The Dial*, 83 (Nov. 1927): 449–50.

[53] Kenneth Macpherson, 'As Is', *Close Up*, 3/1 (July 1928): 7.

[54] Havelock Ellis, letter to the Editor, *Close Up*, 2/2 (Feb. 1928): 75.

[55] H.D., 'The Cinema and the Classics III: The Mask and the Movietone', *Close Up*, 1/5 (Nov. 1927): 23.

[56] Dorothy Richardson, 'Continuous Performance VI: The Increasing Congregation', *Close Up*, 1/6 (Dec. 1927): 64.

[57] Dorothy Richardson, 'Continuous Performance: Narcissus', *Close Up*, 8/3 (Sept. 1931): 183.

encouraging passive reception rather than critical discussion: 'The deprivatized province of interiority was hollowed out by the mass media; a pseudo-public sphere of a no longer literary public was patched together to create a sort of superfamilial zone of familiarity.'[58] In fact, in this period clearly the reverse was true; for these women writers debate around literary texts, as well as the texts themselves, had become a source of sterility and repetition, while the world of cinema opened up a creative forum of experimentation and critical discussion. A meeting of minds around issues of shared concern was able to take place, generating new ideas and spreading interest to many more people; *Close Up* was, then, a space almost paradigmatic of the way in which the ideal public sphere would operate.

H.D.'s interest in cinema seems not only to have formed an outlet for her creative energy, but also to have sustained her on a personal level during this difficult period:

Just at the moment I am involved with pictures. We have almost finished a slight lyrical four reel little drama, done in and about the villages here some of the village people and English friends [*sic*]. The work has been enchanting, never anything such fun and I myself have learned to use the small projector. . . . All the light within light fascinates me, 'satisfies' me, I feel like a cat playing with webs and webs of silver.[59]

The two poems where H.D. deals with cinema have a freshness and sense of clear vision that was otherwise lacking in her poetry; 'Projector II (*Chang*)' describes the experience of the film *Chang* as it takes the audience into the jungle:

> our spirits walk elsewhere
> with shadow-folk
> and ghost-beast,
> we speak a shadow-speech,
> we tread a shadow rock,
>
> . . . . .

---

[58] Habermas, *Structural Transformation*, 162; see also George Anastalpo, 'Education, Television, and Political Discourse in America', *Center Magazine* (July–Aug., 1986): 21, cited in Schudson, 'Was There Ever a Public Sphere? If So, When?: Reflections on the American Case', in *Habermas and the Public Sphere*, ed. Calhoun, 143.

[59] H.D. response to 'Confessions Questionnaire', *The Little Review* [12] (May 1929): 38–9.

with wondrous creatures leap
from tree to tree . . . [60]

Chang was revolutionary in its cinematic techniques, using an 'enlarged screen, which suddenly flashes on three times larger than the normal size, and . . . the use of Vitaphonic record of animal noises' in a story of Northern Siam.[61] The film used a defamiliarization technique combined with documentary realism in a new way. In this respect it points forward to works such as H.D.'s *Trilogy*, which uses juxtapositions of defamiliarized everyday objects and the mystical and spiritual, fusing straight description of the everyday civilian war world with exotic or obscure images.

Cinema also kept alive the possibilities of psychoanalysis that had become dormant in the literary text, partly through the closeness of many films of this time to dream sequences and fantasy, partly too through a deliberate exploitation of psychoanalytic symbolism as a short-hand for conveying feelings and emotions. Hanns Sachs (Freudian analyst, friend of G. W. Pabst) expressed the view of many of those involved in *Close Up*: 'The plot, whether of a novel, play or film, consists of closely interwoven psychological coherencies. The film can be effective only in so far as it is able to make these psychological coherencies visible; in so far as it can externalise and make perceptible—if possible in movement—invisible inward events.'[62] Within *Close Up* film and psychoanalysis were not separated, they were considered part of the same sphere of debate, and *Close Up* included articles and comment by Barbara Low (English Freudian), Havelock Ellis, and Hanns Sachs. In addition, many of the films under discussion were attempts to portray internal and unconscious processes. In 1930 H.D. starred in, and was involved in the production of, Macpherson's experimental psychoanalytic film *Borderline*; she writes of it: 'Borderline is a dream and perhaps when we say that we have said everything.'[63] *Borderline* was described by Macpherson as '*transferential*', its aim being:

[60] H.D., 'Projector II (*Chang*)' *Close Up*, 1/4 (Oct. 1927): 36–47; see also 'Projector' in *Close Up*, 1/1 (July 1927): 46–51.

[61] Anon., 'Films of the Month', review of *Chang*, *Close Up*, 1/4 (Oct. 1927): 83. According to this article the film was 'taken by' Ernest B. Shoedsack and Merian C. Cooper.

[62] Hanns Sachs, 'Film Psychology', *Close Up*, 3/5 (Nov. 1928): 8.

[63] H.D., 'Borderline', 31.

'To take the action, the observation, the deduction, the reference, into the labyrinth of the human mind, with its queer impulses and tricks, its unreliability, its stresses and obsessions, its half-formed deductions, its glibness, its occasional amnesia, its fantasy, suppressions and desires.'[64] There was a sense of film as a site of the exploration of suppressed impulses, allowing both for the creation of images with multiple resonances, and for a Surrealist juxtaposition of disparate images, neither of which were yet being fully achieved in the literary text.

The film generating most discussion in this connection was G. W. Pabst's *Joyless Street* (*Die freudlose Gasse*). Bryher knew Pabst through her psychoanalyst Hanns Sachs, and Sachs was involved in the production of the film.[65] It was set in post-war Vienna, portraying social problems and high inflation, and was censored in many countries due to its portrayal of women forced into prostitution by social deprivation. The film was aimed primarily at a female audience,[66] and told the story of two women, one nearly forced into prostitution, the other a prostitute who is driven to commit murder. The film portrays the women not only as victims but also as aggressors; Patrice Petro notes: 'While the censors fail to mention that Maria and her friend act as much out of anger as they do out of love, the specific amendments they make to the film suggest that the representation of this anger lurked behind their concerns with female spectators "over-identifying" with the film.'[67] *Joyless Street* was not only of particular interest to these women writers due to its focus on female subjectivity and its target audience of women, but also because of its use of psychoanalytic material; Bryher describes the film: 'There was one film that we felt expressed our generation. It was *Die freudlose Gasse* (*Joyless Street*) directed by G. W. Pabst and starring Greta Garbo for the second time in her career. It seemed to us the first picture to use contemporary material with a sense of intelligence and art.'[68] The 'contemporary material' was the most up-to-date psychoanalytic knowledge. Bryher writes: 'It is

[64] Kenneth Macpherson, 'As Is', *Close Up*, 7/5 (Nov. 1930): 296, 294.

[65] Guest, *Herself Defined*, 193.

[66] See Patrice Petro, 'Film Censorship and the Female Spectator: *Joyless Street* (1925)', in *The Films of G. W. Pabst: An Extraterritorial Cinema*, ed. Eric Rentschler (New Brunswick: Rutgers University Press, 1990), 31.

[67] Petro, 'Film Censorship', 39.

[68] Bryher, *The Heart to Artemis*, 252.

the thought and the feeling that line gesture that interest Mr Pabst. And he has what few have, a consciousness of Europe. He sees psychologically and because of this, because in a flash he knows the sub-conscious impulse or hunger that prompted an apparently trivial action, his intense realism becomes through its truth, poetry.'[69] H.D. felt that *Joyless Street* expressed more fully than any other film the depths of an internal reality, a 'meaning that applies to everybody';[70] she was upset that few people wanted to see it—'People won't, they dare not face reality';[71] it confronted, Bryher writes, 'what all if they could, would willingly forget'.[72]

In theory then, cinema made psychoanalytic thought available to people who would be unlikely to read Freud or attend lectures, and part of the excitement of film was this opening up of new understandings to a wider community. However, in practice, *Joyless Street* was unlikely to be seen by the wider public, who in general were exposed to, and enticed by, more 'popular' films from Hollywood. There was heated debate by these women as to whether these more popular films were beneficial to the wider public in exposing them to new influences, or detrimental in encouraging passive reception. Barbara Low saw popular films as psychologically dangerous, because, in contrast to other art forms, they replaced personal responsibility in an engaged creative process with pre-packaged answers; she rejected such cinema because of its 'overpowering appeal to the eye and corresponding small demand upon intellectual processes: its arbitrary, and therefore false, simplification: its confusion of values'. She continues:

. . . the Film's simplifications and problem solving creates the fantasy that the spectator's wishes are or can be, fulfilled, and this helps to maintain his omnipotence and narcissism. . . . That is to say a return to the pleasure-seeking infancy with its magically fulfilled desires, since it is always easier for the Ego to retread known paths which have already yielded pleasure than to go forward on paths yet untried and calling for effort.[73]

[69] Bryher, 'G. W. Pabst: A Survey', *Close Up*, 1/6 (Dec. 1927): 60.

[70] H.D., 'Expiation', *Close Up*, 2/5 (May 1928): 43.

[71] H.D., 'The Cinema and the Classics I: Beauty', *Close Up*, 1/1 (July 1927): 32.

[72] Bryher, 'G. W. Pabst: A Survey', 61.

[73] Barbara Low, 'Mind-Growth or Mind-Mechanization?: The Cinema in Education', *Close Up*, 1/3 (Sept. 1927): 47, 49.

Bryher, Monroe, and H.D. also took this view; Bryher writes that Hollywood produces 'tinned ideas'[74] and that 'the public have surrended [*sic*] logical processes, to them the performance is not pleasure, but dope; they do not reason . . .'.[75] Monroe saw the popularity of mass films as a possible threat to literature: 'Perhaps our own age—this age of a million printing-presses, is yet more bookless than we realize. The great majority, the men and women who do the work of the world and whose votes carry our elections—how many of them ever open a book? Or if by chance they do, how many of the so-called books they open add anything to their store of wisdom and beauty?' She speculates on the possibility in the future of people possessing their own 'cinema' in their homes: 'We may be approaching another bookless age, when art will have to present life in action rather than in print to an audience watching and listening-in from far-away invisible living-rooms.'[76] H.D.'s response to the potentially negative impact of mass film was unambiguous: 'To the people, films stand in many, many instances for poison, for dope in its most pernicious essence, for aphrodisiacs that stupefy and drain the senses and cripple the desires.'[77]

Such a view is very much in line with the kind of anxiety Habermas expresses about the mass media of the twentieth-century: 'Indeed, mass culture has earned its rather dubious name precisely by achieving increased sales by adapting to the need for relaxation and entertainment on the part of consumer strata with relatively little education, rather than through the guidance of an enlarged public toward the appreciation of a culture undamaged in its substance.' He continues:

Under the pressure of the 'Don't talk back!' the conduct of the public assumes a different form. In comparison with printed communications the programs sent by the new media curtail the reactions of their recipients in a peculiar way. They draw the eyes and ears of the public under their spell but at the same time, by taking away its distance, place it under 'tutelage', which is to say they deprive it of the opportunity to say something and to disagree.[78]

---

[74] Bryher, 'The Hollywood Code', *Close Up*, 8/3 (Sept. 1931): 238.
[75] Bryher, 'Dope or Stimulus', *Close Up*, 3/3: 59–60.
[76] H.M., 'Books and Tomorrow', *Poetry*, 32/1 (Apr. 1928): 35, 36.
[77] H.D., 'Russian Films', *Close Up*, 3/3 (Sept. 1928): 21.
[78] Habermas, *Structural Transformation*, 165, 170–1.

The mass media, according to Habermas, undermine the basis of the public sphere by encouraging passive reception, by lowering the level of education and intelligence needed to participate, by removing the amount of choice of material available (only a few films can be offered, as opposed to vast numbers of books), and by failing to encourage discussion or critical interrogation. Many people expressed these kinds of views at this time, including F. R. Leavis who writes that films 'involve surrender, under conditions of hypnotic receptivity, to the cheapest emotional appeals'.[79]

Within the public sphere of modernist women writers, discussion ranged over how to expose the 'masses' to more experimental film, how to encourage discussion about film, how to stop the degeneration of film as a whole into a 'mass' medium, and whether or not 'mass' film could be seen as in any way generative of new thought. In part, of course, the fear of 'mass' film expressed by these writers was yet another manifestation of the general attitude of superiority expressed by writers/intellectuals towards the 'masses', a manifestation of the desire to create or preserve an 'intellectual aristocracy' by keeping cinema as a pure and uncontaminated space. However, as in the early years of this literary public sphere, these anxieties were very much rooted in a desire to protect genuine thought and exploration from a levelling out of ideas to a lowest common denominator, to prevent a replacement of experimentalism with formulaic thought. To a large extent they foresaw what would, in fact, happen: the domination of the cinema by a small number of powerful film companies whose sole motivation would be profit.

Not all women writers opposed the more popular film culture. Several argued that 'mass' cinema and more experimental cinema could exist side by side, as popular literature did with 'serious' literature; Marion Fitz-Simonds made this point in *Close Up*:

Your correspondent [J. A. Hardy] states that a form of entertainment which appeals to the taste of the masses can never become an art. If I may say so prejudice alone can have induced such a remark, certainly not logic. Don't the 'masses' like cheap paintings, cheap illustrations in magazines and books, cheap music, cheap music hall turns, yet

---

[79] F. R. Leavis, *Mass Civilisation and Minority Culture* (Cambridge, UK: The Minority Press, 1930), 10.

does this in any way mean that there cannot be good paintings, good illustrations, good music, good plays?[80]

H.D. made the same point, that 'Because certain inferior bottles have held aphrodisiacs and raw spirits, and even more pernicious dopes, are all the flasks, and jars and bottles in the world to be damned and smashed equally?'[81] This defence rests on an idea that two types of film might exist, the one suitable for 'serious' thought, the other aimed at the 'masses', and that the one did not preclude the other. Popular films were also defended from another angle, that it was desirable for cinema to reach the greatest number of people in order to have the widest beneficial effect. Richardson took this point of view, persuasively and repeatedly protesting against the view that film should be kept for a small group of connoisseurs:

Cut out the good films . . . Leave only the average story-film, sensational or otherwise, the News Reel and the comic strip. Judge, condemn, all these, right and left. Is it possible to deny, even of this irreducible minimum of value, that it supplies to the bookless, thoughtless multitude the majority of whom do not make even that amount of unconscious contact with aesthetic and moral beauty that it is implied [sic] in going to church, a civilising influence more potent and direct than any other form of entertainment available in their leisure hours, and sufficiently attractive to draw them in large numbers?[82]

In part she was advocating a somewhat dangerous colonialism, a 'conversion' of the 'masses' to 'civilising influences'. However, behind her words there was also a more altruistic idea that by presenting the 'masses' with unfamiliar situations and ideas, however stereotyped these might be, film would necessarily enhance the restricted lives of great numbers of people.

In addition to the creative space opened up by *Close Up* around issues of film, one other little magazine, Eugene Jolas's *transition*, demonstrated success in facilitating a development of new ideas in the literary arena as a whole, including for the beleaguered community of women writers. The work that appeared in *transition* was not always successful, but was important in establishing a climate of experimentation that could carry the literary arena forwards in new directions in the

[80] Marion Fitz-Simonds, letter to the editor, *Close Up*, 1/4 (Oct. 1927): 80.
[81] H.D., 'Russian Films', 21.
[82] Richardson, 'Continuous Performance: This Spoon-fed Generation?' 307.

1930s. *transition* was a genuine attempt at the kind of public space that had characterized the *Little Review*, and readers and editors frequently engaged in creative discussion. Jolas and Elliot Paul write:

By making *transition* a meeting-place for the most independent men and women of vision, we have brought continuous news from the regions in which the pioneers of many countries go forward. We have furnished a haven for prude-ridden portrayers of life. We have made possible glimpses into a universe where the 'hallucination of the word' expresses life transmuted into forms of magic wonder.

They felt that 'Standardization produces . . . symmetrical monstrosities' and they therefore concentrated on experimentation for its own sake.[83] *transition* was a space that could enable a transition from older 'high modernist' experimentation towards an incorporation of new currents of thought from philosophy, psychology, and political and social theory. As Bernard Smith observed of the literary arena in general: 'On the surface nothing is happening yet . . . And yet, underneath the surface slime there is bedrock.'[84] Unlike the *Little Review*'s closing editorial, Jolas was able to end *transition* in 1930 with optimism about the future: 'The transitional period of literature appears to be drawing to a close. But our experimental action, I feel sure, will constitute an impulsion, and a basis on which to construct for some time to come.'[85]

transition was very welcoming to Surrealists, though it did not believe Surrealism as such to be the way forward; Jolas, Elliot Paul, and Robert Sage write:

We believe with them that the artist's imagination should be placed above everything else in importance, but we do not hold with them that writing should be exclusively of the interior. In plain and direct words, for the edification of Mr. Lewis we believe in a new romanticism, more volatile than that of the past, which achieves a magic by combining the interior and the exterior, the subjective and the objective, the imaginary and the apparently real.[86]

Such a welding of the external and internal in new ways and with

[83] Eugene Jolas and Elliot Paul, 'A Review', *transition*, 12 (Mar. 1928): 140, 143.
[84] Bernard Smith, 'American Letter', *transition*, 13 (Summer 1928), 246.
[85] Eugene Jolas, 'Announcement', *transition*, 19–20 (June 1930): 369.
[86] Eugene Jolas, Elliot Paul, and Robert Sage, 'First Aid to the Enemy', *transition*, 9 (Dec. 1927): 175.

a deepened awareness of the unconscious was to be central in a new wave of literary projects of the 1930s, and most strikingly in women's writing. Jolas emphasized the importance of dream in fusing the external world with a subjective experience of it: 'For in the dream and the half-dream we find enormous and fantastic affinities which to the rational analysis seem absurd. But they have the magic of transmuting the mediocre values of the real world and of opening up territories which are revelations to the voyager.'[87] In women's writing from the 1930s onwards such use of dream landscapes is central, a shifting, unstable, semi-surreal landscape where psychic disturbance finds objective correlative and where objective disturbance finds psychic correlative.

In exploring dream and the unconscious in relation to the literary text, *transition* published Jung's thoughts about the 'visionary' work of art which arises 'out of timeless depths, a glittering, demonic-grotesque thing, bursting human values and beautiful form, a ghastly-ridiculous skein of the eternal chaos'.[88] Unlike Freud, Jung attached great importance to the work of the artist, crediting him or her with an unusual depth of vision. Jung denied the Freudian purely personal neurotic motivation behind a work of art, believing that the true work of art 'rises far above the personal and speaks out of the heart and mind and for the heart and mind of humanity'. He writes: 'But the poet sees now and then forms of the nocturnal world, the ghosts, the demons, the gods, the secret amalgamation of human destiny with supra-human intention and the intangible things which occur in the pleroma; he sees from time to time something of that psychic world which is the terror of the primitive, barbarian man.'[89] In the 1930s women writers would be involved in portraying exactly such a night world, and in trying to give it shape, a descent back into this primitive state to evoke primal terror, allowing a collective 'suppressed barbarism' to surface and be explored. Jung continues: 'For wherever the collective unconscious forces its way into experience and weds itself to the collective consciousness, there occurs a creative act which concerns the entire contemporaneous epoch. The work emerging from this is, in the deepest sense of the word, a message to the

---

[87] Eugene Jolas, 'Logos', *transition*, 16–17 (June 1929): 29.
[88] C. G. Jung, 'Psychology and Poetry', *transition*, 19–20 (June 1930): 28.
[89] Ibid. 41, 25.

contemporaries.'[90] Again, women's writing of the 1930s would show itself to be 'contemporary' in exactly this way, exploring a collective neurosis resulting from a troubled world climate.

Even in the late 1920s we find isolated expressions by women writers of a broadly Jungian view that would later bear fruit in literary expression. Kay Boyle in particular was experimenting with the semi-surreal, the merging of outer and inner forms to create new images:

> Here is the sweet wine of my knees to be poured for you
> my temples are hollow bowls for the fruit of your mouth
> The waves of the sea pace the shore and bemoan you . . .[91]

Boyle's work dissolves the boundaries of inner and outer world, and between solid and liquid, animate and inanimate, allowing physical objects to take on attributes of psychic processes, to become as mutable as in a dream landscape.

To sum up, the period 1925–31 must be seen as one of incubation and transition for women's writing rather than production. In part the problem was that after an intense period of introspection there was a need to branch outwards to a world beyond the self, but not yet any means of connection to this more public world. It was not so much that the world climate or ideological position of these women writers was radically different to that of earlier periods, but precisely because it was not, and that these writers desperately needed to avoid stagnancy and repetition, that their work lacked the obvious drive and direction of earlier years. However, the magazines *Close Up* and *transition* seem to have offered ways forward into a new period of confident writing and clear direction, and here we find the germination of ideas that would fuel new directions in writing in the 1930s, including the very distinctive projects of modernist women writers. Writers including Kay Boyle and Storm Jameson were beginning to work in new directions towards greater social awareness, while for others, including H.D., an interest was beginning to deepen in psychoanalytically grounded representations of the unconscious mind, building on the earlier foundations discussed in Chapters 2 and 3, and taking this public sphere forward into the 1930s.

---

[90] C. G. Jung, 'Psychology and Poetry', 38.
[91] Kay Boyle, 'And Winter', *transition*, 5 (Aug. 1927): 114.

5

Responses to a World in Crisis
(1932–46)

> I wanted to free myself of repetitive thoughts and experiences—my own and many of my contemporaries. I did not specifically realise just what it was I wanted, but I knew that I, like most of the people I knew, in England, America, and on the Continent of Europe, was drifting. . . . I would (before the current of inevitable events swept me right into the main stream and so on to the cataract) stand aside, if I could (if it were not already too late), and take stock of my possessions.
>
> H.D.[1]

Recent examinations of the literature of the 1930s have typically focused on a small group of almost exclusively male writers— W. H. Auden, Stephen Spender, Cecil Day Lewis, Louis MacNeice, and others in this group.[2] Studies of the early 1940s have been less sure in their focus—critics have turned variously to the work of the older generation (Eliot's *Four Quartets*), the 'war poets' (considered to be primarily men in the armed services),[3] the now more mature and reflective 'Auden Generation' and their young male successors (including Roy Fuller and Julian Symons), or, finally the younger wave of more Romantic, contemplative writers including Dylan Thomas, and Sidney Keyes.[4]

---

[1] H.D., 'Writing on the Wall', *Life and Letters To-Day*, 45/93 (May 1945): 76.

[2] See, for example, Cunningham, *British Writers of the Thirties*; Samuel Hynes, *The Auden Generation*. One notable exception to this tendency is Janet Montefiore's *Men and Women Writers of the 1930s: The Dangerous Flood of History* (London: Routledge, 1996).

[3] In Jon Stallworthy's anthology of war poetry, for example, even though he attempts to include a wider range of poets than men in the armed forces, of the fifty-one Second World War poets included, only four are women. Jon Stallworthy, ed., *The Oxford Book of War Poetry* (Oxford: Oxford University Press, 1988).

[4] See, for example, A. T. Tolley, *The Poetry of the Forties* (Manchester:

Not only have prose writers been to a large extent excluded from both periods, but so have virtually all women. A few of the most politically active women writers have been granted some space in discussion, particularly militant socialist writers such as Storm Jameson, Kay Boyle, and Muriel Rukeyser. Yet even here their very inclusion has often been indicative of a misunderstanding of their work rather than an engagement with it, forcing it into moulds that were created for (and by) a group composed primarily of young, male, Oxbridge graduates.

Critical commentaries on H.D.'s work of the 1930s in general agree that she was not interested in public engagement with her contemporaries. Lawrence Rainey, in an article hostile to H.D.'s work, argues that she was virtually a recluse: 'Her world, in short, was a cocoon, and she neither needed nor pursued the give and take of exchange with others. Nor did she need or seek an audience, be it small or large'.[5] Even critics more sympathetic to H.D. broadly agree with Rainey on this point; according to Barbara Guest, H.D. 'wanted to be left alone to weave her private web, just as she made her tapestries in her own room'.[6] Guest conjures up an impression of H.D. locked away, riddled with anxiety about her divorce from Aldington and other failed relationships, solipsistically nursing her wounds and perhaps occasionally writing an intensely private poem. Again, in Gary Burnett's words, 'except for a few more-or-less obscure publications—[H.D.] was to remain publicly silent until *The Walls Do Not Fall* in 1944';[7] the impression given is that H.D. did not want or achieve any communication with the outside world. Finally, Susan Stanford Friedman asserts that '[H.D.'s] achievement reached an aesthetic dead end in the thirties. With the rise of fascism and the imminence of a second catastrophic war, H.D. wrote far less regularly and published little in any genre'.[8]

None of this is borne out by the evidence. Rainey, for example, seizes on the fact that some of H.D.'s work of the 1930s appeared in private editions to come to his conclusion, ignoring

Manchester University Press, 1985); Robert Hewison, *Under Siege: Literary Life in London 1939–45* (Weidenfeld & Nicolson, 1977; London: Methuen, 1988).

[5] Rainey, 'Canon, Gender, and Text', 107.

[6] Barbara Guest, 'The Intimacy of Biography', *Iowa Review*, 16/3 (Fall 1986): 69.

[7] Burnett, *H.D. between Image and Epic*, 138.

[8] Susan Stanford Friedman, *Psyche Reborn: The Emergence of H.D.* (Bloomington, Ind.: Indiana University Press, 1981), 7.

the fact that these editions nevertheless generated hundreds of copies, each of which could be read by more than one person (H.D. and Bryher, for example, exchanged texts with each other and were sent work by other women writers), that much of H.D.'s work in any case appeared in magazines, including *Life and Letters To-day*, *Pagany*, *The Times Literary Supplement*, *Poetry*, and *Seed*, and finally that she herself sent much of her work directly to her contemporaries, hardly the action of a recluse. H.D. did not withdraw from the public sphere, she re-entered it in a serious way after a more private and contemplative period in the late 1920s, becoming very much interested in communicating with contemporaries and exploring and understanding events beyond her own immediate world. She published several important works during the course of the 1930s, including *Kora and Ka* and *The Usual Star*[9] (both written slightly earlier) and *Nights* and *Euripides Ion* (written and published at this time).[10] She also published several poems, a children's book (*The Hedgehog*),[11] her essay 'A Note on Poetry'[12] and several reviews.[13] In addition, following her period of analysis with Freud in the 1930s she produced two accounts of her visits, one from memory, serialized as 'Writing on the Wall' in *Life and Letters To-day* between 1944 and 1946, the other ('Advent') based substantially on notes taken during the period of analysis.

H.D. was also concerned to maintain and develop links with individual women writers, and in the 1930s was in touch, either by letter or personal contact, with writers including Marianne Moore, Violet Hunt, Ethel Colburn Mayne, Alice Toklas, Ellen

---

[9] H.D., *Kora and Ka* (Dijon: Imprimerie Darantière, 1934; Bios: Berkeley, 1978); H.D., *The Usual Star* and *Two Americans* (Dijon: Imprimerie Darantière, 1934). These are considered in this chapter since both were written in 1930 and were published in the 1930s. The material they deal with is much more in line with H.D.'s work of the 1930s than that of the mid- to late-1920s.

[10] H.D. ('John Helforth'), *Nights* (Dijon, Imprimerie Darantière, 1935; New York: New Directions, 1986); H.D., *Euripides Ion*, trans. with notes by H.D. (London: Chatto & Windus, 1937).

[11] H.D., *The Hedgehog* ([London]: The Brendin Publishing Company, 1936).

[12] H.D., 'A Note on Poetry', in *The Oxford Anthology of American Literature*, vol. 2 (New York: Oxford University Press, 1938, 11th printing, 1956), 1287–8.

[13] See, for example, Sylvania Penn [H.D.], 'Two Englishwomen in Rome (1871–1900)', review of *Two Englishwomen In Rome* by Matilda Lucas, *Life and Letters To-Day*, 20/16 (Dec. 1938): 105–6; Sylvania Penn, 'I Sing Democracy' review of *Whitman* by Edgar Lee Masters, *Life and Letters To-Day*, 17/9 (Autumn 1937): 154–9.

Hart, Jean Starr Untermeyer, and May Sarton, as well as several others indirectly through their correspondence with Bryher. In her exchanges with these writers she discussed literary work in progress (theirs, her own, and that of contemporaries) and engaged in a circulation of manuscripts and published texts. Yet Barbara Guest, usually an authoritative source of information on H.D., asserts that H.D.'s correspondence at this time, 'with a few exceptions such as Marianne Moore and Pound, had been with private friends, not literary peers'.[14] Of course by now many of H.D.'s peers had become friends, yet a great number of the exchanges in these letters are centred on literary texts and problems of publishing, making them very much part of an inter-action of peers; these letters formed a sphere of discussion that complemented that of the little magazines and wider publishing arena and enabled new ideas to be exchanged.[15]

It is also clear from H.D.'s letters that she was reading work by Marianne Moore and Marya Zaturenska, and from her library that she was reading work by Violet Hunt, Mabel Dodge Luhan, and Dorothy Wellesley; she kept herself more informed than at any other stage of her career about the work of her con-temporaries. These contemporaries were of course also reading and reviewing each other's work and corresponding with each other, part of a public sphere by now in a mature stage of development. We can establish, for example, that Dorothy Richardson was reading work by Edith Sitwell, Gertrude Stein, and Virginia Woolf, that Naomi Mitchison was reading H.D., and that Elizabeth Bishop was reading work by Moore and Stein,[16] and from the magazines it is clear that Bryher was read-ing and reviewing work by Richardson, Barbara Low, and Mary Butts. Bryher's 1935 decision to buy the magazine *Life and Letters*, and give it new direction as *Life and Letters To-day*,[17] was a significant boost to this public sphere of women writers;

---

[14] Guest, 'The Intimacy of Biography', 68.

[15] This is in contrast to the exchange of letters discussed in Chapter 6, where there is little if any critical discussion, and where there is an attitude of retreat from, rather than engagement with, the external and socio-political world.

[16] Elizabeth Bishop, *One Art: The Selected Letters*, ed. Robert Giroux (London: Chatto & Windus, 1994), 47, 67 and throughout.

[17] *Life and Letters To-day* managed to maintain production through the war years due to Bryher's perspicacious stockpiling of paper. See Bryher, *The Days of Mars: A Memoir, 1940–46* (London: Calder and Boyars, 1972), 7.

the magazine was transformed from one with sporadic appearances by a few women writers to one with regular appearances by a great many, including H.D., Stein, Edith Sitwell, Moore, Jean Starr Untermeyer, Zaturenska, and Richardson. *Life and Letters To-day* helped to rejuvenate an exchange of ideas related to literature and to encourage a more general discussion about personal and political events.

Many of these writers made statements [re]affirming their commitment to the public sphere,[18] such as Alyse Gregory: 'the basis of happiness rests largely upon our power of earnest and honest communication, one with another'.[19] She attacks people who treat conversation as a 'scrimmage', contribute only 'egotistic utterances' or use it as a chance to show off, arguing in favour of a rational assessment of each utterance, consideration given to all new ideas, and a space with universal access—precisely the values of the public sphere.[20] Dorothy Richardson also reaffirmed the values of the public sphere in terms of equal access, underpinning rationality and a creative generation of ideas through a meeting of minds; she writes of 'creative conversation': 'Primarily it demands of all the participants that none shall be speaking in his own name, none following either the best debating society tradition, including the dodge of restating, with improvements, the statement of another before demolishing it . . . [or] the determination to score at all costs.'[21] She felt that the approaching war would paradoxically help foster the conditions for creative conversation by throwing people onto their own resources and providing the necessary conditions to motivate people into engaging in critical (and recreational) discussion. Laura Riding also expressed a deep commitment to an exchange of ideas, and compiled her collection *The World and Ourselves*,

---

[18] See: Dorothy Richardson to Bryher, May 9 1943, Nov. 1933 and Mar. 12 1937 in *Windows on Modernism*, ed. Fromm, 463, 250, 330; Bryher, review of *Clear Horizon* by Dorothy Richardson, *Life and Letters To-Day*, 13/2 (Dec. 1935; Winter Quarter): 198–9; Bryher, 'Recognition Not Farewell', review of *The Crystal Cabinet* by Mary Butts, *Life and Letters To-Day*, 17/9 (Autumn 1937): 159–64; Naomi Mitchison, 'Those Queer Greeks', including review of *Euripides Ion* by H.D., *Time and Tide*, 17/15 (Apr. 10, 1937): 468; Alyse Gregory, 'Social Relations', *Wheels on Gravel* (London: John Lane The Bodley Head, 1938), 40.
[19] Ibid. 40.
[20] Alyse Gregory, 'In Defence of the Lady', *Wheels on Gravel*, 159.
[21] Dorothy Richardson, 'A Talk about Talking', *Life and Letters To-day*, 23/27 (Dec. 1939): 287.

where she invited writers and others to discuss 'the unhappy outer situations of our time' by commenting on the relation between 'public' crisis and 'private' ways of dealing with this. Of this collection she writes:

In order to test my personal sense of world troubles and approach them with that active certainty which can only come of relating one's sensibilities to the sensibilities of others, I have invited a number of people to state their own attitude to the outer situations of our time. I have wanted to start not with history, not with ready-made theory, not with what I alone have to say—but with what others around me say.[22]

Her volume operated explicitly, then, on the principles of public democratic exchange characteristic of an ideal model of the public sphere.

Throughout the 1930s and even during the war years, the public sphere of modernist women writers continued to operate as an international body of women writers committed to listening to each other's ideas and to offering new contributions, and, in fact, as the world political climate deteriorated maintaining an exchange of ideas acquired a new imperative. Jameson writes: 'Anything that a writer can do, to cheat the dictator's police, he ought. The more difficult it becomes—the difficulties harden in war time, because of censorship and the fact that letters are lost or delayed—the more faithfully he must help the movement of ideas in Europe and between Europe and the rest of the world.'[23] To be part of an exchange of ideas, whether 'literary' or political, was to be part of a resistance to totalitarianism, to participate in keeping up morale, and to affirm community and supportive relationship above sectarianism. During the war H.D. continued to exchange letters and ideas with, amongst others, Richardson, Eliza Sitwell, Faith Compton Mackenzie, Alyse Gregory, Ivy Compton Burnett, May Sarton, Silvia Dobson,[24] Moore, Edith Butler, and Mary Herr. She also read work by Boyle, Stein, and Mary Butts and owned books by writers including Elizabeth Bowen and Vita Sackville-West. Of course the war led to inevitable problems of international communication. Nevertheless, Anglo-American links were main-

---

[22] Riding, 'Foreword', *The World and Ourselves*, p. x.
[23] Storm Jameson, 'Writing in the Margin: 1939', *The Writer's Situation and Other Essays* (London: Macmillan, 1950), 199.
[24] Silvia Dobson was a writer and teacher who arrived in London in the 1930s.

tained, and H.D.'s work was reviewed in *Poetry*, the *New York Herald Tribune Weekly Book Review*, *The New Yorker*, *Sewanee Review*, *Virginia Quarterly Review*, and *Yale Review*, by American writers including Louise Bogan, Jessica Nelson North, Deutsch, and Elizabeth Atkins. H.D. herself maintained links with American periodicals, writing: 'We get Life, Time and the New Yorker and though late, of course, we read up past reports, and find much of intense interest; I feel very well informed on USA life.'[25]

Clearly there was no general collapse of the public sphere in the 1930s or in the war years, nor was H.D. in particular isolated and apart from the network of women writers that had sustained her throughout her career. Nor is it true that H.D.'s output was muted or suffering from a lack of direction in the 1930s. At times she did express an inability to write, as, for example, to Bryher in November 1934: 'Please, for six months or a year do NO[T] probe me about my writing. It's no good and terrible pain to me.'[26] No doubt such expressions have fuelled the belief in H.D.'s failure of creativity. Yet equally often she expressed positive feelings about her work; less than a year later she wrote to Bryher of finding the process of writing *Ion* 'thrilling'[27]: 'I am very happy working at Ion. I have set myself the task of getting it across—and am strangely very glad, as it was a hang-over, now I am free and very happy, serving thus, the gods.'[28] The 1930s do not seem to have been a low point in terms of H.D.'s writing career, but a period of exciting new ideas, paving the way for the most productive period of her career in the early 1940s.

Another myth that needs to be dispelled is that H.D. was largely unconcerned with political issues during the 1930s. Donna Krolik Hollenberg, for example, writes of the 'private nature of much of H.D.'s literary work in the 1930s'.[29] This myth fits into a wider one, that only Auden and his young male contemporaries were seriously engaging in the political situation, in addition to a few of the older generation such as Pound,

[25] H.D. to Gretchen Wolle Baker, November 11, [1941], Beinecke.
[26] H.D. to Bryher, Nov. 24, [1934], Beinecke.
[27] H.D. to Bryher, Aug. 13, [1935], Beinecke.
[28] H.D. to Bryher, Aug. 9, [1935], Beinecke.
[29] Hollenberg, *Poetics*, 97.

and a few of the younger militant socialist women such as Storm
Jameson and Muriel Rukeyser. The work of the vast majority of
women writers of this period has been classified as personal and
apolitical, excluded from being considered alongside serious
politically engaged work by the Auden Generation; the exclusion of these women writers seems to have been on the grounds
of their relatively mature age, their gender, their lack of public
school and Oxbridge education and, in the case of H.D., Moore,
Bishop, and others, also their nationality. In fact, the absence of
these factors did not stop them exploring many of the same
issues and following similar directions, as well as undertaking
very distinctive projects of their own, and a reconsideration of
their work must not only help to recontextualize H.D.'s work,
but must affect the study of 1930s literature more generally.

H.D.'s work of this period was part of the wider move away
both from formal experimentalism and from intense introspection for their own sakes, and a re-contextualization of both
within contemporary socio-political reality; this can be seen
taking place across the board by a great many women writers as
well as by a younger generation of male poets such as Auden and
Day Lewis, though interestingly not to the same extent in the
older generation of male writers. The public sphere of modernist
women writers included many women who had come of age
before the First World War, and yet were now able to engage
with the political events of the 1930s alongside much younger
male contemporaries such as Spender or Auden. H.D. later
writes of her alter-ego, the priestess from *A Dead Priestess
Speaks*:

We are through with experimenting. We are in the mid-thirties, not the
mid-twenties. But there must be a new means of expression, of self-
expression, of world-expression. She has not found it but she goes on
assembling her small treasures. This is done feverishly, through a sort
of compulsion, you might say. It is necessary to tidy-up, to clear the
decks. We are not in the mid-twenties, we are in the mid-thirties. The
storm is coming.[30]

H.D. felt that a new way of writing had to be found that both
avoided experimentation for its own sake but, on the other
hand, did not become the kind of 'documentary' writing that

[30] H.D., 'H.D. by Delia Alton', *The Iowa Review*, 16/3 (Fall 1986): 211.

was developing popularity, as in, for example, some of the work of Storm Jameson and Kay Boyle. She felt that writing needed to be psychologically informed and aware, but connected to the external world, that it needed to be as interesting as literature, but not to the exclusion of external socio-political reality. H.D. writes of the two extremes of experimentalism versus documentary writing with frustration: 'One refused to admit the fact that the flood was coming—the other counted the nails and measured the planks with endless exact mathematical formulas, but didn't seem to have the very least idea of how to put the Ark together.'[31] She sought a middle ground of political writing that was nevertheless of literary interest.

H.D.'s literature and letters show a radical increase in her level of political interest; she wrote in 1935 to Bryher: 'It is the oddest feeling for me, to feel I am swimming WITH the tide, about war matters and so on'[32] while Bryher wrote to H.D. in 1936: 'I'm fundamentally interested in dirt and politics.'[33] Neither H.D. nor Bryher had before demonstrated any serious and conscious engagement with politics. H.D. used her new politicization as a way to re-engage with the public sphere and the world around her; she wrote to Silvia Dobson: 'I have felt very cut-off, but digging deep and reading politics.'[34] Many other writers who had previously shown little if any political awareness, such as Edith Sitwell, Richardson, and Alyse Gregory, now also demonstrated a notable politicizing of their writing. Gregory felt that at such a time: 'Perhaps the wisest course for a "lady" . . . is to inform herself as much as possible on the political and social movements of her generation, sceptical of all propaganda, using her critical intelligence at every turn with an understanding that is able to sift what is base from what is noble, what is false from what is true'. She recognized that narcissistic contemplation could not be defended if this involved ignoring the 'roving frenzy of brutal and irrational wars'.[35] In addition, a younger generation of writers such as Stevie Smith, Kathleen Raine, Boyle, Bowen, Bishop, and others were from the outset very politically

---

[31] H.D., 'Writing on the Wall', *Life and Letters To-Day*, 45/96 (Aug. 1945): 74.
[32] H.D. to Bryher, Oct. 18, [1935], Beinecke.
[33] Bryher to H.D., June 30, 1936, Beinecke.
[34] H.D., quoted in Silvia Dobson, ' "Shock Knit Within Terror": Living Through World War II', *The Iowa Review*, 16/3 (Fall 1986): 233.
[35] Gregory, 'In Defence of the Lady', 157, 155.

engaged and had the energy and commitment to spread their ideas to others.

Though there was no uniform response by this public sphere of women writers to the world political situation, there was a notable move to the Left and a belief in the necessity of abandoning neutrality. Nancy Cunard, canvassing writers on their opinions regarding the Spanish Civil War, writes: 'it is impossible any longer to take no side. . . . The equivocal attitude, the Ivory Tower, the paradoxical, the ironic detachment, will no longer do.'[36] However, to take the side of the Spanish Republic, and against fascism in general, was to become aligned in effect to a 'cause', something this network had avoided from the early days of Suffragism. As a group these women writers had to work out for themselves how it would be possible to maintain rational-critical discussion and opinion formation while aligning themselves to a broadly Leftist movement dominating the Anglo-American literary world—there was a definite and acknowledged danger in being swept away in rhetoric and in abandoning a critical interrogation of new ideas. Alyse Gregory, for example, noted the danger in becoming 'fanatical, unreceptive to life, unaware of other human beings except as they fall in with our aims, lofty or otherwise';[37] she counselled only a cautious embracing of group ideologies, and even then only to the extent that values of free thought and expression were not undermined. These risks were to a large extent avoided, as will be demonstrated later in this chapter, by a searching examination of individual motivations and a refusal to allow morality to crystallize into black and white ideological affiliations and expressions.

The vast majority of women writers who had been pacifists during and following the First World War now abandoned this position in the years leading up to and during the Second World War, including H.D., Storm Jameson, and the British novelist Rosamond Lehmann; the dominant feeling was that war was the lesser of two evils, necessary in order to protect human rights.

---

[36] Nancy Cunard, 'To the Writers and Poets of England, Scotland, Ireland and Wales', quoted in Valentine Cunningham, 'Neutral?: 1930s Writers and Taking Sides', in *Class, Culture and Social Change: A New View of the 1930s*, ed. Frank Gloversmith (Sussex: The Harvester Press, 1980), 45.

[37] Gregory, 'In Defence of the Lady', 155.

Lehmann, typically, writes in 1937: 'Up till now a pacifist in the fullest sense, I have come to feel that non-resistance can be—in this case, is—a negative, a sterile, even a destructive thing.'[38] H.D. expressed similar views in 1941:

No one I believe has hated war more than myself—I suffered terribly in the years 1914–1918, losing one child as a result of that war at birth and nearly losing my second daughter. Yet there is such a thing as morality and it has been impossible for us, who have perhaps still something of the Puritan in us, to bear what we have seen here of the persecution of all intellectual thought by Fascism, unmoved.[39]

Of course this movement away from pacifism had also taken place among many male contemporaries as the choice between fascism and war became ever more stark.[40] However, for women this change of allegiance involved some specific and problematic decisions. Firstly, since women had traditionally been associated with values of peace and nurturance, and particularly motherhood, to advocate involvement in war was to challenge fundamental conceptions of femininity and femaleness.[41] Furthermore, many of the older generation of women, including H.D., Louise Bogan, Sara Bard Field (American poet), and Storm Jameson, had lost sons, brothers, and fathers in the First World War, and now felt inevitable revulsion at the thought of renewed fighting. British women writers had the added knowledge that if war broke out they were likely to be conscripted, and that in any case the 'home front' would be subject to attack.

Yet not only did these writers abandon pacifism almost en masse, their engagement with issues of war was itself not passive. Many, including those who had shown no political interest at all in the First World War, did not merely support the war, but took steps to aid the Allied war effort. These included H.D., who took it upon herself to become actively engaged in attempting to

[38] Rosamond Lehmann, in *Authors Take Sides on the Spanish War*, [ed. Louis Aragon] (London: Left Review, 1937), [16].

[39] H.D., 'A Letter from England', *Bryn Mawr Alumnae Bulletin*, 21/8 (Nov. 1941): 22.

[40] A notable exception, who remained true to pacifism, was of course, Aldous Huxley. See Aldous Huxley, *What Are You Going to Do About It?* (London: Chatto & Windus, 1936).

[41] Virginia Woolf's *Three Guineas*, for example, asserts the more traditional view that women are inherently against war, because of the way they have been conditioned. Virginia Woolf, *A Room of One's Own and Three Guineas*, throughout.

persuade Americans to enter the war; in November 1941, just one month before Pearl Harbor, she published a letter in the *Bryn Mawr Alumnae Bulletin*, the newsletter of her old college, arguing in favour of American involvement in the war:

. . . supposing we are conquered, what then? Germany would control the economic world and would certainly prevent any export of American goods to Europe except under German dictated conditions and there would be nothing to prevent a mass attack being made on the States itself. Perhaps you would be able to resist successfully, but your young people then would be dragged into the war anyhow, and it would be a harder struggle.[42]

H.D. was astute enough to point out the problems that an invasion of Britain by Germany would have on the USA, and also to realize that many Bryn Mawr alumnae would either be in powerful positions, or would be married to people in powerful positions. It is remarkable that this attempt at intervention has been overlooked in commentaries on H.D.'s life and work. Many other women writers, including Jameson and Bryher, also turned their skill as writers to use in political letter-writing, while Rebecca West used her popularity to call for people not to complain about their position: 'If we grizzle and chatter and prefer short term safety from the bomber instead of long term safety from slavery, then we are rubbish'.[43]

One reason why H.D. in particular was compelled into political engagement was her time spent in Vienna as an analysand of Freud in 1933 and 1934; she writes of this period:

Already in Vienna, the shadows were lengthening or the tide was rising. The signs of grim coming-events, however, manifested in a curious fashion. There were, for instance, occasional coquettish, confetti-like showers from the air, gilded paper swastikas and narrow strips of printed paper . . . The party had begun, or this was the preliminary to the birthday or the wedding.[44]

What she saw repulsed her, and brought out a desire to help those worst affected; along with Bryher[45] she became actively

[42] H.D., 'A Letter from England', 22.
[43] Rebecca West, 'If the Worst Comes to the Worst', *Time and Tide*, 21/23 (June 8, 1940): 602.
[44] H.D., 'Writing on the Wall', *Life and Letters To-day*, 45/96 (Aug. 1945): 74; Kay Boyle writes of a very similar experience in her novel *Primer for Combat* (London: Faber and Faber, 1943), 135.   [45] Bryher, *The Heart to Artemis*, 278.

involved in refugee work, helping Jews, students of psycho-analysis and other intellectuals to escape: 'one has been much involved with refugee problems, the group I work with has now been personally responsible for over 100, placed in England and America'.[46] Jameson was also involved in refugee work, and seems to have felt frustration both at a general apathy and at the government policy of refusing access to refugees; the narrator in 'The Children Must Fear' suggests: 'There are still too many refugees, although it is made as hard for them to get into England as if England were a raft and Europe going under. It would be less embarrassing to sensitive people if they would die peaceably and dumbly, and not try to escape.'[47]

H.D. was part, then, albeit in a small way, of active efforts both to help the Allied cause and to rescue those threatened with persecution in Nazi-occupied Europe. She was also involved in another political grouping: along with Bryher, Kathleen Raine, Jameson, and Naomi Mitchison, she was part of the socialist project Mass-Observation, of which about a third of volunteers were women.[48] Mass-Observation was committed to assembling the facts of everyday existence in this period of crisis, an anthro-pology of ordinary lives carried out by ordinary people. It sought to move away from a focus on individual production and to remove a distinction between an intellectual or artistic elite and the 'masses' by gathering the opinions of people from all classes and backgrounds and documenting very ordinary lives. In fact, however, the majority of participants were middle class rather than workers, due in part to the lack of time workers could give to the project,[49] and also to a difficulty in raising the aware-ness of the project among working-class communities. Mass-Observation first appealed for volunteers through a letter in *The New Statesman and Nation*, a magazine that would have had very few working-class readers.[50]

One benefit of Mass-Observation was its role in bringing

---

[46] H.D. to Gretchen Wolle Baker, Aug. 31 [1939], Beinecke.

[47] Storm Jameson, 'The Children Must Fear', *Europe to Let: The Memoirs of an Obscure Man* (London: Macmillan, 1940), 275.

[48] Caroline Lang, *Keep Smiling Through: Women in the Second World War* (Cambridge: Cambridge University Press, 1989), 6.

[49] Cunningham, *British Writers of the Thirties*, 338.

[50] Tom Harrisson, Humphrey Jennings, and Charles Madge, 'Anthropology at Home', *The New Statesman and Nation*, 13/310 (Jan. 30, 1937), 155.

together a community of like-minded people and in raising their political awareness. H.D. had joined Mass-Observation 'at the suggestion of a friend'[51] and in turn she recommended it to her own friends, including some in America.[52] Richardson received a Mass-Observation volume from Bryher, and was immediately enthusiastic: 'Thank you for the M.O. leaflet, read last night & throwing up this morning in my slow-moving mind a few reflections. In terms of utility, this thousand lensed documentary movie-camera promises to be all things to all men.'[53] Mass-Observation offered participants a chance to feel that they were contributing towards stabilizing the world community simply by communicating; if the ordinary lives of ordinary people could be known, perhaps then the kinds of prejudice and partisanship that lead to hostility could be averted. H.D. in particular had utopian hopes that Mass-Observation might 'help to break down these barriers that make eventually for prejudice and at the last analysis for war'.[54] As war looked increasingly inevitable the need to set down the feelings of this age for posterity was felt as imperative; there was a desire to capture the last gasp of a world many felt certain would be annihilated. H.D. expressed this need: 'I liked the feeling of being anonymous, but with a directed purpose, the feeling that in case of war or certain political trouble, I would in some way, have made a statement that linked on the human doctrine and human behaviour.'[55]

There are various other ways to understand the enthusiasm for the Mass-Observation project. For H.D., both the literary dimension (including its interest in Surrealism) and the psychoanalytic dimension of Mass-Observation were of as much interest as the political. Mass-Observation did not set itself up simply as a record of external events, but also as a record of people's conscious and unconscious responses, and it was led not only by the anthropologist Tom Harrisson, but also by the Surrealist

---

[51] H.D. ('CO.11'), 'Mass Observation Report, May 12, 1937', ed. Diana Collecott, *Line*, 13 (1989): 168.

[52] H.D. ('CO.11'), 'Letter and Reply to M.O. Questionnaire, 1937', ibid.

[53] Dorothy Richardson to Bryher, [Summer 1937], in *Windows on Modernism*, ed. Fromm, 336; a letter from H.D. to Bryher indicates that Richardson did become involved, sending Mass-Observation material to Bryher in Sept. 1937. (H.D. to Bryher, Sept. 9, [1937], Beinecke.)

[54] H.D., 'Letter and Reply to M.O. Questionnaire, 1937', 169.

[55] H.D. ('CO.11'), 'Mass Observation Report, May 12, 1937', 168.

poet Charles Madge. For Kathleen Raine the literary took precedence over the political or psychoanalytic: 'The poetic side of Mass-Observation captivated me; but the political side made me shrink and shudder.'[56]

Mass-Observation appealed to many women writers simply because it was a way of speaking out, of having a voice at a time when the values of free speech and expression were so clearly under attack, both in German-occupied countries where books were being burned, and in a Britain increasingly subjecting itself to censorship and nationalist rhetoric. The feelings of women writers on this issue seem to have been similar to those of male contemporaries such as Auden, Spender, and Day Lewis. Spender, for example, felt that: 'Of all evils, tyranny is the most destructive to [the poet's] freedom of expression as a writer, his livelihood and even his life.'[57] The writer found him or herself on the front line in a fight for freedom of expression, and writing became inherently a political act. Rukeyser felt literature to be the only way to resist fascist forces that would oppose thought and life: 'The attitude of poetry is the attitude with which we can face these battles. It is, indeed, much more. It is a technique that may provide the fierce and vivid spirit with its complexity, a many-minded resistance which we need today.'[58] Like many others she was aware that Nazi ideology was against individuality of thought, and it was this, as much as reports of physical persecution, that stirred the political feelings and actions of these women writers. Again, Laura Riding felt that a community of writers could, through their writing, bring about world change, simply by affirming values of communication: 'And as among writers themselves there is a co-operative centrality of communication, so will the entire world become a field of communication'.[59]

Literature became a way of asserting creative language use against propaganda and slogan, of using language not to coerce but to express opinion and personal visions of 'truth'. Of this network of writers only Millay was attracted by writing war

---

[56] Kathleen Raine, *The Land Unknown* (Hamish Hamilton, 1977) in *Autobiographies* (London: Skoob Books Publishing, 1991), 176.

[57] Stephen Spender, 'Poetry', *Fact*, 4 (July 1937): 20.

[58] Muriel Rukeyser, 'The Usable Truth', *Poetry*, 58/4 (July 1941): 207.

[59] Riding, 'Conclusion', *The World and Ourselves*, 419.

propaganda—for most the idea of stifling expression by writing designed to induce feelings of blind patriotism was anathema. Jameson wrote against British propaganda: 'We ought to remember the nature of war, not hide it in phrases. "Peace can only triumph with a sword in its hand" means the child torn by hot steel or crushed in the ruins of his home, the human entrails in the entrails of the missing aeroplane.'[60] While the true horror of war had only really surfaced after World War One rather than during its course, in this war there was less willingness to be taken in by glorifications of fighting. This was a war that people broadly believed in and felt to be 'just', but one also in which the realities of the scale and horror of the loss of life could not be so easily veiled.

In contrast to the First World War, many women involved in this literary public sphere now attempted to use their work to convey the brute reality of the effects of war and to attack all veiling of this in wishful thinking and slogan. Like Auden's 'Refugee Blues'[61] much work by women writers of this time explicitly attempted to counter any self-interested refusal to take an interest in the plight of those being persecuted in occupied Europe, and attacked the rationalizations people were using to justify their apathy. Marghanita Laski's powerful poem 'We Get Used to Atrocities Because—', for example, asserts the absurdity of the kinds of reassurances, palliatives, and excuses people brought into play to console each other and to ignore the reality:

> one hears they never touch women
> of course a good many of the photographs are faked
> the Jews expect it
> * you can't make an omelette without breaking eggs
> after all, what's the League of Nations for?
> they probably get better food in the concentration camps
>   than they would at home
> it doesn't do to think about it . . .[62]

These writers challenged the use of language as a veil for the truth, and even before the war began a battle of words was

[60] Storm Jameson, *The End of this War* (London: Allen & Unwin, 1941), 10.
[61] See, for example, W. H. Auden, 'Refugee Blues' [written 1939], *Selected Poems*, ed. Edward Mendelson (London: Faber & Faber, 1979), 83–4.
[62] Marghanita Laski, 'We Get Used to Atrocities Because—' *Time and Tide*, 17/15 (Apr. 10, 1937): 464.

already under way. Many poems of this period described life for those in concentration camps, or for refugees, or for victims of torture and persecution, feeling the imperative of bringing these to public awareness.

The perceived apathy of the wider population and of the government in the 1930s drove several writers to engage in directly political rather than literary writing. Bryher wrote multiple furious and frustrated political tirades, often published in literary magazines under the guise of reviews or critical comment. She felt incensed at the way people attempted to cover up the truth under bland reassurances and evasions: 'Nothing astonished me so much last month as the way that the English abandoned thought and stuck by slogans. It was common to all political parties. Instead of the traditional calm, they massed themselves together under loose definitions and bolted for cover. This is no way to succeed in war and is, emphatically, not the method to win "Peace".' This is a critique of empty phrases, a literary criticism in a primarily literary journal brought to bear on the political situation. To the public who had believed such reassurances she writes: 'You can blame no government but yourself. You have refused to read the news and as a result you get none in your papers.' Some of Bryher's attacks were directed in particular against those women who claimed their femininity as grounds for lack of interest in politics, or who asserted that the domestic sphere alone was their sphere of interest: 'Every time that you laugh about not having the time nor the brains to bother about foreign affairs, you will just go and water the lupins, you are making it a little more certain that you will lose eventually, your garden, your home, and your life.'[63] Bryher refused to countenance the excuse that women's interests lay elsewhere, in the private rather than the public sphere.

For British women writers, of course, the advent of war made apathy and ignorance no longer possible; many were at direct risk of attack in bombing raids, including H.D., who remained in London in 'Bomb alley or Doodle-bug-alley'.[64] She could have gone to America—many did so, including Auden, Wyndham Lewis, Christopher Isherwood, and Aldous Huxley. But she felt

---

[63] Bryher, 'The Crisis: September', *Life and Letters To-Day*, 19/15 (Nov. 1938): 1, 4, 5.

[64] H.D. to Gretchen Wolle Baker, July 27, [1944], Beinecke.

that it would be weakness to leave London at this time. The first air-raid was experienced as the end to a period of waiting, 'like a thunder cloud bursting',[65] precipitating an enormous release of creative energy. H.D. described her time in London as 'revealing and exciting'[66] and wrote to Moore of London in the war: 'our fervour and intensity give me new life to the very bones'.[67] Writing amidst falling bombs and the noise of the barrage, H.D. produced some of her best work; she wrote and published *Trilogy*,[68] 'Writing on the Wall' and *What Do I Love?*; she wrote, but did not publish at this time, *Within the Walls*, *The Gift*, *By Avon River*, and several stories, and she began 'The Sword Went Out to Sea'.[69]

H.D.'s increased energy was immediately apparent to her critics; Horace Gregory and Zaturenska noted an 'increased intensity' in her recent work,[70] while Louise Bogan observed of *The Walls Do Not Fall*, the first section of *Trilogy*, that it 'shows tenser feeling, writing of more energy, and thought of a larger sweep than has been usual in her poetry for many years'.[71] Again, Ivy Compton Burnett wrote to H.D. of H.D.'s work: 'It makes me thankful that we had the bombs, and thankful that you faced them'.[72] H.D. was not alone in finding this period a catalyst for creative energy. Elizabeth Bowen said later of the war years: 'I would not have missed being in London throughout the war for anything: it was the most interesting period of my life.'[73] Many of these women writers expressed a preference for a universally shared risk as opposed to the relative safety of civilians in World War One; Bryher, long after the war, writes:

[65] H.D. to Howard Clifford, July 20, [1940], Beinecke.

[66] H.D. to Gretchen Wolle Baker, February 14 [1941], Beinecke.

[67] H.D. to Marianne Moore, June 26 1940, Beinecke.

[68] This was published in its three parts; *The Walls Do Not Fall*, *Tribute to the Angels*, and *The Flowering of the Rod*, each appearing in Britain and the USA.

[69] H.D., 'The Sword Went Out to Sea', Beinecke.

[70] Horace Gregory and Marya Zaturenska, *A History of American Poetry 1900–1940* (New York: Harcourt, Brace, 1946), 197; H.D. owned a copy of this edition.

[71] Louise Bogan, 'Verse', including reviews of *Beast In View* by Muriel Rukeyser, *Take Them, Stranger* by Babette Deutsch and *The Walls Do Not Fall* by H.D., *The New Yorker*, 20 (Oct. 21, 1944), 94.

[72] Ivy Compton Burnett to H.D., May 20, 1944, Beinecke.

[73] Victoria Glendinning, *Elizabeth Bowen, A Biography* (New York: Alfred A. Knopf, 1977), 158, quoted in Phyllis Lassner, *Elizabeth Bowen*, Women Writers (Basingstoke: Macmillan, 1990), 21–2.

'in spite of the bombing I found the Second World War so much easier to bear than the First. We were all "in it" and there was not the dreadful gap between soldiers and civilians that had caused so much stress in 1914'.[74]

The surge of creativity precipitated by the war stands in direct contrast to several important and influential accounts of this period. Robert Hewison, for example, writes: 'As—to borrow from Auden—the clever hopes expired of a low, dishonest decade, English literary life fell into a state of shock from which it found little cause to recover during the war years.'[75] Again, Samuel Hynes writes: 'For the writers as writers, the appropriate response to the end of the 'thirties was silence, or a retrospective brooding over what had happened. Some of them would fight in the war, or support it in various other ways, but they would not write much about it'.[76] This is certainly not borne out by a study of this network of women writers, in fact the opposite was very much the case, the war fuelled greater levels of creativity, and it was not until after the war years that such a 'retrospective brooding' would set in.

American women writers, like their British counterparts, found the war a catalyst for creativity, though obviously their removal from danger placed them in a very different position. Nevertheless, physical distance from the effects of the war did not prevent several writing as if from direct experience—an intense empathy sprang up and enabled an identification by women in America with those in Britain. Jean Starr Untermeyer in a later account of this period writes of the personal empathy that she felt at this time:

Even though we in America did not have to meet at first hand the bestiality and violence of the Second World War, the heartbreaking spectacle of displaced peoples in flight, the destruction of cities and their art treasures, nor the ravages of war on our own land, yet no one with imagination, to say nothing of empathy, could shut himself away from the world-pervading horror. Night after night I remained sleepless . . .[77]

---

[74] Bryher, *The Days of Mars*, 7–8; see also Bryher, *The Heart to Artemis*, 172.

[75] Hewison, *Under Siege*, 208.

[76] Hynes, *The Auden Generation*, 382.

[77] Untermeyer, *Private Collection*, 293. Untermeyer, however, was one of the few of these writers who did not find war a catalyst for creativity, but found herself unable to write at this time.

The American poets Muriel Rukeyser and Ruth Lechlitner both wrote of the way the war impacted on domestic life. Rukeyser did have some direct experience of this, as she was in Spain at the start of the Civil War in 1936. In 'The Children's Elegy' she likens evacuation to bereavement; an evacuated child speaks of its loss of the mother:

> War means to me, sings a small skeleton,
> only the separation,
> mother no good and gone,
> taken away in lines of fire and foam.
> The end of war
> will bring me, bring me home.[78]

This is a very different perspective from the one expected of 'war poetry', and one with which many women would have been familiar and with which many more could empathize. Ruth Lechlitner too writes in identification with the experience of British women; in 'Quiz Program' she describes death impacting on a shopping trip, highlighting the dissonance between the everyday lives of women in cities under threat and the death all around them:

> . . . when marketing will you buy
> (Wheat and corn steady, steel closing up fractions, aviation
>   firm)
> Red plum or white cauliflower or the shattered thigh
> Of a woman bombed, or the torn hands of children . . .[79]

Again, it is women and children who are the focus in a vivid portrayal of the effects of war written by an American writer who, as far as it has been possible to determine, had no direct experience of such events.

Though some American women writers, such as Rukeyser and Kay Boyle, did have direct experience of events in Europe, the majority of course did not, and in general they sought a different way to write of war, one that did not require a direct experience they did not have; Rukeyser more often wrote not of an external experience of war, but of war transposed onto an internal scenario, such as in her 'Letter to the Front':

[78] Muriel Rukeyser, 'The Children's Elegy', *Poetry*, 63/4 (Jan. 1944): 180.
[79] Ruth Lechlitner, 'Quiz Program', *Poetry*, 58/3 (June 1941): 133.

> Wars of the spirit in the world
> Make us continually know
> We fight continually to grow.[80]

The war here is as fierce as that in the external world, but is fought by the self against the self. Her speaker writes *to* rather than *from* the front, an assertion of the importance of her own internal battles. Internal battles are also the focus of Moore's 'In Distrust of Merit', just one of many poems of this period in which she examines issues of the war and its internal roots and manifestations:

> There never was a war that was
> not inward; I must
> fight till I have conquered in myself what
> causes war, but I would not believe it.[81]

The poem supports the widely shared view by women writers of this period that the forces behind war could be found in a microcosm in the self, and that it was as necessary to resolve these on the personal level as on the global. Elizabeth Bishop, very much influenced by Moore, also wrote poems where the external event of war or a troubled world was internalized and explored on an internal level. In 'Sleeping Standing Up', for example, the speaker finds herself implicated in a world at war by her dream of driving a tank in a night world where the 'dangerous thing' is acted out.[82] Again, in Bishop's 'Roosters' the rooster, representing the aggression and violence of war, dominates the lives of the people, represented on a weather vane and entering people's consciousness through its crowing. The poem demonstrates an awareness that there will be a betrayal of fundamental human values, as violence is present within every individual, inextricably intertwined with that of the external, public world at war.[83] In fact, it was not only American writers who transferred or extended the external war into explorations of internal wars;

---

[80] Muriel Rukeyser, 'Letter to the Front', *Beast In View* (New York: Doubleday, Doran, 1944), 57.

[81] Marianne Moore, 'In Distrust of Merit', *Nevertheless* (New York: Macmillan, 1944), 14.

[82] Elizabeth Bishop, 'Sleeping Standing Up', *Life and Letters To-day* 19/15 (Nov. 1938); repr. *The Complete Poems* (London: Chatto & Windus, 1970), 33.

[83] Elizabeth Bishop, 'Roosters', *New Republic* (Apr. 21, 1941): 547–8; repr. *The Complete Poems* (London: Chatto & Windus, 1970), 39–45.

many women writers in Britain, including H.D., wrote primarily of the internal conflicts, battles, and aggression that were felt to underlie this particular external manifestation. Laura Riding expresses this in her 1938 *The World and Ourselves*: 'The outer problems are not the serious ones. They are sportive diversifications of the inner problems'. Riding blames the world situation precisely on the fact that 'circumstances have been over-externalised and isolated from their influence'.[84]

Both the approach of war and its actuality inevitably made deep impacts on a sense of stable self or secure world, and led many into profound anxiety or internal crisis. It is possible to trace a spate of breakdowns, suicides, and attempted suicides by women in this period that we find in no other period covered in this study. Elizabeth Bishop suffered serious depression in 1931; In 1931 and 1933 Louise Bogan had a serious breakdown and reflected: 'The thought of my own possible suicide, under certain conditions, is becoming more and more clear in my mind';[85] Sara Teasdale committed suicide in 1933; Richardson suffered a breakdown in 1935; Woolf committed suicide in 1941; Millay had a breakdown at the end of the war; Anna Wickham committed suicide in 1947. H.D. also had a major breakdown in 1934 and again as the war ended, and wrote during the war: 'there is almost the hope—God forgive us—that the bomb that must fall on someone, would fall on me'.[86] Of course personal issues were involved in all these cases, but in this period more than any other the personal could not be separated from the political, with private neurosis borne out and inflamed by public event. Interestingly, instances of breakdown seem to be evenly split between Britain and the USA and occurred more frequently in the years immediately preceding the war than during the war itself, indicating that personal risk was not the primary factor.

A great number of writers, both male and female, documented this period in metaphors of darkness or night landscapes, as, for example, Auden's 'September 1, 1939'.[87] In her journal Alyse

[84] Riding, 'Introduction', *The World and Ourselves*, 18, 27.
[85] Louise Bogan, *Journey Around My Room: The Autobiography of Louise Bogan*, ed. Ruth Limmer (New York: The Viking Press, 1980), 83.
[86] H.D., *The Gift* (New York: New Directions, 1982), 137.
[87] W. H. Auden, 'September 1, 1939', *Selected Poems* (London: Faber and Faber, 1979), 86.

Gregory expresses her sense of the world: 'Darkness surrounds us, perfidy is in our hearts through the variable days, nor do we lose it in the night's fantastic quagmires. Puppets are we on the edge of an abyss.'[88] Many writers presented disturbed inner landscapes in Surreal and semi-Surreal writing. Though women writers were generally (though not exclusively) marginalized as subjects in both French and British Surrealism in terms of the publication of officially affiliated Surrealist work (or exhibition of Surrealist art),[89] and though Surrealist groups tended to include women in their ranks as object rather than subject, much women's writing of this period was Surrealist in all but official affiliation.[90] None of the women writers in this particular literary public sphere of women writers were much involved in official Surrealist groups, but many felt the attraction of its ethos and were able to make use of its principles in their work while keeping some degree of distance from full immersion in it as a movement. Surrealism took as a starting point Freud's assertion that 'the ego's cognizance of itself is subject to disturbance, and the boundaries between it and the outer world are not immovable.'[91] This, of course, had long been H.D.'s view, and with an awareness of world instability and personal vulnerability many more women writers were exploring this idea.

The world that emerges in these semi-Surrealist texts by women writers is one of shifting realities, a disturbed psyche, and a loss of the ability of the human subject and human rationality to control experience. In Muriel Rukeyser's 'For Fun', for example, the buildings speak out while the human subject is unable to engage in anything meaningful:

[88] Alyse Gregory, *The Cry of a Gull: Journals 1923–1948* (Brushford, Somerset: Out of the Ark Press, 1973), 77–8.

[89] Of the twenty-four Surrealists in *New Directions 1940*, for example, none are women, nor are any of the thirteen 'Pre-surrealists'. *New Directions in Prose and Poetry 1940*, ed. James Laughlin (Norfolk, Conn.: New Directions, 1940); H.D owned a copy of this edition.

[90] Many seem to have resisted a Surrealist identification, and in the case of Edith Sitwell vigorously defended their independence from it. See Paul Ray, *The Surrealist Movement in England* (Ithaca: Cornell University Press, 1971), 271.

[91] Sigmund Freud, *Civilization and its Discontents*, trans. Joan Riviere (London: The Hogarth Press, 1930), 11. Translation from *Das Umbehagen in der Kultur* (Vienna, 1929).

It was long before the city was bombed I saw
fireworks, mirrors, gilt, consumed in flame,
we show you this said the flames, speak it speak it
but I was employed then making straw oranges.
Everything spoke: flames, city, glass, but I
had heavy mystery thrown against the heart.[92]

This meaningless human activity, as contrasted to the activity
and speech of inanimate objects, is reminiscent of activities given
to the mad in asylums for the insane, the implication being that
humanity was experiencing a mass insanity. Many texts by
women writers of this period are peopled by subjects who have
lost any clear morality, intellectual authority, or religious conviction; they are reduced to random, bizarre, and meaningless
behaviour or animal instinct. So in Storm Jameson's *Love in
Winter* the city is populated by people 'looking to each other like
maggots'[93] while in Margaret Fraser's 'Delicate Destruction'
maggots eat away at the human brain and 'Industrious destruction gnaws'.[94]

As moral values were revealed as disposable, so these texts
entered into the black spaces left behind. In subject matter they
are very similar to work done by Surrealists such as Thomas
McGreevy or Hugh Sykes Davies,[95] whose texts are populated
with the rats, weevils, and worms that represent the disturbance
of the collective unconscious.

Unlike Surrealists within the official groups, however, in
general women writers who used Surrealist techniques in this
period tended to see these as a supplement to, rather than
replacement for, existing writing techniques. There are no
comparable texts by women writers to, say, Benjamin Péret's
'Making Feet and Hands' or Harry Crosby's 'Telephone
Directory'[96] with their far more extreme entry into the irrational

---

[92] Muriel Rukeyser, 'For Fun', *Life and Letters To-day*, 23/27 (Nov. 1939): 195.

[93] Storm Jameson, *Love in Winter* (London: Cassell, 1935; London: Virago,
1984), 28.

[94] Margaret Fraser, 'Delicate Destruction', *Poetry*, 47/1 (Oct. 1935): 18.

[95] See, for example, Thomas McGreevy, 'Homage to Hieronymus Bosch', and
Hugh Sykes Davies, 'Music in an Empty House', both in *Surrealist Poetry in English*,
ed. Edward B. Germain (London: Penguin, 1978), 76–7, 102–3.

[96] Benjamin Péret, 'Making Feet and Hands', trans. David Gascoyne, in *Surrealist
Poetry in English*, 124–5; Harry Crosby, 'Telephone Directory', in *Surrealist Poetry
in English*, 75.

and incongruous; instead women writers tended to maintain links with the conscious and rational. Also, like organized British Surrealism, for these women writers the work of art was not merely a contingent outlet for the all important 'expression', but the whole point of the exercise. These women were writers first and Surrealists second. Finally, again in common with British Surrealism and differing from the fundamental principles of French Surrealism, there was a belief in the potentially therapeutic value of the text through allowing an exploration of dark and irrational aspects of the mind.[97] The dark regions of the psyche were not of interest in and of themselves, but were very clearly part of a process oriented towards understanding these aspects, and thereby towards undermining their destructive potential. The ethos behind such work by these women was in line with the writing of the psychoanalyst W. R. D. Fairbairn, who argued: 'Art-work thus provides the means of reducing psychical tension in the artist's mind by enabling his repressed urges to obtain some outlet and satisfaction without unduly disturbing his equanimity'.[98] Fairburn felt that Surrealism was flawed because no repression at all was exercised, and that the work of art needed to find a medium between allowing a therapeutic release and some level of containment. It is this kind of middle position that much work by these modernist women writers occupied.

Of course the interest by modernist women writers in Surrealism does raise issues about the centrality of rationality as a basis of this literary public sphere. In understanding how Surrealism can be compatible with a concept of public exchange rooted in rationality, firstly it is necessary, as it was in relation to the historical avant-garde, to distinguish between the critical discussion around the literary text and the text itself; clearly an irrational subject matter does not necessarily undermine a process of rational critical discussion around the literary text. Secondly, the conscious 'argument' of the text still remained a relevant issue in work by these women writers; they were able to

---

[97] For a discussion of the therapeutic aspect of the Surrealist text to the British Surrealists Hugh Sykes Davies and Herbert Read, see Ray, *The Surrealist Movement in England*, 145, 194–5.

[98] W. R. D. Fairburn, 'Prolegomena to a Psychology of Art', *The British Journal of Psychology*, 28/3 (Jan. 1938): 294.

discuss their work in progress and to be influenced by each other's ideas, maintaining a 'conversation' through, as well as around, the literary text.

One text that epitomizes the impact of the irrational in semi-Surreal dark landscapes of shifting values is Djuna Barnes's *Nightwood*. The novel charts a constant endeavour by several characters (Nora, Felix, Jenny, and others) to protect themselves from all that is 'base' and irrational, yet also reveals their attraction to these impulses and desires. They fight against all knowledge of the 'night', afraid of the surfacing of the repressed, yet are all desperately attracted to Robin, the epitome of night values, as well as having an acute desire to save her and bring her back into the day. This sense of a battle against and attraction to the base and seamy side of life is epitomized in the doctor's description of 'Nikka, the nigger', a circus performer: 'Over his *dos*, believe it or not and I shouldn't, a terse account in early monkish script—called by some people indecent, by others Gothic—of the really deplorable condition of Paris before hygiene was introduced, and nature had its way up to the knees.'[99] It does not matter if the story is 'true', what matters is that Nikka becomes a symbol of the struggle to remind the self both of the human elevation from all that is base, primitive, filthy, and yet also of humanity's inability to escape from these and its fascination with them. The doctor sees an elemental violence in all people that they fight against but are drawn towards: 'There is not one of us who, given an eternal incognito, a thumbprint nowhere set against our souls, would not commit rape, murder and all abominations.'[100]

Many of the characters in *Nightwood* demand to be hurt, they thrive on their own pain. Felix is able to articulate this: 'The unendurable is the beginning of the curve of joy.' But it is Robin who lives out this life as victim or masochist most fully, drawn to the 'night', lowering herself down to, eventually, the level of a dog. Robin demands to be abandoned or hurt by all she comes into contact with and induces both Jenny and Nora to be physically violent towards her. Nora realizes the dimension of masochism/sadism in their relationship and the universality of the appeal of this: 'It flashed into Nora's head: "God, children

---

[99] Djuna Barnes, *Nightwood* (London: Faber and Faber Ltd., 1936), 32–3.
[100] Ibid. 128.

know something they can't tell, they like Red Riding Hood and the wolf in bed!" '[101] *Nightwood* dares to enter the night-side of the self where violence is not 'out there' but inside; futile attempts to deny this side of the self are demonstrated to be as destructive as Robin's embracing of it.

Text after text by women writers of this period enters the realm of the sadistic or masochistic, often graphically described, searching to understand or explore the human motivation to become the victim or aggressor (usually both). Women's writing of this period is bound up in fascism and gratuitous violence, but generally related to personal relationships and internal drives rather than as acted out on the world stage. In Kathleen Raine's 'Invocation' the speaker imagines tortures exacted on her body as the price for creativity, almost revelling in alternative ways in which her body could be mutilated. The speaker calls for snakes to 'torment her breast', for her uterus to be 'cut out', her belly to be 'slashed', her tongue to be 'slivered into thongs of leather' and to have 'rain stones' placed into her breasts.[102]

It is not, of course, that male writers of this period did not write about self-directed violence, but that for this particular group of women writers the focus is so dominated by internalized violence; again and again it is the self that is the victim and/or aggressor rather than external figures. This is in contrast to another group of writers, those adopting a journalistic style and writing in a more polarized way that tends to depict good (us) against evil (them). Kay Boyle, for example, whose powerful novels focus on violence and fascism in the external world, writes: 'For the first time since we were children we again believe in right and wrong and in absolute good and evil'.[103] The internalized perspective of the group of women writers under consideration also stands in contrast to many of the texts by the Auden Generation such as Auden's 'September 1, 1939' where the violence is 'out there', it is in the actions of 'dictators' which the innocent must suffer, or in 'Imperialism', not, it seems, within the speaker.[104]

---

[101] Ibid. 168, 117.
[102] Kathleen Raine, 'Invocation', *Stone and Flower: Poems 1935–43* (London: Nicholson & Watson, 1943), 10.
[103] Boyle, *Primer for Combat*, 42.
[104] Auden, 'September 1, 1939', 87.

For the majority of women writers under study here, even where the external war world is present in a text, it is generally not this that is the primary focus. So in Stevie Smith's *Over the Frontier*, though the frontier marks the transition to both external, legitimized acting out of aggression in war conditions and a release of personal sadistic desires, it is the latter that are the novel's focus. Pompey is brought face to face with her own sadism, and she attempts to resist it:

I am in despair for the racial hatred that is running in me in a sudden swift current, in a swift tide of hatred, and Out out damned tooth, damned aching tooth, rotten to the root.
Do we not always hate the persecuted?

Pompey asks fundamental questions about the role of 'victim' and 'aggressor' and realizes that these are far from clear-cut— even what appears to be altruism may be infected with currents of sadism. She also hypothesizes that the 'victim' may to some extent choose to be in the victim position, that he or she may be infected with as much aggression as the 'aggressor', but that this is manifested very differently; she speculates about the persecution of the Jews in a way very difficult to contemplate or countenance today, given a knowledge of the holocaust: 'Only a people hungry and ripe for persecution would have inspired and survived such a history.'[105] In part what Pompey recognizes in even raising this issue, is that it is only by interrogating the human tendency to enact both positions of aggressor and victim that these patterns can ever be dealt with. However, by asking this question Pompey is also attempting to remove the blame for her own aggressive and persecutory feelings from herself and displace it onto those she wishes to attack. The novel depicts her increasing closing-off to an awareness of her own internal reality, and her increasing susceptibility to an ideology of destruction and aggressive militarism. The novel is clear about the harm that unthinking participation in such a system does not only to its 'victims', but to the aggressors who lose touch with their own internal worlds.

Such a widespread examination of internal drives, privileged over external event, is not simply an expression of narcissism, but shows a profound awareness of a need to combat external

---

[105] Stevie Smith, *Over the Frontier* (London: Jonathan Cape, 1938), 158, 198.

violence at its source. Writing by many of the women of this period is very clearly 'war writing', yet deals remarkably little with battles, bombing raids, Nazism, or even life on the home front. Anaïs Nin's comments are enlightening here, in expounding a view that seems to have been fairly universally shared amongst women writers in this public sphere: 'The inner hatreds of men are now projected outside. There are fights in the streets. Revolution in France, they say. Men did not seek to resolve their own personal revolutions, so now they act them out collectively.'[106] For many women writers of this period, there is less an interest in the way that these inner difficulties are being acted out than in turning to their source—in the self—and examining the nature of these darkest impulses.

H.D.'s work of this period, then, can be placed in a wider context of women writers whose interest lay in exploring the masochistic and sadistic within the self. Later, reflecting on her work, H.D. writes: 'am I a masochist? Up to a point, it must have been my Will to be deserted. It must have been my will to be destroyed, so that I could go on to the star-nebula, H.D.–H.D. It is all in my Trilogy, 1945–1950'.[107] Again, in a letter to Bryher in 1932 she admitted, albeit jokingly, that she possessed a 'low sadistic side',[108] and it is largely such a sadism that formed the basis of her explorations in her work throughout the 1930s and early 1940s.

At this time, then, H.D. turned inwards to find the source of events that were shaking the world, and her work is correspondingly disturbing and disturbed. In *Nights*, for example, the novel centres on a relationship rooted firmly in bed, in sadistic attack and masochistic desire; Natalia enjoys sex with David only for its threat of annihilation: 'She let go, let drown in her blackness, she couldn't say it was all right, she was so frightened simply.' This relationship gradually swamps Natalia with darkness until the only choice left is her suicide, the ultimate outcome of attacks on the self. The text is insistent that Natalia's masochism is as

---

[106] Anaïs Nin, *The Journals of Anaïs Nin*, vol 1, ed. Gunther Stuhlmann (London: Owen, 1966), 316. Though Nin was highly marginal to this public sphere, her comments here articulate very well what was indeed the consensus within the public sphere.

[107] H.D., 'Thorn Thicket: Bosquet', second typed draft [?], carbon, 1960, p. 32, Beinecke.

[108] H.D. to Bryher, Jan. 4, [1932], Beinecke.

destructive as David's sadism, that the 'victim' role is to some extent a choice that has appeal to both victim and aggressor. Natalia is absorbed in her own annihilation, she visualizes death all around her and is ultimately overwhelmed by the self-attack that had begun as a sexual game:

She would get out, under that kiss. It was possible that it would kill her. It was one of the Major Arcana of the Tarot. It might be 13, her favourite almost, Death and the other more intense meaning that the 13 gave it. She believed that David's kiss was death because there was only blackness as she dropped under it and it spread (when she stopped breathing) a black canopy over her head.[109]

H.D. is concerned not only with spiritual heights, but with the darkest impulses of the psyche, examining the fascist within as well as without, and *Nights* is one of the clearest manifestations of this.

In H.D.'s *Kora and Ka* similar issues are acted out, centred on John Helforth's difficulty in resolving the conflict between the attractions of death/hate and life/love, in a classic Freudian division of self into Thanatos and Eros; unable to cope with this division, he rejects the 'feminine', nurturing side: 'I want to be John Helforth, an Englishman and a normal brutal one.'[110] He therefore splits off his feminine side into his 'Ka', a feminine spirit that both plagues him and gives him transcendent vision, and into his lover, Kora, forcing her into the role of female nurturer. The text is insistent that such a splitting off is dangerous, that love and hate, life and death, aggression, and the nurturing instinct, are part of the human condition. H.D. was heavily influenced by Denis De Rougemont's *L'Amour et L'Occident* at this time, and in particular, the evidence of her texts suggest, by his ideas on the fusion of love and death: 'The Eros of death and the Eros of life—each conjures up the other, and each has no true end or ending but the other, which it has been striving to destroy! And so everlastingly till all life and all spirit shall have been consumed.'[111] By ignoring the death-centred part of the self, the risk is taken that this will be acted out

---

[109] H.D., *Nights*, 84, 79.

[110] H.D., *Kora and Ka*, 23.

[111] Denis De Rougemont, *Passion and Society*, trans. Montgomery Belgion (London: Faber and Faber, 1940), 242. Trans. of *L'Amour et L'Occident* (Paris: Librarie Plon, 1939).

in sadism or masochism. For Helforth the result is a sadistic attitude towards his lover: 'I will break through Kora for I hate her.'[112] H.D.'s texts subscribe to the Freudian/Jungian view that masochistic feelings do not exist without the presence of sadistic feelings, and vice versa.[113]

H.D. also explored the root cause of these sadistic/masochistic impulses in her writing, generally following psychoanalytic theory in linking them to infant jealousy. So in H.D.'s 'Electra-Orestes' Electra recognizes that her hostility towards her mother, Clytemnestra, is the universal feeling of the child towards the parents who have excluded it from their relationship with each other, an instance of a universal archetype such that 'Clytemnestra, Electra and Death | are burnt like star-names in the sky . . . '.[114] Electra shows a jealousy of the parental couple that according to both Freud (child's jealousy of the partner of the same sex) and Klein (child's jealousy of one or both of the parental couple, usually the mother) is a key source of aggression.[115] Electra remembers her childhood jealousy:

ELECTRA   I was the sister, I was the priestess, I was alone.
ORESTES   No, you were never alone. You had my father. You had protection.
ELECTRA   Mother had him
ORESTES   But you saw him.
ELECTRA   I saw *them.*

('Electra-Orestes', *Collected Poems 1912–1944*)

Electra remembers only her exclusion, not the protection offered, and comes to see too late that this is the root of her aggression. Friedman's assertion that 'H.D. connected aggres-

---

[112] H.D., *Kora and Ka*, 31.

[113] Sigmund Freud, 'Three Essays on the Theory of Sexuality', *A Case of Hysteria: Three Essays on Sexuality and Other Works*, The Standard Edition of the Complete Psychological Works of Sigmund Freud, translation James Strachey, vol. 7 (London: The Hogarth Press and the Institute of Psycho-analysis, 1953), 159. Translation of 'Drei Abhandlungen zur Sexualtheorie' (Leipzig & Vienna: Deutlicke, 1905); C. G. Jung, *Analytical Psychology: Notes of the Seminar Given in 1925 by C. G. Jung*, ed. William McGuire (Princeton: Princeton University Press, 1989; London: Routledge, 1990), 77.

[114] H.D., 'Electra-Orestes', *Collected Poems 1912–1944* (New York: New Directions, 1983), 383.

[115] See, for example, Melanie Klein, 'Love, Guilt and Reparation', *Love, Guilt and Reparation and Other Works* (The Hogarth Press, 1975; London: Virago, 1988), 310.

sion with patriarchy'[116] seems to be a misreading; H.D. gave equal consideration to female aggression, and connects it as much to the infant's aggression towards the mother as any dynamics of the father–child relationship. The violence is inside the self, though potentially projected onto, or recognized in, others.

In her novel *The Gift* H.D. again explores the violence in close family relationships, particularly of the child towards the parents that do not include it in their close (sexual) relationship. Both parents become demonized in the child Hilda's mind as she projects her own aggression onto them, becoming the 'bad' parents that she imagines retaliating against her infantile attacks. Her father then becomes 'Bluebeard' in her mind, though she represses this association: 'I can not say that a story called Bluebeard that Ida read us from one of the fairy tales, actually linked up in thought—how could it?—with our kind father. There was a man called Bluebeard, and he murdered his wives. How was it that Edith and Alice and the Lady (the mother of Alfred and Eric) all belonged to Papa and were there in the graveyard?' The mother, likewise, becomes a 'witch', the 'bad' mother, who 'was going to stick the little girl right through with her long pointed stick and that was what would happen in the night'. As a child Hilda cannot understand the internal attacks she makes on her parents, but as an adult she can both understand their origin and begin to relate these to the externally acted out violence of the Second World War. She finds the present threat to her life less terrifying than her inner aggression had been before she began to come to terms with and understand it. In a bombing raid she is relieved that: 'The noise was outside. Death was outside. The terror had a name. It was not inchoate, unformed.'[117]

By understanding first her own innate hostility, and then the ways in which such hostility has been enacted throughout history, the war loses its terrifying incomprehensibility and can be understood as a mass acting-out of internal drives; as Freud explained it to her, related in 'Writing on the Wall': *'the child-hood of the individual is the childhood of the race—or is it the*

---

[116] Friedman, *Penelope's Web*, 340.
[117] H.D., *The Gift*, 7, 59, 140.

other way round?'[118] In *The Gift* Mamalie, Hilda's grand-mother, relates to Hilda the story of *Wunden Eiland*, the island of wounds where a long time ago the Indian and Moravian beliefs had met, first in a moment of unity, and later in a massacre at *Gnadenhuetten*. This massacre of church members has haunted Mamalie as if it were her own memory, which she now passes on to Hilda; Hilda realizes this is 'not just a thing that had happened even in the days of Papalie's grandfather, it was something that might still happen'. This is not only a pre-monition of the holocaust and bombing campaigns, but also an awareness that violence is inside every person, including herself. Only by understanding the origins of violence in herself and by coming to terms with this can she begin to handle the external threat, otherwise perceived as retaliation. The experience of confronting personal responsibility for this is difficult but ulti-mately rewarding: 'I had gone down, been submerged by the wave of memories and terrors repressed since the age of ten and long before, but with the terrors, I had found the joys, too'.[119]

The 'all clear' that sounds at the end of *The Gift* is more than a physical removal of external threat, it represents the under-standing, and therefore the removal of threat from, Hilda's innate sadism. The purpose of exploring these aggressive internal forces, then, does not seem to have been simply an acceptance of a loss of values, but an idea that through bringing repressed desires into a personal and collective awareness, change on both a personal and collective level could come about. A. T. Tolley asserts that 'In the thirties, the emphasis had been on the manipulation and improvement of the world: in the forties, in the face of the enormities of the war, it was on acceptance.'[120] This misses out the fundamental drive in much women's writing precisely on 'manipulation and improvement', on an internal rather than external level. As Edward Glover wrote in 1933: '*the first effective step towards abolishing war must be the most complete investigation and individual understanding of the nature of sadistic impulses, their original form, strength and depth, the history of their modification and inhibition.*'[121]

---

[118] H.D., 'Writing on the Wall', *Life and Letters To-day*, 45/93 (May 1945): 76.

[119] H.D., *The Gift*, 96, 139.

[120] Tolley, *The Poetry of The Forties*, 34.

[121] Edward Glover, *War, Sadism and Pacifism* (London: Allen & Unwin, 1933; extended series [1947]), 29.

Such a delving down into self-motivation for the sake of its therapeutic value is, of course, the quest of psychoanalysis, and many women writers turned to psychoanalysis or psychoanalytic thought in this period, seeking help for a shared neurosis rather than for purely personal problems. Bryher, for example, gave substantial amounts of money to the psychoanalytic movement in order to allow its work to develop, and used *Life and Letters To-day* to publish Barbara Low, Hanns Sachs, Melitta Schmideberg (daughter of Melanie Klein), Walter Schmideberg (Austrian psychoanalyst, husband of Melitta Schmideberg), and Havelock Ellis. In this way she was able to give a great number of readers and contributors access to contemporary psychoanalytic understandings. For H.D. the 1930s were dominated by her periods of psychoanalysis with several eminent psychoanalysts—Hanns Sachs (1931–2 in Berlin), Freud (1933 and 1934 in Vienna)[122] and Walter Schmideberg (1936 and 1937 in Switzerland). Psychoanalysis became a way of subjecting irrational internal violence to rational scrutiny, and therefore of undermining its power, a 'cure' that H.D. undertook for the community, not just for herself. She reflects in 'Writing on the Wall' on her reasons for consulting Freud:

I wanted to free myself of repetitive thoughts and experiences—*my own and many of my contemporaries*. I did not specifically realize just what it was I wanted, but I knew that I, *like most of the people I knew, in England, America, and on the Continent of Europe*, was drifting . . . . I would (before the current of inevitable events swept me right into the main stream and so on to the cataract) stand aside, if I could (if it were not already too late), and take stock of my possessions.[123] [italics mine]

Bryher too saw her psychoanalysis not as a purely personal project, but said also: 'It enabled me to help others who had gone temporarily over the borderline.'[124] She felt that the psychoanalysis was 'releasing a dynamo of electric energy on the world'.[125]

Many of these women writers wrote of their creative work as part of both a personal and collective healing process; Alyse Gregory, for example, writes: 'I would like to write something

---

[122] H.D. and Bryher were both also reading Freud's work and attending lectures.
[123] H.D., 'Writing on the Wall', *Life and Letters To-day*, 45/93 (May 1945): 76.
[124] Bryher, *The Heart to Artemis*, 256.
[125] Bryher to H.D., Nov. [11?], 1935, Beinecke.

that would bring consolation to the despairing or to the sensitive, self-distrustful, lonely people, or young people who are unfulfilled; and I would like to harmonize and make clear what I have learned from life, deepen my vision, and strengthen my intellect.'[126] The writing undertaken for Mass-Observation was a special case of this, a collective project closely allied to psychoanalysis; a typist from London described this: 'A psychological approach to the neurosis of civilisation is needed, and this is the line that Mass Observation is taking, and this is what I think it is for.'[127] Through Mass-Observation the individual experience and motivations could be compared to those of others, and the collective mood uncovered, and through this uncovering, deprived of its destructive force. H.D. too felt Mass-Observation to be part of a therapeutic process: 'Astrologists tell us, whether we discount their theory or not, that we are moving forward in a great age of "friends". M.O. and psycho-analysis seem part of this so-called Aquarian age movement, the moving forward where we are all in a whirl of unity, not of disruption'.[128] Individuals could be reassured by their participation in a larger process and by the similarity of the responses of others to their own. Again, Naomi Mitchison took this view, explicitly comparing Mass-Observation to psychiatry: 'Earlier Rosemary had been writing to a friend who is very unhappy; I suggested Mass-Obs. Of course, one realises that Mass-Obs is a kind of God-Figure—one confesses, one is taken an interest in, encouraged. Will Mass-Obs supersede psychiatry? I always recommend it myself.'[129]

It was not only the special case of Mass-Observation that enabled writers to take part in the healing process; writing in general was perceived as offering a space not only for an engagement with the depths of the psyche, but also for healing vision and regeneration through personal exploration and participation with others. However draining the process of artistic

---

[126] Gregory, *The Cry of a Gull*, 70.

[127] Miss Earnshaw, in *Wartime Women: An Anthology of Women's Wartime Writing for Mass-Observation*, ed. Dorothy Sheridan (London: Mandarin, 1990; 1991), 20.

[128] H.D., 'Letter and Reply to M.O. Questionnaire, 1937', 168.

[129] Naomi Mitchison, diary entry June 26, 1941, in *Among You Taking Notes: The Wartime Diary of Naomi Mitchison 1939–45*, ed. Dorothy Sheridan (London: Victor Gollancz, 1985),154.

creation could be, however much it drew on the whole resources of the individual and at times demanded more than could be given, in essence it also opened up a way out of the confusion by allowing the expression of what would otherwise remain at an internal level. As Fairburn writes in 1938: 'If art provides a channel of expression for sadistic phantasies, we have equal reason to believe that it provides a channel of expression for phantasies of restitution.'[130] Such an idea of art as potentially able to heal stands in contrast to the accounts given of this period as a time of absolute despair for artists; Robert Hewison, for example, writes:

What is important is that the extreme subjectivity, the retreat into personal concerns—elevated by some into the philosophy of 'personalism'—is indicative of the erosion of confidence in the power of artists to be shapers of circumstances, rather than victims. It is further evidence of the decline in morale felt to a greater or lesser degree by many writers during the war.[131]

There are many different ways in which texts of the period, in fact, very deliberately participated in a healing process. The 1940s are of course most often associated with the neo-religious writing of Auden and, most famously, Eliot's *Four Quartets*. The work of Edith Sitwell of this period came closest to this, using conventional Christian symbolism to write of resurrection and regeneration, part of the wave of writers turning to religious symbolism and Romantic forms in their writing, including Kathleen Raine, David Gascoyne, George Barker, and Dylan Thomas. H.D. too drew on Christian symbolism, however, her work is far more eclectic than that of Sitwell, Raine, Eliot, or Auden. Her *Trilogy* fused conventional Christian symbolism with mysticism, astrology, and hermeticism—different belief systems were brought together in a quest towards healing. *Trilogy* both presents the problem and, as *The Gift* does, works to heal. The first section, *The Walls Do Not Fall*, is H.D.'s most sophisticated and thorough exploration of the anger and aggression inside all people; there is no 'they' who are violent as against an 'us' who are not:

---

[130] Fairburn, 'Prolegomena', 297.
[131] Hewison, *Under Siege*, pp. xvi–xvii.

> We have seen how the most amiable,
> under physical stress,
>
> become wolves, jackals,
> mongrel curs;
>
> We know further that hunger
> may make hyenas of the best of us;[132]

One of the speakers desires to be eaten by the god *Amen*, to allow a masochistic fantasy to be acted out as a religious rite.[133] The lowest and the highest of humanity's desires become inextricably fused; there must be a painstaking examination of motive and symbolism in order to begin to separate these out. Meanwhile, the subconscious landscape is one of fish devouring fish, and of threat from octopus or shark and other 'incongruent monsters'.[134] By understanding personal aggression, the aggression of the 'enemy' becomes better understood, and *Trilogy* allows for development and progress towards healing rather than simply charting the problem. Out of suffering new understanding can emerge; the worm 'profit[s] | by every calamity'[135] and is able to draw life and creativity—however fevered and momentary—out of destruction, in a process akin to Eliot's redeeming and purifying fire:[136]

> in the rain of incendiary,
> other values were revealed to us,
>
> other standards hallowed us;
> strange texture, a wing covered us,
>
> and though there was a whirr and roar in the high air,
> there was a Voice louder,
>
> though its speech was lower
> than a whisper.[137]

In the second section, *Tribute to the Angels*, the process of

---

[132] H.D, *The Walls Do Not Fall* (London: Oxford University Press, 1944), 39; Susan Edmunds makes interesting connections between such expressions of female aggression and Kleinian theories in her 'Stealing from "Muddies Body": H.D. and Melanie Klein', *H.D. Newsletter*, 4/2 (Winter 1991): 17–30.

[133] H.D., *The Walls Do Not Fall*, 29.

[134] Ibid. 36, 37.

[135] Ibid. 14.

[136] T. S. Eliot, 'Little Gidding', *Four Quartets* (first publ. Harcourt, Brace, 1943) in *Collected Poems*, 221.

[137] H.D, *The Walls Do Not Fall*, 19.

healing is directed towards a sublimation of personal aggression and violence that transforms it into something more positive. H.D.'s view of alchemy is very Jungian, symbolic of the attempt to reconcile the 'unsatisfied duality'[138] of opposites in the self,[139] the victim and aggressor, sadist and masochist, communist and fascist that are at war. In *Tribute to the Angels* the alchemist attempts to take the sickness and evil of the recent past and turn it into a new substance. Though there have been 'seventy-times-seven | bitter, unending wars' there can be forgiveness and a new start. War is revealed to be only one of seven aspects of God, not the whole story. The sadism/violence is not destroyed, but transmuted, and thereby both understood and made new. All the aspects of God, all God's 'colours', if brought together will make white, a new purity.[140]

Finally, in the third section, *The Flowering of the Rod*, there can be resurrection, as characters leave behind all that has weighed them down and find new ways, imperfect and difficult, out of the darkness they have inhabited. H.D. writes:

The last [section of Trilogy] deals with resurrection—a good theme for the after-war or the end of the war. I had started making it a Victory poem but Victory is such a problem—I mean, there is so little real victory—a great deal, yes, but I mean there is the devastation everywhere. So I just thought the best thing was resurreuction [*sic*]—a rising-out or above all the dreary waste and sorrow.[141]

To be healed is to learn how to turn destruction and personal destructive capacities to creative use. The speaker renounces 'iron, steel, metal', the materials of war, for more organic materials of sea plants and wood. Destruction by fire is replaced by a cyclic death and rebirth that is not 'a heap of skulls' but a 'lily, if you will'. Mary rejects the masochistic position for one of healing, of myrrh:

> I am that myrrh-tree of the gentiles,
> the heathen; there are idolaters,

---

[138] H.D., *Tribute to the Angels* (London: Oxford University Press, 1945), 15.
[139] C. G. Jung, *Psychology and Alchemy*, trans. R. F. C. Hull (London: Routledge and Kegan Paul, 1953; 2nd edn., 1968), 37. Translation of *Psychogie und Alchemie* (Zurich: Rasher Verlag, 1944; 2nd edn., 1952).
[140] H.D., *Tribute to the Angels*, 11, 41.
[141] H.D. to Gretchen Wolle Baker, Dec. 20, [1944], Beinecke.

even in Phrygia and Cappadocia,
who kneel before mutilated images
and burn incense to the Mother of Mutilations . . .[142]

Trilogy as a whole, then, points to a way out of war by attempting the fullest examination of the forces that lead to war, and, ultimately, the forces that can lead to peace, of any work by any woman writer of this period. It is part of a wave of poems attempting to come to terms with a world appearing to have lost all moral values and stability. Norman Pearson viewed *Angels* as the first of the peace poems even before peace had been achieved, recording a 'reblossoming in a new springtime'.[143] The speaker is always 'surrounded by companions'; it is the 'us' that is important, the community that is able to pull itself up again out of destruction and begin to rebuild. A community has endured fire together and participated in the same revelation, they are:

> born of one mother,
>
> companions
> of the flame.[144]

Together they can work towards a cure, if they can accept their shared responsibility. There is seen to be a way out of destruction that involves human thought and reason (and specifically psychoanalysis) rather than the divine and incomprehensible intervention of the *Four Quartets*.[145] For H.D., then, writing was a way through the war, a means of survival and attempt at something more than this, a healing vision for herself and for others. Despite the fact that the effort of dealing with the war drained all her energies, she found herself able to harness the fevered energies of the war to her writing as long as the immediate pressures of the war continued. As long as the war continued she seemed unaware of the toll that harnessing it for positive energies and healing vision was demanding.

[142] H.D., *The Flowering of the Rod* (London: Oxford University Press, 1946), 15, 17, 23–4.

[143] Norman Pearson, review of *Tribute to the Angels* by H.D., *Life and Letters To-Day*, 46/95 (July 1945): 58.

[144] H.D., *The Walls Do Not Fall*, 20, 21.

[145] For a comparison of H.D.'s *Trilogy* with Eliot's *Four Quartets* see Cyrena N. Pondrom, '*Trilogy* and *Four Quartets*: Contrapuntal Visions on Spiritual Quest', *Agenda*, 25/3–4 (Autumn/Winter 1987/8): 155–65.

Numerous other texts of this period undertake a healing process, the most notable of which is Rukeyser's 'Ajanta'. In 'Ajanta' the speaker enters a cave in order to undertake a search for self and to gain a moment's respite from the forces assailing her. What she seeks—and finds—are 'connections', both to the past and to herself:

> The space of these walls is the body's living space;
> Tear open your ribs and breathe the color of time
> Where nothing leads away, the world comes forward
> In flaming sequences.

To come to this cave is to return to an infant state, the cave is the 'painted space of the breast'; in this female space the distortions of patriarchy are removed and power is seen for what it is.[146] However, unlike the New Apocalypse writers, Rukeyser, and most other women writers of this period, do not accept a fantasy world of politics-free organic wholeness.[147] 'Ajanta' does not offer, or even seek, a permanent escape, but a moment of wholeness following which the speaker will be newly empowered to return to the real world:

> World, not yet one,
> Enters the heart again.
> The naked world, and the old noise of tears,
> The fear, the expiation and the love,
> A world of the shadowed and alone.[148]

Her work admits tension and difficulty, and offers only partial solutions, not simplistic total vision.

Of course, any idea that art could provide release and healing from aggression understood on an individual and internal level does pose problems when set against a reality of the persecution of Jews and other groups in Europe, the mass loss of life in battle and in bombing raids. Though work by these women writers deals skilfully with internal scenarios of violence, their

---

[146] Muriel Rukeyser, 'Ajanta', *Beast in View*, 4, 7.

[147] The New Apocalypse writers included Dorien Cooke, J. F. Hendry, Norman McCaig, Robert Melville, Nicholas Moore, Philip O'Connor, Dylan Thomas, and Henry Treece. The work of Sitwell to some extent shares their simplistic vision of organic wholeness and non-problematized Romanticism.

[148] Rukeyser, 'Ajanta', 8.

work does not deal satisfactorily with the reality of the external-
ized sadism, and this must perhaps be seen as a blindness and a
shortcoming of these texts. This is a point that Victoria Harrison
makes about the work of Elizabeth Bishop, and which has a far
wider applicability to these women writers:

When one refuses to isolate a world war from the destructiveness lurking in the unconscious or from the potential warring of lovers in bed,
one distorts history at the same time as one revises one's perception of
it. Lovers in bed, one might argue, have not slaughtered millions; on the
other hand, one might respond, if we do not insist on understanding
ourselves where we are, we will not know what is alive, once we have
counted the losses of war.[149]

For these writers, knowing 'what is alive' was the imperative of
the 1930s and early 1940s. To explore the self in this way did
not preclude a more direct engagement with the war, such as
refugee work or political campaigning, nor was it in itself only of
marginal importance. To find out what was 'alive' was to make
life more than a struggle for survival, and was to make surviving
the war of the utmost importance.

The amount of energy invested in visions of restoration and
regeneration during the war by many women writers was
enormous. However, conversely, with the end of the war there
was a feeling of collapse and lack of any energy to face a difficult
new age of rebuilding, not only the war torn landscape but the
world of literature that had been so concerned with issues of war
and world conflict. Immediately the war ended H.D. experienced a breakdown, and she was not alone. In August 1945, as
she began to suffer the after-effects of the war, she wrote to
Gretchen Wolle Baker: 'So many of my London friends have
broken down, in various forms of nervous reaction, since V.E.
Day. . . . I have an excellent doctor & he gave me injections for
extreme fatigue'.[150] That several of these writers did experience a
collapse at, or in the decade following, the end of the war
(including Wickham and Stevie Smith) has perhaps most to do
with the amount of energy invested during the war in relentless
explorations of the psyche in order, almost, to stay sane, and the
relaxing of this energy once the war ended. H.D. had been able

---

[149] Harrison, *Elizabeth Bishop's Poetics of Intimacy*, 78.
[150] H.D. to Gretchen Wolle Baker, Aug. 2, 1945, Beinecke.

to muster huge amounts of energy during the course of the war, living with a new level of intensity through the worst years, but such a huge input of energy was non-sustainable once the war ended and 'normal' life looked set to resume.

H.D.'s degree of collapse reflected the amount of creative energy she had invested in fighting off defeatism during the war years. All that had been repressed in the war connected with the sheer terror of her position was now able to surface. She had written to Molly Hughes during the war: 'One can be very brave on the surface and some imp of distress or disgust or real downright biological or racial TERROR may grub down into the depth of ones mind, pushed down there by ones very best qualities of fortitude and courage, and there it or he may srpout [*sic*] into some real terror or "phobia"'.[151] At the end of the war H.D. was removed to Switzerland without her knowledge; on regaining an awareness of the world she felt this as a hostile abduction, and saw persecution all around her. Her letters to Bryher of the period reflected her enormous anxiety: 'Tell the Bear [Schmideberg] to bring his gun and some extra gun-men, if necessary.' She believed that her room was 'wired' and that 'they spotted my sheets with some sort of real or chemical "urine". I did not find this till long after mid-night, when I opened the bed. ... I got the sheets off but the shutter was locked, so I sat up all night, breathing this filthy "gas."'[152]

The period ended for H.D., then, not with a 'bang', but definitely a 'whimper'.[153] However, this does not in any way undermine the importance of her work as pursued throughout the pre-war and war years. The work of this period demonstrates the successful culmination of the interests of earlier years, such as an interest in internal reality, in personal violence, in the unconscious and in the public and private; her work also capitalizes on the gains made in terms of formal experimentation of the earlier years, both her own and that of her contemporaries. H.D. was able to demonstrate her immense versatility as a writer, in successful prose work such as *Nights* and *Kora and Ka* and in her immense *Trilogy* poem-sequence where her early Imagist work, with its evocation of internal and external 'experience' through

---

[151] H.D. to Molly Hughes, Nov. 14, [1943], Beinecke.
[152] H.D. to Bryher, [Sept. 21, 1946], Beinecke.
[153] T. S. Eliot, 'The Hollow Men', *Collected Poems*, 92.

the exact image, and her later more complex experiments, find their ultimate culmination.

Her work shared with many other women writers a relentless energy to get towards 'truth', however uncomfortable this might be. Clearly the women within this literary public sphere were generally not writing 'war poetry' as it is usually understood, and yet this global, public event can be found underlying their writing. That they tended to examine personal violence, masochism, and the corresponding therapeutic processes rather than battles and bombing raids both makes their work more private than that of the few clearly identifiable [male] war poets, yet far more public than either the neo-Romanticism of the New Apocalypse writers or the later work of Auden and Dylan Thomas. In a Habermasian context, the work emerging from the literary public sphere of women writers during this period was certainly not concerned merely with the 'good life' or exclusively centred on the lifeworld, yet it was certainly oriented towards protecting these spheres from all forms of systemic intrusion. The work of modernist women writers at this time demands a challenging of the concepts of 'public' and 'private', a realization that the 'public' may find internal representation and the 'private' external manifestations. For many modernist women writers these years mark the high point of their careers as writers, and for the community as a whole this was a time when the public sphere operated to its optimal capacity, generating heated and fully engaged discussion in areas of fundamental human importance, and resulting in texts that are of the highest literary merit.

6

Postscript

> So one by one they plunge into the labyrinthine forest
> and vanish down solitary paths, with no guide but their
> sorrows, no companions but their own voices. Their ways
> cross and re-cross yet never once do they meet though now
> and then one catches somewhere not far off a brief snatch
> of another's song.
>
> W. H. Auden, *The Age of Anxiety*[1]

Following the end of the war, the public sphere of modernist women writers was never again to regroup as a dynamic network. Though several individual writers produced interesting texts, the sense of a collective and co-operative endeavour was lost. In place of a public exchange of ideas, interactions between writers now took place within a much smaller arena oriented towards support and encouragement and rooted in private friendships rather than a more public interaction of contemporaries. For some this was simply a retreat into a more private space needed for reflection in old age, out of the fray of the public arena; for some this was connected to a sense of despair in an age of nuclear threat and social hardship, coupled with an awareness of the evil that had surfaced in the war years; for others there was a sense that a readership had vanished, their minds now occupied either by political issues or by the work of a much younger literary generation; for others still there was more simply a sense of nothing to say in a post-war world, nothing to contribute to a world from which they felt alienation.

By 1947 H.D., aged 61, had recovered from her breakdown, but was to remain in Switzerland for much of the rest of her life, predominantly at the Küsnacht clinic where she need do nothing but reflect and write. She wrote of her life there: 'I am ashamed almost, to stay on here, but it is beautifully warm & I have my

---

[1] W. H. Auden, *The Age of Anxiety* (London: Faber and Faber, 1948), 85.

books & MSS & work always, mornings in bed!'[2] H.D. had retreated into a protected space that was removed from contact with the external world, where she could read endlessly over her older work and write new texts that were largely disengaged from external reality. She was not entirely cut off from the outside world or from the literary community—her letters demonstrate her continued communication with a group of women writers including Sitwell, Richardson, Eliza Butler, Moore, Sylvia Beach, Alyse Gregory, Elizabeth Bowen, Rosemary Sutcliffe, Silvia Dobson, Marya Zaturenska, and Mary Herr, together with whom she engaged in a circulation of manuscripts. However, though there was some discussion of completed work and work in progress, these letters do not evidence a dynamic exchange of ideas spilling over from a vibrant engagement in the public sphere, but a network of private support and encouragement, replacing rather than complementing a more public engagement.

This period marks, then, the end of a 'public sphere' and its transformation into an arena of much more private exchanges involving a relatively small number of women writers. The new writing tended not to be offered as a contribution to a public dialogue, but instead to be sent, most often unpublished, to a small and select group of readers from whom the author could count on support and appreciation. Most of H.D.'s work had a readership limited to a close network of friends and friends-of-friends and existed only as two or three manuscript copies. Publication had become increasingly irrelevant in a network where the intended readership was so limited. H.D. now saw her contact with her contemporaries not as an active arena of challenge and discussion, but as a space of withdrawal. She saw her reading not as a place where she could come into contact with new ideas, but, for example, as 'a sort of sedative', and describes her vision of ideal interaction with her contemporaries: 'When I think of these, my contemporaries, I dream of a sort of retreat, a Magic Mountain where they could come and stay, rest, have proper food, books, all the attractions of our buzzing little metropolis, specialists, at beck and call.'[3] 'Retreat' is a key word

---

[2] H.D. to Richard Aldington, Jan. 13 [1959], Beinecke.
[3] H.D., 'Compassionate Friendship', second draft [?], typescript, with corrections by H.D., 1955, 7, 21, Beinecke.

here; H.D. now actively desired a close world of mutual support rather than the difficult criticism and disagreement that might generate new growth. In place of engagement with the external world, and in place of experimentalism and openness to the influence of contemporaries, H.D.'s work of this period was oriented towards what was for her a vital process of resolution and understanding, making it entirely appropriate to have discussion restricted to a small group of confidants whose loyalty and interest had already been tested.

Several of these women writers explicitly linked a retreat into the personal to the difficulties of the post-war era. Amy Bonner, for example, writes of the effects on a mind no longer able to cope with an engagement with the external world:

> I pull down the blinds of my mind like the lidded turtle
> To draw within, within deep caverns of thought,
> The subjective retreat of the tired, the wan, the worn,
> The grief-stricken.[4]

This poem spells out the trend of introspection and retreat observable across the literary sphere, and links it to a post-diluvian world decimated by all that has taken place. Instead of critical engagement with the contemporary world there was 'prayer', the development of a personal vision expressed as a religious conviction—or silence. There was a feeling that the mind could no longer take on board anything of the reality around it and specifically that the writer could no longer write anything meaningful about the external landscape. Again, Storm Jameson writes: 'In an age of faith, a writer adds himself, his work, to the living growing civilisation he has been born into. In a dying civilisation, he can only try to detach himself, to free himself from the weariness creeping over his age, by withdrawing from it into his own words.'[5]

Instead of looking to the future then, or even to the present, much of the work of this period looked backwards. Many of these writers wrote memoirs and accounts of recent literary history at this time, looking back on earlier, less troubled years. Memoirs included Sylvia Beach's *Shakespeare and Company*

---

[4] Amy Bonner, 'Curve of Quiet', *Poetry*, 72/5 (Aug. 1948): 246.
[5] Storm Jameson, 'W. H. Auden: The Poet of Angst', (1947) *The Writer's Situation*, 87.

and Bryher's *The Days of Mars*,[6] while other texts looked backwards over the dynamic literary community which had now ceased to exist, such as Babette Deutsch's *Poetry in Our Time*, Storm Jameson's *The Writer's Situation and Other Essays*, Louise Bogan's *Achievement in American Poetry*, Horace Gregory and Marya Zaturenska's *A History of American Poetry*, and Katherine Anne Porter's *The Days Before*.[7] For others there was a need to look back on a more personal history in an attempt to resolve past conflicts or to find some kind of synthesis or resolution. Djuna Barnes's *The Antiphon* is an extreme case, where the text was used to express a personal desire for revenge against family members. Barnes herself wrote of this text: 'If ever a thing were truly written for the writer this is it.'[8]

Marianne Moore's writing of this period shows several features that are characteristic of much of the work by this group at this time; her work was increasingly abstract and concerned with internal reflection and the ineffable rather than the more public issues that had been implicit in earlier work such as 'In Distrust of Merits'. In poems of the late 1940s such as 'By Disposition of Angels' she abandons the concrete and external, or even internalizations of shared public event and meaning, now reflecting on 'unparticularities praise cannot violate' and 'Mysteries [that] expound mysteries'.[9] Her 1958 poem 'In the Public Garden', while ostensibly set in a very public space, looks inward to speculate on values such as self-discipline, and concludes that 'Art, admired in general, | is always actually personal.'[10] Like many of her contemporaries, Moore had turned

[6] Sylvia Beach, *Shakespeare and Company* (New York: Harcourt, Brace, 1956); Bryher, *The Days of Mars: A Memoir*.

[7] Babette Deutsch, *Poetry in Our Time* (New York: Columbia University Press, 1952); Jameson, *The Writer's Situation*; Louise Bogan, *Achievement in American Poetry* (Chicago: Henry Regnery, 1951); Gregory and Zaturenska, *A History of American Poetry 1900–1940*; Porter, *The Days Before*.

[8] Djuna Barnes to Willa Muir, Aug. 20, 1962, quoted in Phillip Herring, *Djuna: The Life and Work of Djuna Barnes* (New York: Viking, 1995), 281.

[9] Marianne Moore, 'By Disposition of Angels', first published in *Quarterly Review of Literature* IV (ii) (1948): 121; repr. *The Complete Poems of Marianne Moore* (London: Faber and Faber, 1967), 142.

[10] Marianne Moore, 'In The Public Garden', first published in *The Boston Globe* (June 15, 1958): 6; repr. *The Complete Poems of Marianne Moore* (London: Faber and Faber, 1967), 190–2.

towards personal vision and away from the concrete or issues of collective importance. For this reason her later work often presents a high level of difficulty to the reader, focused on abstract philosophical considerations or personal references that are far removed from a shared or public world.

For H.D. the primary purpose of writing in the years after the war was to look back on her life and seek resolution or an overarching vision, to find meaning to set against a seemingly senseless and chaotic external environment. In short, her work was centred on healing her wounds through a process of therapeutic mulling over past events. In letters to friends she described how her writing allowed her to find personal resolution; she wrote to Bryher of *Helen in Egypt*,[11] for example: 'When Achilles asks which was the dream, which the "veil", it is my own effort to re-adjust or get the two together yet separate.'[12] She used her work to reflect back on her whole writing career, sometimes overtly, as in *Vale Ave*:

> I transcribed the scroll, I wrote it out
> and then I wrote it over, a palimpsest of course,
>
> but it came clear, at last, I had the answer
> or the seven answers to the seven riddles,
>
> the why and why and why—the meeting and the parting
> and his anger—it took some time, though five years is not long
>
> to write a story, set in eternity but lived in—England;
> I left of course; I traveled [*sic*] to Tessin from Lausanne,
>
> to Zürich and around and back again,
> and I wrote furiously; he got the last of this prose Trilogy,
>
> this record, set in time or fancy-dressed in history,
> five years ago, then I had five years left
>
> to break all barriers, to surpass myself
> with Helen and Achilles . . .
>
> an epic poem? unquestionably that . . .[13]

To mull over the past was for H.D., as for many of her contemporaries, a crucial stage in assimilating the events of her life.

---

[11] H.D., *Helen in Egypt* (Grove Press, 1961; Manchester: Carcanet Press, 1985).
[12] H.D. to Bryher, Oct. 11, [1952], Beinecke.
[13] H.D., *Vale Ave: a poem by H.D.* (Redding Ridge: Black Swan Books, 1992), 49.

H.D.'s transcript of 'Compassionate Friendship' is largely a reflection back on her career as a writer in order to find cohesion and clarity, to make her work fit into some kind of overall pattern: 'I find myself caught back into these periods, poetry and prose and want to go over everything.'[14]

H.D. certainly felt her work of this period to have been highly valuable in offering her relief from troubled states of mind, and described this work as amongst her best as far as an achievement of personal clarity was concerned. She wrote to Bryher: 'as I said of SYNTHESIS and as I now say of the ROSE book [White Rose and the Red], I have satisfied myself, and after nearly a life-time of "writing," that is, I suppose, something'.[15] In other letters to Bryher she wrote: 'I am so happy about GUEST'[16] and of *White Rose and the Red* 'not that I MYSELF don't think the book is marvellous, I do';[17] she described this novel and 'The Sword Went Out to Sea' as her 'MAGISTER LUDI'[18] and 'The Mystery' as 'the perfect formula'.[19] And again: 'The Sword traces my intellectual and emotional life to its conclusion or rather to its fulfilment. The Sword is the crown of all my effort, the final version or rather the new version of the Greek novel that I had written, revised, discarded and re-written, ever since the time of the actual experience in the spring of 1920.'[20]

That critics of this period often did not agree with such a positive valuation is symptomatic of a clash of purposes here; H.D. seems to have found important 'answers' and 'vision'—but does not describe her writing as successful in terms of its formal structure or linguistic interest, nor does she describe it as providing answers for the community; these seem to have lost their priority against more pressing personal needs. Many critics saw this work as failed attempts to communicate, when, in fact, it is doubtful if communication was her primary objective. Critics were baffled by her use of various thought systems, which included Jungian, Kleinian and Freudian psychoanalysis, hermeticism, kabbalism, myth, and myth theory. Josephine Jacobsen, for

[14] H.D., 'Compassionate Friendship', 26, Beinecke.
[15] H.D. to Bryher, Aug. 5, [1948], Beinecke.
[16] H.D. to Bryher, Aug. 1, [1947], Beinecke.
[17] H.D. to Bryher, Aug. 5, [1948], Beinecke.
[18] H.D. to Bryher, July 15, [1951], Beinecke.
[19] H.D. to Bryher, June 1, [1954], Beinecke.
[20] H.D., 'H.D. by Delia Alton', 190.

example, wrote in 1962 of *Helen in Egypt*: 'Her experience with Freud had a profound impact on H.D.'s poetry, and Helen in Egypt is in part the poetically hapless result, since the psychoanalysis, untransmuted, has swamped the poetry.'[21] What Jacobsen was observing was symptomatic of the process that H.D. herself had described, of allowing her writing to take place in an almost 'automatic' way, with minimum conscious intervention, and to trust that her comprehensive understanding of different psychoanalytic theories and other systems of thought would bring to the surface the most relevant and pressing issues to be resolved.

To criticize her writing for its impenetrability, then, as many critics did, is perhaps to approach the text as a contribution to a public discourse that it was not intended to be. Richard Eberhart criticized H.D.'s work of this period: '[Religious] troubles knot her later pages, where she loses edge trying words upon the ineffable.'[22] H.D. does 'try out' ideas, she does attempt to deal with highly complex systems of thought and to test these out against each other, invoking religious figures and systems including Christianity (and therefore a whole host of angels),[23] the god Amen, Isis (and the 'cult of Isis' as a religion),[24] various Egyptian goddesses, Hectate (and the 'witch-cult'),[25] occultism, hermeticism, Moravian theology, and a 'secret cult of the Night'.[26] H.D. writes that 'the mythical or religious love-story continues through all the writing.'[27] However, this religious quest was part of her wide-ranging search for understanding, not a 'public' contribution to a discourse into which she had no interest in entering, and to criticize her work for 'losing edge' therefore misses the point.

Many other writers of the older generation found that their work was misunderstood in this way, that critics were baffled by its highly personal focus and its very personal meanings. Critics

---

[21] Josephine Jacobsen, 'H.D. in Greece and Egypt', *Poetry*, 100/3 (June 1962): 188.

[22] Richard Eberhart, 'Hölderlin, Leopardi, and H.D.', including review of *Selected Poems* by H.D., *Poetry*, 91/4 (Jan. 1958): 265.

[23] See, for example, H.D., *Hermetic Definition* (Oxford: Carcanet Press, 1972), 19–21 and 57–84.

[24] Ibid. 8.

[25] H.D., *Helen in Egypt*, 26.

[26] H.D., *Vale Ave*, 24.

[27] H.D., 'H.D. by Delia Alton', 180.

demanded more clues than they were given, and found them-selves left adrift in texts of personal association to which they had no key. Deutsch complained of Sitwell's work of this period: 'The trouble with Miss Sitwell's perfumes, sounds, and colors is that their correspondences are sometimes overly private.'[28] Kenneth Allsop complained of the older generation as a whole:

Wincing with distaste, mournful and puzzled, they have withdrawn to a remote and musty fantasy life among their woodland temples. Their considerable talent is absorbed into the construction of elaborate, private languages, elegiac remembrance of things past, reveries that are passed like an empty parcel around an ever diminishing circle. Their writing becomes more and more heavily wrought with convoluted scrollwork, or more and more allusive, quivering with nuance, gauzy with conventional subtleties that taper-off into the raising of an eye-brow.[29]

The criticism here was not just that texts were 'difficult', as earlier avant-garde work had been, but that they did not seem to be a recognizable 'communication' at all. These were not texts that were intended to raise questions in the reader's mind about the nature of writing, the role of art, the possibilities of language and so on—their difficulty arose because of the inaccessibility of entirely private landscapes which entailed a whole network of references and correspondences unavailable to any reader not on intimate terms with the writer's life. Further, in the case of many, as diverse as H.D., Muriel Rukeyser, Eliza Butler, Kathleen Raine, and Silvia Dobson, the reader was called on to be familiar with multiple difficult, often obscure systems of thought and philosophical theories that formed a barrier to all but the most determined. These are texts with far less accessibility than earlier avant-garde experiments such as those by Freytag-Loringhoven or Mina Loy, since they refuse to be placed in a wider literary community or to be interpreted by current issues of shared interest. Their difficulty is not in any sense a public statement, but almost incidental, a result of the reader's lack of clues to an internal world; this work represents, then, either the logical conclusion to, and most extreme point of, avant-gardism, or its ultimate disintegration.

---

[28] Deutsch, *Poetry in Our Time*, 221.
[29] Kenneth Allsop, *The Angry Decade* (Peter Owen, 1958; Wendover: John Goodchild Publishers, 1985), 25.

Many of these writers had no desire to get their work of this period published. H.D. certainly seems not to have attempted publication of the majority of her texts, including 'The Sword Went Out to Sea', 'White Rose and the Red', 'The Mystery', 'Magic Mirror', 'Compassionate Friendship', and 'Thorn Thicket',[30] while others were not published until well after her death, such as 'Advent',[31] 'H.D. by Delia Alton', *Vale Ave*, *End to Torment*,[32] and *Hermetic Definition*. In fact, only *By Avon River*[33] and *Helen in Egypt* were written and published at this time. However, in the case of several of her unpublished texts she may have sought publication without success, rejected by a publishing arena that wanted to look forwards and outwards rather than backwards and inwards. Susan Friedman in her authoritative list of H.D.'s publications cites 'White Rose and the Red' as 'probably rejected'.[34] The highly personal and reflective nature of her work of this time was no doubt the reason for this.

H.D.'s contemporaries also experienced difficulties in getting published that they had not previously encountered, and turned to each other for affirmation and consolation; Jean Starr Untermeyer wrote to H.D.: 'I, too, have put together a rigidly selected Poems; but so far no publisher. I broke with Viking after so many years. But I shall go on till some publisher sees the light. Ha!'[35] Eliza Butler too found it hard to get her work published, and wrote to H.D. in 1953: 'I <u>do</u> need encouragement at the moment, as the agent has returned Byron and Goethe saying it is of no interest! I'm trying the Hogarth Press with it'.[36] The next month she wrote that Hogarth Press had also rejected it,[37] and in February 1955 that it had been rejected by Murray;[38] it was

---

[30] All these manuscripts are held at the Beinecke Library (The Yale Collection of American Literature).

[31] H.D., 'Advent' in *Tribute to Freud* (New York: Pantheon Books, 1956; With 'Advent', Boston, Mass.: David R. Godine, 1974; Manchester: Carcanet Press, 1985), 113–87.

[32] H.D., *End to Torment* (New York: New Directions, 1979); H.D., *Hermetic Definition*.

[33] H.D., *By Avon River* (New York: Macmillan, 1949).

[34] Susan Stanford Friedman, 'H.D. Chronology: Composition and Publication of Volumes', *The H.D. Newsletter*, 1/1 (Spring 1987): 14.

[35] Jean Starr Untermeyer to H.D., Nov. 10, 1956, Beinecke.

[36] Eliza M. Butler to H.D., June 30, 1953, Beinecke.

[37] Eliza M. Butler to H.D., July 19, 1953, Beinecke.

[38] Eliza M. Butler to H.D., Feb. 20, 1955, Beinecke.

finally accepted for publication in January 1956.[39] When she did manage to get her work published it received a great many exceptionally negative reviews. She wrote to H.D. in 1952:

You ask about reviews of <u>Silver Wings</u>. The one in the Listener was mild indeed compared with some of the others. It's had a <u>very</u> bad reception on the whole; and the worst of it is that the publishers . . . completely agree with the reviewers & didn't want to publish it; [Leonard Woolf] made them. Very few of my friends like it either; so that it if werent [*sic*] for you, and just one or two others, I should be frightfully discouraged. Also, my big book <u>The Fortunes of Faust</u> has had a very bad press, when it has not been altogether ignored.[40]

Silvia Dobson's letter to H.D. in 1956 gives a clue to as to why so many of these writers might have been experiencing their difficulties in getting published: 'Gollancz didn't take my book, but that chief reader's report was helpful. He thought it "was intenesely [*sic*] interesting and rang true completely . . . . . until it soared into a most unexpected realm of fancy and fantasy"'.[41] Dobson's work was rejected, then, for being too intensely personal and inaccessible, for being, essentially, to do with processes of personal reflection above public communication.

Interestingly, the same reasons that caused several critics to write negative reviews of H.D.'s work at this time (as that of her contemporaries), seem to underlie the high critical acclaim in which it is held today. H.D.'s work of this period, with its characteristic lack of formal structure and ability to allow a 'free play' of ideas, makes it of particular interest to a current within feminist theory that celebrates such work as representing a challenge to 'patriarchal' discourse. Again and again H.D.'s work of her last years has been embraced as refusing the constraints of the 'symbolic order', and for demonstrating a return to the 'pre-oedipal', a transcendence; Friedman tells us that H.D. 'resurrects matriarchal values';[42] Hollenberg writes that 'the chain of word origins and word-sound associations afford[s] H.D. a liberating departure from the male symbolic order';[43] Deborah Kelly

---

[39] Eliza M. Butler to H.D., Jan. 14, 1956, Beinecke.

[40] Eliza M. Butler to H.D., Aug. 25, 1952, Beinecke.

[41] Silvia Dobson to H.D., Oct. 20, [1956?], Beinecke.

[42] Susan Friedman, 'Creating a women's mythology: H.D.'s *Helen in Egypt*', *Women's Studies*, 5/2 (1977): 165.

[43] Hollenberg, *Poetics of Childbirth and Creativity*, 218.

Kloepfer writes of *Helen in Egypt*: 'Perhaps a "matricentric" text relies on a riddle, relies on riddling in both its senses—posing puzzling questions and piercing holes, "impair[ing] [the symbolic] as if by puncturing" '.[44]

It would seem, then, that H.D.'s use of her writing in her last years to reflect in a less formally structured and far more personal space has led to a posthumous critical acclaim in a climate that finds in this evidence of resistances to 'patriarchal' authority and values. In particular *Helen in Egypt* is held, for these reasons, to be her *magnum opus*, its labyrinthine structure and involutions taken to be an entirely positive development within her work. The very private text paradoxically becomes central in a public sphere of feminist critics to the extent that these critics are able to enter into a critical dialogue about the multiple meanings which it can produce; the lack of guidance given to the reader results in endless speculation of the various readings and different theoretical interpretations that are possible.

For the purpose of a study of this public sphere of modernist women writers whose course has been charted over a thirty-three-year time-span, the crucial point to notice is simply that the writing of this period, by H.D. and others, had stepped outside the bounds of the more public exchange of ideas evident in earlier years, and that it therefore needs to be understood within a different framework from that offered by a broadly Habermasian model. Any approach to the work of this period needs to focus more firmly on the work of individuals and their intensely personal agenda, rather than on a public exchange that no longer existed.

---

[44] Deborah Kelly Kloepfer, *The Unspeakable Mother: Forbidden Discourse in Jean Rhys and H.D.* (Ithaca: Cornell University Press, 1989), 169–70. Kloepfer is quoting from Naomi Schor, 'Eugenie Grendet: Mirrors and Melancholia', in *The (M)other Tongue: Essays in Feminist Psychoanalytic Interpretation*, ed. Shirley Nelson Garner, Claire Kahane, and Madelon Sprengnether (Ithaca, NY: Cornell University Press, 1985), 217.

Conclusion

By examining the operation of this (counter-)public sphere over thirty-three years it has been possible to form an understanding of its internal operating principles, the ways in which it functioned to allow for a dissemination and exchange of ideas; Craig Calhoun's questions about the formation of any given counter-public sphere as discussed in Chapter 1 bear repetition here:

> For any such cluster we must ask not just on what thematic content it focuses but also how it is internally organized, how it maintains its boundaries and relatively greater internal cohesion in relation to the larger public, and whether its separate existence reflects merely sectional interests, some functional division of labor, or a felt need for bulwarks against the hegemony of a dominant ideology.[1]

It is now possible to return to Calhoun's questions and to summarize the principles underlying this counter-public sphere of women writers.

Over the years, then, this public sphere developed a complex internal organization that was initially, in the years 1913–17, centred around a core group of three little magazines all edited by women: the *Egoist*, *Little Review*, and *Poetry*. In these magazines a literary community was able to come together as equals, with well-established writers (Amy Lowell, Edith Wyatt) participating alongside the young and inexperienced (H.D., Bryher, Moore). Discussion groups sprang up around these magazines where ideas could be voiced and critically interrogated, and where personal contacts and friendships were formed. The magazine editor was particularly important in the development of the public sphere and in establishing its underlying principles, and the democratic convictions of editors such as Harriet Monroe and Margaret Anderson were crucial in setting out the terms on which this network would operate. H.D.'s

---

[1] Craig Calhoun, 'Introduction', *Public Sphere*, 38.

editorship of the *Egoist* for one year (1916–17), and her involvement in *Close Up* in the 1920s, gave her the opportunity to help shape the course of debate. She and other magazine editors were instrumental in establishing and maintaining conditions whereby only the relative worth of the texts appearing in the magazines, as assessed by other readers, contributors, and writer-critics, would determine whose voices would become important.

As the public sphere developed in confidence between 1918 and 1924 and became established as a coherent network, its base spread out over a much wider group of magazines, and into a much more competitive arena. The women participating in this public sphere no longer required the nurturing and relatively protected space of the female-edited journals, but were able to make their voices heard within male-dominated publications where their work was immediately subject to more potentially hostile criticism. In addition, with the growing confidence of these writers there was scope for increased disagreement and more heated exchange, allowing new ideas to be thoroughly tested and a 'fast track' of writers to separate itself out from the many hundreds publishing in the magazines. Outside of the magazines, their work developed into longer published texts including novels, plays, and collections of poems, as well as films, theoretical material, memoirs, and treatises. From 1918 it was evident that a new wave of writers had been influenced by the early work of, in particular, H.D., Lowell, and Moore, and their work poured into the public sphere, giving it greater diversity and scope. Other writers who had been outside this public sphere also became involved, most notably Mina Loy, bringing new influences into this network. It was increasingly evident that the ideas emerging in the writing of this period originated not with any one writer, but were the result of the radical potential of this melting pot of new thought.

Of the mass of material coming into the public sphere, it was the critical and theoretical work that became most crucial in a dissemination and exchange of ideas. These writers were in a position to spell out the changes being observed in the literary text, and to discuss the importance and relative merits of these changes. Over the years, stylistic developments included the *vers libre* and Imagist poems, the stream of consciousness novel, 'automatic' and pseudo-psychotic writing, avant-garde forms, and the Surrealist form. Increasingly, new areas of thought from outside of this public sphere, particularly in psychoanalysis, fuelled critical and theoretical discussion, and allowed the public sphere critically to interrogate its own utterances. H.D. was involved in criticism and reviews, as well as writing several theoretical texts, and participated in an extended discussion of these issues in letters between herself and her contemporaries. Her 1919 theoretical work *Notes on Thought and Vision*, for example, brought psychoanalytic ideas further into this literary arena and raised important questions about an understanding of literary creativity and in particular the relation of creativity to the body and to sexuality.

One reason why discussion flourished and why so many new ideas came into the public arena was that the critical discussion was conducted primarily between the writers and readers themselves rather than by specialist 'critics'. Very few of these women were involved in academia, nor were there any pre-established critical norms; this was a field wide open to new ideas, fuelling a dynamic wave of experimentation in all directions, thematic and stylistic. Whereas today a (feminist) critic must tread warily so as to avoid being accused of 'essentialism' or of making 'naïve' connections between signifier and signified, and must hedge any statements of connection between the life and the work of a writer with multiple disclaimers, in this newly emergent critical community no such curbs were in place, and critical discussion could accommodate a variance of opinion. As far as was possible then, this arena functioned in a way close to the Habermasian model of the ideal public sphere; only the worth of the opinion offered, divorced from narrow confines as to what might constitute an acceptable utterance, determined the extent to which it would be taken on board by this public sphere of women writers.

In addition to the 'rational' theoretical and critical discussion, individual literary texts participated in 'discussion' by positioning themselves in relation to shared critical ideas, in testing and expanding the frontiers of the written form, in experimenting with ways of representing the human psyche and specifically women's experience (particularly in the early 1920s), in questioning boundaries between 'literature' and 'politics' (particular-

ly in the 1930s), and in multiple other challenges to conventions
of representation and the scope of the literary text. For any
individual literary text it was possible to identify a sub-text
behind it that was implicitly offering comment or asking questions; these included questions such as 'can the self be expressed
like this . . . ?' or statements such as 'it is not possible to express
this idea or emotion in more conventional forms'. These implicit
questions and statements were recognizable to the reader and
could be responded to either in critical discussion of the text
concerned, or by new writing that implicitly accepted or refuted
these earlier statements (or answered these questions) and might,
ideally, develop these ideas further and carry the literary arena in
a new direction. H.D.'s writing was so important in this literary
public sphere precisely because it raised so many questions and
ideas, questions of style, questions around women's identity,
questions of consciousness and unconsciousness, questions of
the boundary of the public and private, the political and personal. Even the more avant-garde work can be understood as
part of such discussion, then, since it caused critics and reviewers
to ask fundamental questions about the written form. Though
the forms of these texts often departed from 'rationality', they
could nevertheless serve as conversational utterances broadly in
line with the principles set out by Habermas. Any narrow understanding of rationality, or an idea that the literary text is in
any sense a 'flawed' utterance that fails to live up to the ideal
rational utterance, clearly needs to be modified to take account
of this much more complex rational exchange of ideas.

One reason why H.D.'s work was central to this network of
women writers, then, was because of its refusal to be limited by
conventions of form or subject matter, and its constant willingness to open itself to new influence. In each of the major stages
of change in women's writing of these years—the challenge to
sentimentality, the experiments in *vers libre*, the interest in internal reality, the stream of consciousness novel/use of interior
monologue, the opening up of issues of women's sexuality, the
interest in psychoanalytic theory, and the increasing interest in
the political world and examinations of this on an internal
level—H.D.'s work was at the forefront of change and development. She was willing to abandon early modes of expression and
to allow her work to develop through influence and through

her assessment of, and interest in, the critical and theoretical discussion into which she entered.

Calhoun also raises the issue of the 'boundaries' of the counter-public sphere—what it is that determines who can participate, how the identity of the public is understood, and how this is compared and contrasted to that of the dominant arena. As has been demonstrated, this public sphere maintained its boundaries in part through a rigorous self-regulation that brought it at times close to a 'literary aristocracy'. H.D. had the financial freedom that was almost a prerequisite for participation, and was later supported substantially by Bryher's more significant wealth. Though some early attempts were made to support the less wealthy in order to enable them to play an equal role in the public sphere, the vast majority of women involved in this network were upper-middle or upper class. They were free to travel, and often exiles (as H.D. was); they were generally well educated, either at home or, increasingly, at college or university (H.D., Bishop, Eudora Welty, Josephine Miles, Jameson, Moore, Mary Renault, and others). This was the necessary background that could grant these women their freedom, and though several expressed condescending attitudes towards the 'masses' this was less to do with class snobbery as such than a recognition that the less educated were often unable to participate at a high level of literary and critical discussion. To participate in this public sphere also required a level of income sufficient to guarantee independence to travel and to have the leisure to write.

To return again to Calhoun, it is certainly possible to establish that there was in this counter-public sphere a 'relatively greater internal cohesion in relation to the larger public'. An ideal of a community fighting for the same ends led to very strong bonds between many of these writers and it was out of such bonds that much of the best work emerged, buoyed up by a sense of an 'us' that pervaded much of the work. Again and again these women asserted the values of the literary community and make strong claims for the work emerging out of this. Storm Jameson writes:

The isolation of writers from each other is almost as deadly as their isolation from the life of farmers, labourers, miners and the other men on whom the life of the nation depends. If something of this unnatural apartness can be broken down, by writers working together, by their coming into relation with their fellow-men and women, they may, between them, provide the conditions, the warmth, for a new literature.[2]

Jameson was aware that a 'new literature' could not evolve out of the work of an individual, however committed, and that movements dominated by the views of one charismatic leader generally had a short lifespan and limited following. In addition, the community could support its members through personal and collective difficulties and help the individual to position herself in relation to events in the wider world.

Laura Riding in particular was able to articulate many of the fundamental principles of the literary public sphere in her 1938 *The World and Ourselves*; she writes, for example, of the discussion of an ideal community centred around an issue of mutual importance: 'Talk is profitable when there is a subject of common interest that needs enlargement to include the greatest possible variety of individual interests, so that mistaken assumptions or incomplete definitions shall not weaken its general appeal.'[3] Again, Riding theorizes the manner in which such a public sphere might come into existence:

Let us imagine a company in operation—or, rather, in the process of being formed. We begin with a group of people who know one another 'through' one another and among whom a general devotion prevails. They rarely meet all at the same time, and perhaps only a few live in the same neighbourhood; and there is more positive intimacy between some than between others. But a thread of common interest is drawn from one to the other . . .[4]

Riding articulates the necessity of 'speak[ing] only as you have some living interest in your subject, only as it is in some way yours' and of 'finding the words which are truest to the occasion or the subject at that moment of your interest in it'.[5] Whether this was the avant-garde form or the Imagist poem, the stream of consciousness novel, or the theoretical text, women involved in this network were very clearly trying to find the form that was 'theirs' and words that were 'true to the occasion', rather than relying on more traditional forms. To have some 'living interest'

[2] Storm Jameson, 'Documents', *Fact*, 4 (July 1937): 17–18.
[3] Riding, 'Introduction', *The World and Ourselves*, 13.
[4] Riding, 'Conclusion', *The World and Ourselves*, 452.
[5] Riding, ibid. 514.

in the subject approximates the Habermasian requirement of a 'private interest', this being the motivation that will bring the speaker into dialogue and cause him or her to engage with others both in defence of personal convictions and in a willingness to have these ideas modified by the views of others. There was a desire to express the idea in the way that best communicated that particular idea, and a resistance to any convention or tradition that would restrict honest, open, and above all new, expression. Riding sets out the necessity of abandoning all dogma and convention: 'Do not speak on any subject through a previous opinion of it: this always makes a preliminary tightening of the mind. Let the material rise fresh before you, and you rise fresh to it. . . . Let each occasion of language be a new occasion.'[6] To approach these writers as a 'public sphere', then, is not to impose an arbitrary theoretical system of thought from outside, but to understand the ways in which these writers understood their own interaction.

To some extent this community of writers certainly did involve Calhoun's 'felt need for bulwarks against the hegemony of a dominant ideology'; women had been to a large extent excluded from the dominant literary public sphere, and needed to establish their work and their projects as being of an equal validity and interest to those of other more 'dominant' groups. In the earliest years, from 1913 to 1917, they needed to assert their difference from a perceived tradition of women's 'sentimental' writing, the 'pretty' and 'feminine' that were felt to be stifling expression. They had also to counter an expectation that their work be contained within the private sphere as letters and journals, or that it appear in contained spaces within the public sphere (the anthology of 'lady poets'). From 1918 to 1924 in particular, breaking down expectations of women's writing often involved radical challenge, the presentation of the ugly, the sexually explicit, the vocal demand for public voice. In fact, then, this community was less a reassuring space, a 'bulwark' to provide shared security, than a highly hazardous space where they risked ridicule (Amy Lowell in particular fell victim to this), rejection (the work of Dorothy Richardson and May Sinclair was dismissed by many as trivial) or censorship (Margaret

---

[6] Riding, ibid.

Anderson's *Little Review* and Radclyffe Hall's *Well of Loneliness*, for example).

These women were also not only implicitly reacting against a tradition of establishment (male) writers who were educated at public schools and at Oxbridge, and who were publishing in the most prestigious magazines and wielding a great deal of literary power, but also against the male-dominated avant-garde that had set itself up in opposition to such an establishment tradition. They had to stand up against the rhetoric that gave them only secondary positions in the new movements, the myth that modernism created of itself and which has been handed down in critical accounts of the period. As has been seen again and again throughout this study, these women did not position themselves at the margins of the modernist projects that have been written into literary history as the 'important' projects, but followed often very different trajectories, ones which at times overlapped with, and at times diverted from, those of male contemporaries. If these writers are to be included in studies of modernism, it is not enough simply to slip them into existing narratives; the narratives themselves must be rewritten to take account of something far more complex than an existing understanding of the 'key movements' (Imagism, Futurism, Vorticism, the Auden Generation and so on) allows for.

An analysis of this counter-public sphere of modernist women writers has also demonstrated that any idea of art as confined to the Habermasian 'lifeworld', set apart from the political or social, is erroneous. The literary work of these writers was bound up in important social and political issues of its time, engaging with early feminist arguments, issues around a growing commercialism, a troubled political climate, and the brute reality of the Second World War. Only in the early years of this public sphere, when the operative structures were being established and principles of exchange experimented with, and the last years, in which there was a retreat into the private, did these writers avoid contact with a wider reality and new systems of thought. It is impossible to distinguish between a purely aesthetic realm and a realm of socio-political events, and at times, and particularly in the 1930s, these two 'spheres' were closely intertwined, with modernist women writers engaged in exploring important issues within the wider socio-political public sphere, as well as taking more direct political action.

In particular, the work of these writers was in touch with contemporary developments in psychoanalytic theory, and was part of the first wave of literary texts to make use of these understandings. These women were writing at a time when woman's identity was coming under radical question: woman's sexual identity, her political identity, her relation to war, to commercialism, and to mass media. Psychoanalysis provided them with new tools with which to understand the self and relationships, and played a central part in allowing their work to develop complex understandings of the psyche. In the earliest years, 1913–17, this manifested itself as explorations of internal landscapes, privileged above external reality. Later, psychoanalysis was crucial in explorations of sexual identity, and for examinations of the creative process and the relation of the unconscious to literature; in the late 1920s psychoanalysis proved vital again in an examination of the role of the cinema, connecting film to dream, and providing a vital interpretative framework; and again, in the 1930s, sophisticated psychoanalytic understandings allowed these women writers to explore issues of personal aggression and sadistic/masochistic fantasy in relation to a world-wide enactment of violence.

In addition to entering into explorations of the internal world, these women writers were questioning the boundaries of internal and external, of the 'public' and 'private', and many of the individual issues that have been explored can be placed in the context of these questions. In the earliest years of this public sphere, women's confinement in the 'private' sphere was challenged by entry into the literary public sphere itself and by powerful assertions of a woman's strength and capability, strong feminist statements, and oppositional writing. These women brought into the public sphere 'private' questions around women's sexuality, lesbian relationships, the experience of giving birth, and women's sexual experiences in general, treating these with unprecedented openness. As this public sphere developed in confidence from 1918 onwards, the relatively confined spaces of women-edited journals (*The Egoist, The Little Review, Poetry*) were exchanged for, or supplemented by, more 'public' spaces of the more competitive male-dominated journals (*The Adelphi, The North American Review, The Dial, Rhythmus, The Double Dealer, The Nation and the Athenaeum, The Transatlantic Review, Sphere,* and others), and women writers entered more fully into the publishing arena. Women writers were critically discussing the meaning of these changes and were experimenting with different modes of exchange and discussion, from heated argument and deliberate provocation to facilitate discussion, to a more conciliatory and harmonious exchange rooted in support and encouragement. Through the 1930s and the war years the intensely 'private' issues of personal motivation became of public significance as personal aggression and sadomasochistic desires were transposed onto the world stage, and conversely the public and political were seen to be played out on an internal and personal level.

To conclude, then, the period 1913–46 is one of enormous change and development within this network of women writers. Yet despite massive changes in the literary form and in the central topics of discussion and the ways in which these were understood, despite journals folding and new journals taking their place, and despite the loss of older writers and the introduction of younger ones, a coherent network of writers with identifiable projects can be traced across this period. This was a network, a public sphere, not located in a single place, or grouped around a single issue, but a diverse international public sphere rooted in the expression of a great number of writers. It has been necessary to take such a wide scope in terms of years, location of writers, and type of writing in order to demonstrate the coherence of this network; it has also been possible to challenge the narrow confines within which the work of these writers has been more often approached—'women writers of the first world war', 'women of the 1930s', 'women of the Left Bank' and so on. Useful as such studies are, they tend to obscure the huge amount of exchange and interaction between women in different communities and locations, and the ways in which their work developed over time through mutual influence in a dynamic literary public sphere. Laura Riding expresses the difference between an associative network based on shared interests and a more localized and focused 'movement', as well as the benefits of community:

. . . it is a test of First-Order quality whether a person chooses to work in isolated individualism or seeks to associate himself and his work with others, and other work for the integration of life as truth personally lived. This is a very different basis of association from that by which literary or artistic people commonly form themselves into 'groups' or 'movements'. In most cases these are aggressive or defensive alliances against other groups or movements, and the works so conceived are propaganda for competing forms of literary or artistic individualism, rather than acts of communication with all the good minds there may be.[7]

Several of these writers looked back on their years of engagement in the public sphere and attempted to convey the experience of participation. There are numerous memoirs, personal reflections and reminiscences in letters. There is a general acknowledgement of the enormity of the changes in writing over the years, and of the energy and excitement of participating in a public exchange of new ideas. Katherine Anne Porter sums up half a century of her own participation:

. . . you look back through all the fury you have come through, when it seemed so much, and so dismayingly, destruction, and so much just the pervasively trivial, stupid, or malignant-dwarfish tricks: fur-lined cups as sculpture, symphonies written for kitchen batteries, experiments of language very similar to the later Nazi surgical experiments of cutting and uniting human nerve ends never meant to touch each other: so many perversities crowding in so close you could hardly see beyond them. Yet look, you shared it, you were part of it, you even added to the confusion, so busy being new yourself. The fury and waste and clamor was, after all, just what you had thought it was in the first place, even if you had lost sight of it later—life, in a word, and great glory came of it, and splendid things that will go on living cleared of all the rubbish thrown up around their creation.[8]

H.D. was central to such 'life' in the public sphere, and also, at times, to the 'confusion'. An understanding of her work as located at the centre of this network both sheds light on her own development as a writer, and demonstrates some of the ways in which one individual was affected by, and was a force within, a literary community. Her connections with writers in Britain, the

---

[7] Riding, ibid. 375.
[8] Katherine Anne Porter, 'Reflections on Willa Cather', (1952) in *The Days Before*, 68.

USA, and the Paris Left Bank placed her right at the heart of this network, and her willingness to get involved in numerous projects, magazines, and discussions makes her work of fundamental interest in an analysis of this grouping. Her work was often at the forefront of exchanges in the public sphere of modernist women writers, leading the way in challenges to the written form and in discussions around issues of shared importance. Both her published work and her private letters reveal her to have been fully committed to a public exchange and interaction with her contemporaries.

By the time of her death in 1961 H.D. had become an established figure, no longer marginalized by the establishment, and becoming the first woman to receive an Academy of Arts and Letters award in 1960. She was certainly in no way a marginal figure, but one whose influence had spread to a great many others. Bryher felt that H.D. had been important as a leader: 'Teach, yes, Hilda was as great a teacher as she was a poet. So many letters reached me after she died both from friends and strangers whom she had met perhaps once, all saying "she showed me my way in life." '[9]

It is as such a vital influence in a public sphere of modernist women writers that H.D. should be remembered, and it is in this context that her work needs to be considered.

[9] Bryher, *The Heart to Artemis*, 195.

Bibliography

I. WORK BY H.D.

'Acon'. *Poetry*, 3/5 (Feb. 1914): 165–6. Reprinted in: [Ezra Pound, ed.] *Des Imagistes: An Anthology*. London: The Poetry Bookshop, 1914, 26; H.D., *Sea Garden* [1916], *Collected Poems 1912–1944*, ed. Louis L. Martz, 31–2.

'After Troy'. *Transatlantic Review*, 1/2 (Feb. 1924): 5.

Asphodel. Durham: Duke University Press, 1992.

Bid Me to Live. New York: Grove Press, 1960; London: Virago, 1984.

'Borderline'. Page proofs with corrections by H.D., 1930. The Yale Collection of American Literature, Beinecke Rare Book and Manuscript Library.

By Avon River. New York: Macmillan, 1949.

'The Cinema and the Classics I: Beauty'. *Close Up*, 1/1 (July 1927): 22–33.

'The Cinema and the Classics III: The Mask and the Movietone'. *Close Up*, 1/5 (Nov. 1927): 18–31.

'Cities'. *The Egoist*, 3/7 (July 1, 1916): 102–3.

Collected Poems 1912–1944, ed. Louis L. Martz. New York: New Directions, 1983.

'Compassionate Friendship'. Second draft [?], typescript, with corrections by H.D., 1955. The Yale Collection of American Literature, Beinecke Rare Book and Manuscript Library.

End to Torment. New York: New Directions, 1979.

Euripides Ion. Translation with notes by H.D. London: Chatto & Windus, 1937.

'Expiation'. *Close Up*, 2/5 (May 1928): 38–49.

The Flowering of the Rod. London: Oxford University Press, 1946.

'Fragment XXXVI'. *Poetry*, 19/1 (Oct. 1921): 26–9.

The Gift. New York: New Directions, 1982.

'H.D. by Delia Alton'. *The Iowa Review*, 16/3 (Fall 1986): 179–221.

The Hedgehog. London: The Brendin Publishing Company, 1936.

Hedylus. Oxford: Basil Blackwell, 1928.

Helen in Egypt. Grove Press, 1961; Manchester: Carcanet Press, 1985.

HERmione. New York: New Directions, 1972; (as *Her*) London: Virago, 1984.

'Hermes of the Ways'. *Poetry*, 1/4 (Jan. 1913): 118–20.

Hermetic Definition. Oxford: Carcanet Press, 1972.

'Hermonax'. *Poetry*, 3/5 (Feb. 1914): 164–5. Reprinted in: *The Glebe*, 1 (1914): 28–9; *Des Imagistes*, ed. Pound, 28–9; *Heliodora and Other Poems* (London: Jonathan Cape, 1924), 87–8.

'Hippolytus Temporizes'. *The Bookman*, 56 (Oct. 1921): 123.

Hymen. London: The Egoist Press, 1921.

'Hymen'. *Poetry*, 15/3 (Dec. 1919): 117–29.

('Sylvania Penn'). 'I Sing Democracy'. Review of *Whitman* by Edgar Lee Masters. *Life and Letters To-Day*, 17/9 (Autumn 1937): 154–9.

Kora and Ka. Dijon: Imprimerie Darantière, 1934; Bios: Berkely, 1978.

'The Last Gift'. *The Egoist*, 3/3 (Mar. 1, 1916): 35.

('CO. 11'). 'Letter and Reply to M.O. Questionnaire, 1937', ed. Diana Collecott. *Line*, 13 (1989): 168–9.

'A Letter from England'. *Bryn Mawr Alumnae Bulletin*, 21/8 (Nov. 1941): 22–3.

'Magic Mirror: Part I–VII'. Second typed draft [?] carbon, c.2, corrected by H.D. The Yale Collection of American Literature, Beinecke Rare Book and Manuscript Library.

'Marianne Moore'. *The Egoist*, 3/8 (Aug. 1916): 118–19.

('CO.11'). 'Mass Observation Report, May 12, 1937', ed. Diana Collecott. *Line*, 13 (1989): 162–7.

'Mid-Day'. *The Egoist*, 2/5 (May 1, 1915): 74.

'The Mystery'. Third draft, typescript, n.d. The Yale Collection of American Literature, Beinecke Rare Book and Manuscript Library.

('John Helforth'). *Nights*. Dijon: Imprimerie Darantière, 1935; New York: New Directions, 1986.

'A Note on Poetry'. The *Oxford Anthology of American Literature*, vol. 2. New York: Oxford University Press, 1938, 11th printing, 1956, 1287–8.

Notes on Thought and Vision and *The Wise Sappho*. San Francisco: City Lights Books, 1982.

Paint It Today. New York: New York University Press, 1992.

Palimpsest. Paris: Contact Editions, 1926.

'Projector'. *Close Up*, 1/1 (July 1927): 46–51.

'Projector II (*Chang*)'. *Close Up*, 1/4 (Oct. 1927): 36–47.

Red Roses For Bronze. London: Chatto & Windus, 1931.

'Russian Films'. *Close Up*, 3/3 (Sept. 1928): 18–29.

Sea Garden. London: Constable, 1916.

'The Sword Went Out to Sea'. Third typed draft, n.d. The Yale Collection of American Literature, Beinecke Rare Book and Manuscript Library.

'Thorn Thicket: Bosquet'. Second (?) typed draft, carbon, 1960. The

Yale Collection of American Literature, Beinecke Rare Book and Manuscript Library.

'The Tribute'. *The Egoist*, 3/11 (Nov. 1916): 165–7.

Tribute to Freud. New York: Pantheon Books, 1956; With 'Advent': Boston: David R. Godine, 1974; Manchester: Carcanet Press, 1985.

Tribute to the Angels. London: Oxford University Press, 1945.

('Sylvania Penn'). 'Two Englishwomen in Rome (1871–1900)'. Review of *Two Englishwomen In Rome* by Matilda Lucas. *Life and Letters To-Day*, 20/16 (Dec. 1938): 105–6.

The Usual Star and *Two Americans.* Dijon: Imprimerie Darantière, 1934.

Vale Ave: A Poem by H.D. Redding Ridge: Black Swan Books, 1992.

The Walls Do Not Fall. London: Oxford University Press, 1944.

'White Rose and the Red'. Typescript, fourth draft, 1948. The Yale Collection of American Literature, Beinecke Rare Book and Manuscript Library.

'Writing on the Wall'. *Life and Letters To-Day*, 45/93 (May 1945): 67–98; 45/94 (June 1945): 137–54; 45/96 (Aug. 1945): 72–89; 46/97 (Sept. 1945): 136–51; 47/101 (Jan. 1946): 33–45.

[Untitled]. Response to 'Confessions Questionnaire'. *The Little Review*, [12] (May 1929): 38–40.

2. LETTERS FROM H.D.

To Richard Aldington: Jan. 13, [1959].

To Bryher: Aug. 23, [1924], Sept. 18, [1924], Jan. 4, [1932], Nov. 24, [1934], Aug. 9, [1935], Aug. 13, [1935], Oct. 18, [1935], Sept. 9, [1937], [Sept. 21, 1946], May 12, [1947], Aug. 1, [1947], Aug. 5, [1948], July 15, [1951], Oct. 11, [1952], June 1, [1954].

To Howard Clifford: July 20, [1940].

To Harold Collins: Mar. 4, [1925].

To John Cournos: [Aug. 9, 1916].

To F. S. Flint: Mar. 22, 1916.

To Molly Hughes: Nov. 14, [1943].

To Amy Lowell: [Nov. 23, 1914], Jan. 20, 1916, Feb. 22, 1916, Aug. 10, [1917], [Sept. 1918]. All typed transcripts.

To Marianne Moore: June 26, 1940.

To Gretchen Wolle Baker: Aug. 31, [1939], Feb. 14, [1941], Nov. 11, [1941], July 27, [1944], Dec. 20, [1944], Aug. 2, 1945.

(All in the Yale Collection of American Literature, Beinecke Rare Book and Manuscript Library.)

3. PRIMARY MATERIAL AND CRITICISM BY H.D'S
CONTEMPORARIES

ALDINGTON, RICHARD. 'Books and Papers'. *The Egoist*, 1/3 (Feb. 2, 1914): 49–50.

ALDIS, MARY. 'Some Imagist Poets, 1916'. *The Little Review*, 3/4 (June–July 1916): 26–31.

ANDERSON, MARGARET C. 'Announcement'. *The Little Review*, 1/1 (Mar. 1914): 1–2.

—— 'The Artist in Life'. *The Little Review*, 2/4 (June/July 1915): 18–20.

—— ['M.C.A'.]. [Untitled]. Announcement in *The Little Review*, 7/3 (Sept.–Dec. 1920): 59.

—— 'Editorial'. *The Little Review* [no issue no.] (May 1929: Spring Number): 3–4.

—— *My Thirty Years' War*. London: Alfred A. Knopf, 1930.

—— 'What We Are Fighting For'. *The Little Review*, 2/3 (May 1915): 3–4.

'Another Athens'. Including review of *Heliodora* by H.D. *The Times Literary Supplement*, 1172 (July 3, 1924): 416.

[ARAGON, LOUIS, ed.] *Authors Take Sides on the Spanish War*. London: Left Review, 1937.

AUDEN, W. H. *The Age of Anxiety*. London: Faber and Faber, 1948.

—— *Selected Poems*, ed. Edward Mendelson. London: Faber and Faber, 1979.

BARNES, DJUNA. *Nightwood*. London: Faber and Faber, 1936.

BEACH, SYLVIA. *Shakespeare and Company*. New York: Harcourt, Brace, 1956.

BISHOP, ELIZABETH. *One Art: The Selected Letters*, ed. Robert Giroux. London: Chatto & Windus, 1994.

—— *The Complete Poems*. London: Chatto & Windus, 1970.

BOGAN, LOUISE. *Achievement in American Poetry*. Chicago: Henry Regnery, 1951.

—— *Journey Around My Room: The Autobiography of Louise Bogan*, ed. Ruth Limmer. New York: The Viking Press, 1980, 83.

—— 'Verse'. Including reviews of *Beast In View* by Muriel Rukeyser, *Take Them, Stranger* by Babette Deutsch, and *The Walls Do Not Fall* by H.D. *The New Yorker*, 20 (Oct. 21, 1944), 91–4.

BONNER, AMY. 'Curve of Quiet'. *Poetry*, 72/5 (Aug. 1948): 246.

BOYLE, KAY. 'And Winter'. *transition*, 5 (Aug. 1927): 114.

—— *Primer for Combat*. London: Faber and Faber, 1943.

BRYHER (WINIFRED). 'Thought and Vision'. Review of *Hymen* by H.D. *The Bookman* [New York], 56/2 (Oct. 1922): 225–6.

——*Amy Lowell: A Critical Appreciation*. London: Eyre and Spottiswoode, 1918.

——*Development*. London: Constable, 1920.

——'Spear-Shaft and Cyclamen Flower'. Review of *Hymen* by H.D. *Poetry*, 19/6 (Mar. 1922): 333–7.

——*Arrow Music*. [London: J & E Bumpus, 1922].

——*Civilians*. Territet: Pool, 1927.

——'The Crisis: September'. *Life and Letters To-Day*, 19/15 (Nov. 1938): 1–6.

——*The Days of Mars: A Memoir, 1940–46*. London: Calder and Boyars, 1972.

——'Dope or Stimulus'. *Close Up*, 3/3 (Sept. 1928): 59–60.

——'G. W. Pabst: A Survey'. *Close Up*, 1/6 (Dec. 1927): 59–61.

——*The Heart to Artemis: A Writer's Memoirs*. London: Collins, 1963.

——'The Hollywood Code'. *Close Up*, 8/3 (Sept. 1931): 234–8.

——'My Introduction to America'. *Life and Letters To-Day*, 26/37 (Sept. 1940): 233–8.

——'Recognition Not Farewell'. Review of *The Crystal Cabinet* by Mary Butts. *Life and Letters To-Day*, 17/9 (Autumn 1937): 159–64.

——*Two Selves*. Contact Publishing Co., [1923].

——[Untitled]. Review of *Clear Horizon* by Dorothy Richardson. *Life and Letters To-Day*, 13/2 (Dec. 1935; Winter Quarter): 198–9.

——to H.D.: Nov. (11?), 1935, Apr. 12, 1935, June 30, 1936. Beinecke Rare Book and Manuscript Library, Yale University.

BURNETT, IVY COMPTON to H.D., May 20, 1944. The Yale Collection of American Literature, Beinecke Rare Book and Manuscript Library.

BUTLER, ELIZA M. to H.D.: Aug. 25, 1952, June 30, 1953, July 19, 1953, Feb. 20, 1955, Jan. 14, 1956. The Yale Collection of American Literature, Beinecke Rare Book and Manuscript Library.

'A Change of Price'. *The Little Review*, 1/5 (July 1914): 67.

COLUM, PADRAIC. 'Chap Books and Broadsheets'. Including review of *The Contemplative Quarry* by Anna Wickham. *Poetry*, 6/5 (Aug. 1915): 252–6.

CONKLING, GRACE HAZARD. 'Spring Day'. *Poetry*, 10/1 (Apr. 1917): 20.

——'The Little Rose is Dust, My Dear'. *Poetry*, 7/2 (Oct. 1913): 71.

COURNOS, JOHN. 'The Death of Futurism'. *The Egoist*, 4/1 (Jan. 1917): 6–7.

DEAN, HARRIET. 'Silhouettes'. *The Little Review*, 3/4 (June–July 1916): 13.

DEUTSCH, BABETTE. 'Freedom and the Grace of God'. *The Dial*, 67 (Nov. 15, 1919): 441–2.

DEUTSCH, BABETTE. *Poetry in Our Time*. New York: Columbia University Press, 1952.

—— 'The Romance of the Realists'. *The Dial*, 66 (May 31, 1919): 560–1.

DOBSON, SILVIA. ' "Shock Knit Within Terror": Living Through World War II'. *The Iowa Review*, 16/3 (Fall 1986): 232–45.

—— to H.D., Oct. 20, [1956?]. The Yale Collection of American Literature, Beinecke Rare Book and Manuscript Library.

EASTON, DOROTHY. 'Moments'. In *The Golden Bird and Other Stories*. London: Heinemann, 1920, 222–9.

EBERHART, RICHARD. 'Hölderlin, Leopardi, and H.D'. Including review of *Selected Poems* by H.D. *Poetry*, 91/4 (Jan. 1958): 260–5.

ELIOT, T. S. *Collected Poems 1909–1962*. London: Faber and Faber, 1963; new ed., 1974, 13–22.

—— 'Tradition and the Individual Talent'. *Selected Essays*. London: Faber and Faber, 1932; 3rd enlarged edn., 1951, 13–22.

'Films of the Month'. Review of *Chang*. *Close Up*, 1/4 (Oct. 1927): 82–4.

FITTS, DUDLEY. 'The Verse of Evelyn Scott'. Review of *The Winter Alone* by Evelyn Scott. *Poetry*, 36/6 (Sept. 1930): 338–43.

FITZ-SIMONDS, MARION. Letter to the editor. *Close Up*, 1/4 (Oct. 1927): 80–1.

FLETCHER, JOHN GOULD. 'Miss Lowell's Discovery: Polyphonic Prose'. *Poetry*, 6/1 (Apr. 1915): 32–6.

FRANK, FLORENCE KIPER. 'Psychoanalysis: Some Random Thoughts'. *The Little Review*, 3/4 (June–July 1916): 15–17.

FRASER, MARGARET. 'Delicate Destruction'. *Poetry*, 47/1 (Oct. 1935): 18.

FREYTAG-LORINGHOVEN, ELSE VON. ' "The Art of Madness": III'. *The Little Review*, 6/9 (Jan. 1920): 28–9.

—— 'Mineself—Minesoul—and—mine—Cast-iron Lover'. *The Little Review*, 6/5 (Sept. 1919): 3–11.

—— 'Selections from the Letters of Elsa Baroness von Freytag-Loringhoven,' ed. Djuna Barnes. *transition*, 11 (Feb. 1928): 19–30.

GERMAIN, EDWARD B. *Surrealist Poetry in English*. London: Penguin, 1978.

GLOVER, EDWARD. *War, Sadism and Pacifism*. London: Allen & Unwin, 1933; extended series [1947].

GREGORY, ALYSE. *The Cry of a Gull: Journals 1923–1948*. Brushford, Somerset: Out of the Ark Press, 1973.

—— 'A Poet's Novel'. Review of *Palimpsest* by H.D. *The Dial*, 82/5 (May 1927): 417–19.

—— *Wheels on Gravel*. London: John Lane The Bodley Head, 1938.

GREGORY, HORACE and MARYA ZATURENSKA. *A History of American Poetry 1900–1940*. New York: Harcourt Brace, 1946.

GROFF, ALICE. Letter to the editor. *The Egoist*, 2/2 (Feb. 1, 1915): 31.

HALL, RADCLYFFE. *The Well of Loneliness*. London: Jonathan Cape, 1928; London: Virago, 1982.

HARRISSON, TOM, HUMPHREY JENNINGS, and CHARLES MADGE. 'Anthropology at Home'. *The New Statesman and Nation*, 13/310 (Jan. 30, 1937), 155.

HEAP, JANE ['jh']. 'Eat 'em Alive!' Review of *Mary Olivier* by May Sinclair. *The Little Review*, 6/8 (Dec. 1919): 30–2.

—— 'The Episode Continued'. *The Little Review*, 5/6 (Oct. 1918): 35–7.

—— 'Lost: A Renaissance'. *The Little Review*, [12] (May 1929): 5–6.

—— 'Pounding Ezra'. *The Little Review*, 5/6 (Oct. 1918): 37–41.

—— Reply to 'Concerning Else von Freytag-Loringhoven' by Lola Ridge. *The Little Review*, 6/6 (Oct. 1919): 56.

—— Reply to 'The Art of Madness' by Evelyn Scott. *The Little Review*, 6/8 (Dec. 1919): 48–9.

—— 'Wreaths'. *The Little Review*, [12] (May 1929): 60–2.

'HEDYLUS. By H.D.'. Review of *Hedylus* by H.D. *The Spectator*, 5, 254 (Mar. 9, 1929): 396–7.

HELLER, HELEN WEST. 'Alone in the House'. *The Little Review*, 6/3 (July 1919): 63–4.

HENDERSON, ALICE CORBIN ['A.C.H'.]. 'Imagism: Secular and Esoteric'. *Review of Some Imagist Poets, 1917*. *Poetry*, 11/6 (Mar. 1918): 339–43.

—— 'A Jitney-Bus among the Masterpieces'. *Poetry*, 9/1 (Oct. 1916): 39–41.

—— 'Lazy Criticism'. *Poetry*, 9/3 (Dec. 1916): 144–9.

—— 'Mannerisms of Free Verse'. *Poetry*, 14/2 (May 1919): 95–8.

HERR, MARY to H.D., June 1 [1960]. The Yale Collection of American Literature, Beinecke Rare Book and Manuscript Library.

HUGHES, GLENN. 'Foreword'. *Imagist Anthology 1930*. London: Chatto & Windus. 1930, pp. xvii–xviii.

HULME, T. E. 'Searchers after Reality: Haldane'. *New Age*, 5 (Aug. 19, 1909): 315–16; repr. *Further Speculations*, ed. Samuel Hynes. Minneapolis: University of Minnesota Press, 1955, 7–14.

HUXLEY, ALDOUS. *What Are You Going to Do About It?* London: Chatto & Windus, 1936.

JACOBSEN, JOSEPHINE. 'H.D. in Greece and Egypt'. *Poetry*, 100/3 (June 1962): 186–9.

JAMESON, STORM. 'Documents'. *Fact*, 4 (July 1937): 9–18.

—— *The End of this War*. London: Allen & Unwin, 1941.

JAMESON, STORM. 'The Children Must Fear'. *Europe to Let: The Memoirs of an Obscure Man*. London: Macmillan, 1940, 227–82.

—— *Love in Winter*. London: Cassell, 1935; London: Virago, 1984.

—— *The Writer's Situation and Other Essays*. London: Macmillan, 1950.

JOLAS, EUGENE. 'Announcement'. *transition*, 19–30 (June 1930): 369.

—— 'Enter the Imagination'. *transition*, 7 (Oct. 1927): 157–60.

—— 'Logos'. *transition*, 16–17 (June 1929): 25–30.

—— and ELLIOT PAUL. 'A Review'. *transition*, 12 (Mar. 1928): 139–47.

—— —— and ROBERT SAGE. 'First Aid to the Enemy'. *transition*, 9 (Dec. 1927): 161–76.

JOYCE, JAMES. *A Portrait of the Artist as a Young Man*. First published in the *Egoist* 1914–15; London: Penguin, 1992.

KENTON, EDNA. 'May Sinclair's "Mary Olivier"'. Review of *Mary Olivier* by May Sinclair. *The Little Review*, 6/8 (Dec. 1919): 29–30.

KREYMBORG, ALFRED, ed. *Others: An Anthology of the New Verse*. New York: Alfred A. Knopf, 1916.

LASKI, LOUISE. 'We Get Used to Atrocities Because—'. *Time and Tide*, 17/15 (Apr. 10, 1937): 464.

LAUGHLIN, JAMES, ed. *New Directions in Prose and Poetry 1940*. Norfolk, Conn.: New Directions, 1940.

LAWRENCE, D. H. *Sons and Lovers*. London: Heinemann, 1913; Heinemann Educational Books, 1963.

—— *Women in Love*. New York, 1920; Ware: Wordsworth Editions, 1992.

LEAVIS, F. R. *Mass Civilisation and Minority Culture*. Cambridge, UK: The Minority Press, 1930.

LECHLITNER, RUTH. 'Quiz Program'. *Poetry*, 58/3 (June 1941): 132–3.

LEE, AGNES. 'The Silent House'. *Poetry*, 1/6 (Mar. 1913): 175.

LOWELL, AMY. 'In a Garden'. *The New Freewoman*, 1/6 (Sept. 1, 1913): 114. Also published in *The Little Review*, 1/5 (July 1914): 38–9.

—— 'Jean Untermeyer's Book'. *Poetry*, 14/1 (Apr. 1919): 48.

—— 'Middle Age'. *The Egoist*, 2/7 (July 1, 1915): 113.

—— 'Miscast: I'. *The Egoist*, 1/15 (Aug. 1, 1914): 298.

—— 'Miscast: II'. *The Egoist*, 1/15 (Aug. 1, 1914): 298.

—— 'The Precinct. Rochester'. *The Egoist*, 1/4 (Feb. 16, 1914): 69.

—— 'Spring Day'. *The Egoist*, 2/5 (May 1, 1915): 76–7.

—— *Tendencies In Modern American Poetry*. New York: Macmillan, 1917.

—— [Untitled]. Review of *Flashlights* by Mary Aldis, *Poetry*, 8/6 (Sept. 1916): 318–21.

—— (ed.), *Some Imagist Poets: An Anthology*. Boston and New York: Houghton Mifflin, 1915, 1916, and 1917.

LOY, MINA. 'Anglo-Mongrels and the Rose'. *The Little Review* [9/1–3] (Spring 1923): 10–18.

—— 'Anglo-Mongrels and the Rose: Continued'. *The Little Review* [no issue no.] (Autumn and Winter 1923–4): 41–51.

—— 'Brancusi's Golden Bird'. *The Dial*, 73/5 (Nov. 1922), 507–8.

—— 'John Rodker's Frog'. *The Little Review*, 7/3 (Sept.–Dec. 1920) [no issue no.]: 56–7.

—— *The Lost Lunar Baedeker*, ed. Roger L. Conover. Manchester: Carcanet, 1997.

LYON, MINNIE. [Untitled]. *The Little Review*, 1/10 (Jan. 1915): 61–2.

MACPHERSON, KENNETH. 'As Is'. *Close Up*, 3/1 (July 1928): 5–10.

—— 'As Is'. *Close Up*, 7/5 (Nov. 1930): 293–8.

MANSFIELD, KATHERINE. 'The New Infancy'. Review of *Mary Olivier: A Life* by May Sinclair. In *Novels and Novelists*. London: Constable, 1930; Boston: Beacon Press, 1959.

MARSDEN, DORA. 'Notes of the Week'. *The Freewoman*, 1/2 (Nov. 30, 1911): 23–4.

—— 'Views and Comments'. *The Egoist*, 1/14 (July 15, 1914): 263–6.

—— 'Views and Comments'. *The New Freewoman*, 1/1 (June 1913): 3–5.

—— 'Views and Comments'. *The New Freewoman*, 1/7 (Sept. 15, 1913): 123–6.

—— to Harriet Shaw Weaver, Feb. 25, 1913. The Harriet Shaw Weaver archive, Add. MS 57354, British Library Department of Manuscripts.

'M.H.P'. 'The Critic's Critic'. *The Little Review*, 1/1 (Mar. 1914): 20–2.

'Minutes of Meeting of Directors held at Oakley House, Bloomsbury, on Thursday, Sep. 10th 1913, after shareholders' meeting'. The Harriet Shaw Weaver Archive, Add. MS 57358, British Library Department of Manuscripts.

MITCHISON, NAOMI. *Among You Taking Notes: The Wartime Diary of Naomi Mitchison 1939–45*, ed. Dorothy Sheridan. London: Victor Gollancz, 1985.

—— 'Those Queer Greeks'. Including review of *Euripides Ion* by H.D. *Time and Tide*, 17/15 (Apr. 10, 1937): 468.

MONROE, HARRIET ('H.M'.). 'Another Birthday'. *Poetry*, 27/1 (Oct. 1925): 32–6.

—— 'Books and Tomorrow'. *Poetry*, 32/1 (Apr. 1928): 35.

—— 'Christmas Again'. *Poetry*, 37/3 (Dec. 1930): 150–2.

—— 'Comments and Reviews: The Audience II'. *Poetry*, 5/1 (Oct. 1914): 31–2.

—— 'Editorial comment: "The Tradition—Sobriety and Earnestness"'. *Poetry*, 3/4 (Jan. 1914): 141–4.

MONROE, HARRIET ('H.M'.). 'Editorial Comment: The New Beauty'. *Poetry*, 2/1 (Apr. 1913): 22–5.

—— 'Edna St. Vincent Millay'. *Poetry*, 24/5 (Aug. 1924): 260–6.

—— 'Guide to the Moon'. Review of *Lunar Baedeker* by Mina Loy. *Poetry*, 23/2 (Nov. 1923): 100–3.

—— 'Imagism Today and Yesterday'. *Poetry*, 36/4 (July 1930): 213–18.

—— 'Its Inner Meaning'. *Poetry*, 6/6 (Sept. 1915): 302–5.

—— 'News Notes'. *Poetry*, 28/1 (Apr. 1926): 58–60.

—— 'Of Two Poets'. *Poetry*, 21/5 (Feb. 1923): 262–7.

—— 'Pan-American Concord'. *Poetry*, 26/3 (June 1925): 155–8.

—— 'Personality Rampart'. Review of *My Thirty Years War* by Margaret Anderson. *Poetry*, 37/2 (Nov. 1930): 95–100.

—— *A Poet's Life: Seventy Years in a Changing World*. New York: Macmillan, 1938.

—— 'The Procession Moves'. *Poetry*, 30/5 (Sept. 1927): 270–3.

—— 'Reviews'. Review of *Some Imagist Poets: An Anthology*. *Poetry*, 6/3 (June 1915): 150–3.

—— '*Sword Blades and Poppy Seed*'. Review of *Sword Blades and Poppy Seed* by Amy Lowell. *Poetry*, 5/3 (Dec. 1914): 136–8.

—— 'A Symposium on Marianne Moore'. *Poetry*, 19/4 (Jan. 1922): 208–16.

—— [Untitled]. Review of *Crack o' Dawn* by Fannie Stearns Davis. *Poetry*, 6/1 (Apr. 1915): 45–6.

—— and ALICE CORBIN HENDERSON, eds. *The New Poetry*. New York: Macmillan, 1917.

MOORE, MARIANNE. 'Comment'. *The Dial*, 83 (Nov. 1927): 449–50.

—— *The Complete Poems of Marianne Moore*. London: Faber and Faber, 1967.

—— 'In Distrust of Merit'. *Nevertheless*. New York: Macmillan, 1944, 12–14.

—— 'Poetry'. *Poems*. London: The Egoist Press, 1921, 22.

—— 'To a Steam Roller'. *The Egoist*, 2/10 (Oct. 1, 1915): 158.

'M.S.F'. 'Criticism'. *The Little Review* [4] (11) (Mar. 1918): 59–60.

MURRY, JOHN MIDDLETON. 'The Cause of it All'. *The Adelphi*, 1/1 (June 1923): 1–11.

NIN, ANAÏS. *The Journals of Anaïs Nin*, vol. 1, ed. Gunther Stuhlmann. London: Peter Owen, 1966.

NORTH, JESSICA NELSON. 'The Late Rebellion'. *Poetry*, 22/3 (June 1923): 153–6.

'Our Contemporaries'. *Poetry*, 8/1 (Apr. 1916): 52–3.

PATMORE, BRIGIT to H.D., Sept. 10, 1925. The Yale Collection of American Literature, Beinecke Rare Book and Manuscript Library.

PEARSON, NORMAN. Review of *Tribute to the Angels* by H.D. *Life and Letters To-Day*, 46/95 (July 1945): 58–62.

'Poems by H.D.'. Review of *Heliodora and Other Poems* by H.D. *The Boston Evening Transcript* (Aug. 16, 1924): 3.

PORTER, KATHERINE ANNE. *The Days Before*. London: Secker & Warburg, 1953.

POUND, EZRA. 'Editorial'. *The Little Review*, 4/1 (May 1917): 3–6.

—— 'A Few Don'ts By An Imagiste'. *Poetry*, 1/6 (Mar. 1913): 200–6.

—— *The Letters of Ezra Pound to Alice Corbin Henderson*. Austin: University of Texas Press, 1993.

—— *The Selected Letters of Ezra Pound 1907–1941*, ed. D. D. Paige. London: Faber and Faber, 1950, 9–10.

—— *Des Imagistes*: An Anthology. London: The Poetry Bookshop, 1914.

RAINE, KATHLEEN. *The Land Unknown*. Hamish Hamilton, 1977. In *Autobiographies*. London: Skoob Books Publishing, 1991.

—— *Stone and Flower*: *Poems 1935–43*. London: Nicholson & Watson, 1943, 10.

RICHARDSON, DOROTHY. 'Continuous Performance VI: The Increasing Congregation'. *Close Up*, 1/6 (Dec. 1927): 61–5.

—— 'Continuous Performance: Narcissus'. *Close Up*, 8/3 (Sept. 1931): 182–5.

—— 'Continuous Performance: This Spoon-fed Generation?' *Close Up*, 8/4 (Dec. 1931): 304–8.

—— *Pilgrimage*, 4 vols. London: Duckworth, 1915–31 and London: J. M. Dent & Cresset Press, 1935. Collected editions: J. M. Dent & Cresset Press/New York: A Knopf, 1938 (excluding *March Moonlight*); London: Virago, 1979.

—— 'A Talk about Talking'. *Life and Letters To-day*, 23/27 (Dec. 1939): 286–8.

RIDGE, LOLA. 'Concerning Else von Freytag-Loringhoven'. *The Little Review*, 6/6 (Oct. 1919): 56.

—— to jh [Jane Heap]. *The Little Review*, 5/9 (Jan. 1919): 63.

RIDING, LAURA. 'The Damsel Thing'. *Anarchism is not Enough*. London: Jonathan Cape, 1928, 187–208.

—— 'The New Barbarism, and Gertrude Stein'. *transition*, 3 (June 1927): 153–68.

—— ed. *The World and Ourselves*. London: Chatto & Windus, 1938.

RODKER, JOHN. 'The "Others" Anthology'. *The Little Review*, 7/3 (Sept.–Dec. 1920): 53–6.

ROUGEMONT, DENIS DE. *Passion and Society*, trans. Montgomery Belgion. London: Faber and Faber, 1940. Trans. of *L'Amour et L'Occident*. Paris: Librarie Plon, 1939.

RUKEYSER, MURIEL. 'Ajanta'. *Beast in View*. New York: Doubleday, Doran, 1944, 3–8.

—— 'The Children's Elegy'. *Poetry*, 63/4 (Jan. 1944): 179–83.

—— 'For Fun'. *Life and Letters To-day*, 23/27 (Nov. 1939): 194–5.

—— 'Letter to the Front'. *Beast In View*. New York: Doubleday, Doran, 1944, 57–67.

—— 'The Usable Truth'. *Poetry*, 58/4 (July 1941): 206–9.

RUSSELL, DORA. *Hypatia: Or Woman and Knowledge*. London: Kegan Paul, Trubner, [1925], 24–5.

SANDERS, EMMY VERONICA. 'Adelaide Crapsey'. *Poetry*, 17/5 (Feb. 1921): 249.

—— 'Driftwood'. *Poetry*, 17/5 (Feb. 1921): 251–2.

—— 'Hill Speech'. *Poetry*, 20/6 (Sept. 1922): 305.

SCOTT, EVELYN. 'The Art of Madness'. *The Little Review*, 6/8 (Dec. 1919): 48–9.

—— 'Rainy Season'. *Poetry*, 15/2 (Nov. 1919): 71.

—— ' "The Art of Madness": I'. *The Little Review*, 6/9 (Jan. 1920): 25–7.

—— 'The Last Word'. *The Little Review*, 6/10 (Mar. 1920): 43–7.

SHANAFELT, CLARA. 'Caprice'. *Poetry*, 3/1 (Oct. 1913): 16.

—— 'Ego'. *The Egoist*, 2/1 (Jan. 1915): 11.

—— 'July Morning'. *The Egoist*, 3/2 (Feb. 1, 1916): 30.

SHERIDAN, DOROTHY, ed. *Wartime Women: an Anthology of Women's Wartime Writing for Mass-Observation*. London: Mandarin, 1990; 1991.

SHERRY, LAURA. 'Light Magic'. *Poetry*, 20/6 (Sept. 1922): 297–8.

SINCLAIR, MAY. *Far End*. London: Hutchinson, [1926].

—— *Mary Olivier: A Life*. Macmillan, 1919; London: Virago, 1980.

—— 'The Novels of Dorothy Richardson'. Review of *Pointed Roofs, Backwater*, and *Honeycomb* by Dorothy Richardson. *The Egoist*, 5/4 (Apr. 1918): 57–9.

—— 'The Poems of H.D.'. *The Dial*, 72/2 (Feb. 1922): 203–7.

—— 'The Poems of "H.D." ' *The Fortnightly Review*, 723 (Mar. 1927): 329–45.

—— 'The Reputation of Ezra Pound'. *The North American Review*, 211/774 (May 1920): 658–68.

—— 'Symbolism and Sublimation: II'. *The Medical Press and Circular*, 102/4,032 (Aug. 9, 1916): 142–5.

—— 'Two Notes'. *The Egoist*, 2/6 (June 1, 1915): 88–9.

SITWELL, EDITH. 'Of the Clowns and Fools of Shakespeare'. *Life and Letters To-Day*, 57/124 (May 1948): 102–9.

SMITH, ALICE A. 'Some English Women Novelists'. *The North American Review*, 213/793 (Dec. 1921): 799–808.

SMITH, BERNARD. 'American Letter'. *transition*, 13 (Summer 1928): 245–7.

SMITH, STEVIE. *Over the Frontier*. London: Jonathan Cape, 1938.

SPENDER, STEPHEN. 'Poetry'. *Fact*, 4 (July 1937): 18–30.

STALLWORTHY, JON, ed. *The Oxford Book of War Poetry*. Oxford: Oxford University Press, 1988.

STEARNS, MARY ADAMS ['M.A.S']. 'Unfulfilled Expectations'. Review of *A Lady of Leisure* by Ethel Sidgwick. *The Little Review*, 1/10 (Jan. 1915): 48–9.

STROBEL, MARION. 'Encounter'. *Poetry*, 21/6 (Mar. 1923): 291–3.

SWAWITE, MARGUERITE. 'I Am Woman'. *The Little Review*, 1/10 (Jan. 1915): 40–1.

TAPPERT, KATHERINE. Letter to the editor. *The Little Review*, 1/2 (Apr. 1914): 50.

TEASDALE, SARA. *Flame and Shadow*. London: Jonathan Cape, 1924.

TIETJENS, EUNICE. *Body and Raiment*. New York: Alfred A. Knopf, 1919.

—— 'Fire'. *Poetry*, 19/5 (Feb. 1922): 262–5.

—— *Private Collection*. New York: Alfred A. Knopf, 1965.

—— 'The Spiritual Dangers of Writing Vers Libre'. *The Little Review*, 1/8 (Nov. 1914): 25–9.

'To Serve an Idea'. *The Little Review*, 1/7 (Oct. 1914): 58.

UNTERMEYER, JEAN STARR to H.D., Nov. 10, 1956. The Yale Collection of American Literature, Beinecke Rare Book and Manuscript Library.

[Untitled]. Advertisement for Leona Dalrymple, *Diane of the Green Van*. *The Little Review*, 1/1 (Mar. 1914): 64.

[Untitled]. Advertisement for *The Little Review*. *The Egoist*, 1/17 (Sept. 1, 1914): 339.

[Untitled]. Announcement in *The Little Review*, 1/5 (July 1914): 67.

[Untitled]. Appeal for subscribers. *Poetry*, 3/1: (Oct. 1913): unnumbered page at back of issue.

[Untitled]. Circular for *The New Freewoman*, [1913]. The Harriet Shaw Weaver archive, Add. MS 57355, British Library Department of Manuscripts.

[Untitled]. List of Thousand Club Members. The Harriet Shaw Weaver archive, Add. MS 57357, British Library Department of Manuscripts.

[Untitled]. Review of *Hedylus* by H.D. *The Dial*, 86/3 (Mar. 1929): 264.

[Untitled]. Review of *Hymen* by H.D. *The Times Literary Supplement*, 1032 (Oct. 27, 1921): 702.

[Untitled]. Review of *Hypatia: or Woman and Knowledge* by Dora Russell. *The Adelphi*, 3/2 (July 1925): 151.

[Untitled]. Statement of editorial policy. *The Chapbook*, 1/1 (July 1919): unnumbered page inside front cover.

WALTON, EDA LOU. 'The Poetic Method of H.D.'. *The Nation*, 134 (Mar. 2, 1932): 264.

WEAVER, HARRIET SHAW. 'Views and Comments'. *The Egoist*, 3/1 (Jan. 1, 1916): 1–3.

—— to multiple recipients, [1913]. The Harriet Shaw Weaver archive, Add. MS 57354, British Library Department of Manuscripts.

WEST, REBECCA. 'If the Worst Comes to the Worst'. *Time and Tide*, 21/23 (June 8, 1940): 601–2.

—— *The Judge*. Hutchinson, 1922; London: Virago, 1980.

—— *The Return of the Soldier*. Nisbet, 1918; London: Virago, 1980.

WICKHAM, ANNA. 'The Egoist'. *The Contemplative Quarry*. London: The Poetry Bookshop, 1915, 8.

[WILLIAMS, WILLIAM CARLOS and ROBERT McALMON, eds.] *Contact Collection of Contemporary Writers*. Dijon: Maurice Darantière, 1925.

WINTERS, YVOR. 'A Woman with a Hammer'. Review of *The Contemplative Quarry and the Man With a Hammer* by Anna Wickham. *Poetry*, 20/2 (May 1922): 93–5.

WOOLF, VIRGINIA. *The Diary of Virginia Woolf* vol. 1, ed. Anne Olivier Bell. London: The Hogarth Press, 1977.

—— *A Room of One's Own and Three Guineas*. London: The Hogarth Press 1929 (*A Room of One's Own*) and 1938 (*Three Guineas*); London: Penguin, 1993.

—— 'The Tunnel'. Review of *The Tunnel* by Dorothy Richardson. *The Times Literary Supplement*, 891 (Feb. 13, 1919): 81.

4. SECONDARY MATERIAL

ALLSOP, KENNETH. *The Angry Decade*. Peter Owen, 1958; Wendover: John Goodchild Publishers, 1985.

ARMSTRONG, ISOBEL. *Victorian Poetry: Poetry, Poetics and Politics*. London: Routledge, 1993.

BALDICK, CHRIS. *The Concise Oxford Dictionary of Literary Terms*. Oxford: Oxford University Press, 1990.

BENHABIB, SEYLA and DRUCILLA CORNELL, eds. *Feminism as Critique: Essays on the Politics of Gender in Late-Capitalist Societies*. Cambridge, UK: Polity Press, 1987.

BENNETT, PAULA. 'Late Nineteenth-Century American Women's Nature Poetry and the Evolution of the Imagist Poem'. *Legacy*, 9/2 (1992): 89–103.

—— ed. *Nineteenth-Century American Women Poets: An Anthology*. Malden, Mass: Blackwell Publishers, 1998.

BENSTOCK, SHARI. *Women of the Left Bank: Paris, 1900–1940*. Austin: The University of Texas Press, 1986; London: Virago, 1987.

BLOOM, HAROLD. *The Anxiety of Influence: A Theory of Poetry*. Oxford: Oxford University Press, 1973.

BORNSTEIN, GEORGE, ed. *Representing Modernist Texts: Editing as Interpretation*. Ann Arbor: The University of Michigan Press, 1991.

BRYER, JACKSON R. and PAMELA ROBLYER. 'H.D.: A Preliminary Checklist'. *Contemporary Literature*, 10/3 (Autumn 1969): 632–75.

BURKE, CAROLYN. *Becoming Modern: The Life of Mina Loy*. Berkeley: University of California Press, 1997.

BURNETT, GARY. *H.D. between Image and Epic: The Mysteries of Her Poetics*. Ann Arbor: UMI Research Press, 1990.

CALHOUN, CRAIG, ed. *Habermas and the Public Sphere*. Cambridge, Mass.: MIT Press, 1992.

CHISHOLM, DIANNE. *H.D.'s Freudian Poetics*. Ithaca: Cornell University Press, 1992.

COLLECOTT, DIANA. 'H.D. & Mass Observation'. *Line*, 13 (1989): 153–61.

CONNOR, STEVEN. *Theory and Cultural Value*. Oxford: Blackwell Publishers, 1992.

CUNNINGHAM, VALENTINE. *British Writers of the Thirties*. Oxford: Oxford University Press, 1989.

—— 'Neutral?: 1930s Writers and Taking Sides'. In *Class, Culture and Social Change: A New View of the 1930s*, ed. Frank Gloversmith. Sussex: The Harvester Press, 1980, 45–69.

DAMON, S. FOSTER. *Amy Lowell: A Chronicle*. Boston, Mass.: Houghton Mifflin, 1935.

DAY, GARY. 'The Poets: Georgians, Imagists and Others'. In *Literature and Culture in Modern Britain. Vol. 1: 1900–1929*, ed. Clive Bloom. London: Longman, 1993, 30–54.

DIETZ, MARY G. 'Context is All: Feminism and Theories of Citizenship'. *Dædalus*, 66/4 (Fall 1987): 1–24.

DUPLESSIS, RACHEL BLAU. *Writing Beyond the Ending: Narrative Strategies of Twentieth-Century Women Writers*. Bloomington: Indiana University Press, 1985.

EDMUNDS, SUSAN. 'Stealing from "Muddies Body": H.D. and Melanie Klein'. *H.D. Newsletter*, 4/2 (Winter 1991): 17–30.

ELLIS, HAVELOCK. Letter to the editor. *Close Up*, 2/2 (Feb. 1928): 75.

—— *Man and Woman: A Study of Human Secondary Sexual Characters*. London: Walter Scott, 1894.

ELLIS, HAVELOCK. *Studies in the Psychology of Sex.* London: The University Press, 1897.

FAIRBAIRN, W. R. D. 'Prolegomena to a Psychology of Art'. *The British Journal of Psychology,* 28/3 (Jan. 1938): 288–303.

FARR, JUDITH. *The Life and Art of Elinor Wylie.* Baton Rouge: Louisiana State University Press, 1982.

FREUD, SIGMUND. *Civilization and its Discontents,* trans. Joan Riviere. London: The Hogarth Press, 1930. Translation of *Das Umbehagen in der Kultur.* Vienna, 1929.

—— *The Interpretation of Dreams,* trans. A. A. Brill. London: Allen & Unwin, 1913. Translation of *Die Traumdeutung.* Vienna, 1900.

—— *Introductory Lectures on Psycho-Analysis,* trans. and ed. James Strachey. London: Allen & Unwin, 1922; New York: W. W. Norton, 1966. Translation of *Vorlesungen zur Einführung in die Psychanalyse.* Leipzig and Vienna: Heller, 1917.

—— 'Three Essays on the Theory of Sexuality'. *A Case of Hysteria: Three Essays on Sexuality and Other Works.* The Standard Edition of the Complete Psychological Works of Sigmund Freud, trans. James Strachey, vol. 7 (1901–5). London: The Hogarth Press and the Institute of Psycho-analysis, 1953, 123–245. Translation of 'Drei Abhandlungen zur Sexualtheorie'. Leipzig & Vienna: Deutlicke, 1905.

FRIEDMAN, SUSAN STANFORD. 'H.D. Chronology: Composition and Publication of Volumes'. *The H.D. Newsletter,* 1/1 (Spring 1987): 12–16.

—— 'Creating a women's mythology: H.D.'s *Helen in Egypt*'. *Women's Studies,* 5/2 (1977): 163–97.

—— *Penelope's Web: Gender, Modernity and H.D.'s Fiction.* Cambridge, UK: Cambridge University Press, 1990.

—— *Psyche Reborn: The Emergence of H.D.* Bloomington: Indiana University Press, 1981.

FROMM, GLORIA G, ed. *Windows on Modernism: Selected Letters of Dorothy Richardson.* Athens: The University of Georgia Press, 1995.

GLENDINNING, VICTORIA. *Rebecca West.* London: Weidenfeld and Nicolson, 1987; London: Papermac, 1988.

GOLDMAN, DOROTHY. *Women Writers and the Great War.* New York: Twayne Publishers, 1995.

GRICE, H. P. *Studies in the Way of Words.* Cambridge, Mass.: Harvard University Press, 1989.

GUEST, BARBARA. *Herself Defined: The Poet H.D. and Her World.* New York: Doubleday, 1984.

—— 'The Intimacy of Biography'. *Iowa Review,* 16/3 (Fall 1986): 58–71.

HABERMAS, JÜRGEN. *Knowledge and Human Interests*, trans. Jeremy J. Shapiro. London: Heinemann, 1972. Translation of *Erkenntnis und Interese*. Suhrkamp Verlag, 1968.

—— *The Structural Transformation of the Public Sphere: An Inquiry into a Category of Bourgeois Society*, trans. Thomas Burger. Cambridge, UK: Polity Press, 1989. Translation of *Strukturwandel Der Öffentlcihkeit: Untersuchungen zu einer Kategorie der bürgerlichen Gesellschaft*. Darmstadt: Hermann Luchrehand Verlag, 1962.

—— *The Theory of Communicative Action*, 2 vols., trans. Thomas McCarthy. Cambridge, UK: Polity Press, 1984, 1987. Translation of *Theorie des Kommunikativen Handelns*. Frankfurt am Main: Suhrkamp Verlag, 1981, 1987.

HANSCOMBE, GILLIAN and VIRGINIA L. SMYERS. *Writing for their Lives*. London: The Women's Press, 1987.

HARRIS, SHARON M. 'Origins, Revolutions, and Women in the Nations'. In *American Women Writers to 1800*, ed. Sharon M. Harris. New York: Oxford University Press, 1996, 161–72.

HARRISON, VICTORIA. *Elizabeth Bishop's Poetics of Intimacy*. Cambridge, UK: Cambridge University Press, 1993.

HERRING, PHILLIP. *Djuna: The Life and Work of Djuna Barnes*. New York: Viking, 1995.

HEWISON, ROBERT. *Under Siege: Literary Life in London 1939–45*. Weidenfeld & Nicolson, 1977; London: Methuen, 1988.

HOFFMAN, FREDERICK J., CHARLES ALLEN, and CAROLYN F. ULRICH. *The Little Magazine, A History and a Bibliography*. Princeton, NJ: Princeton University Press, 1946.

HOLLENBERG, DONNA KROLIK. *H.D.: The Poetics of Childbirth and Creativity*. Boston: Northeastern University Press, 1991.

HOLLEY, MARGARET. *The Poetry of Marianne Moore: A Study in Voice and Value*. Cambridge, UK: Cambridge University Press, 1987.

HYNES, SAMUEL. *The Auden Generation: Literature and Politics in England in the 1930s*. London: The Bodley Head, 1976.

JONES, ERNEST. *The Life and Work of Sigmund Freud*, 3 vols. London: The Hogarth Press, 1953–7.

JUNG, C. G. *Analytical Psychology: Notes of the Seminar Given in 1925 by C. G. Jung*, ed. William McGuire. Princeton: Princeton University Press, 1989; London: Routledge, 1990.

—— *Collected Papers on Analytical Psychology*, trans. Constance E. Long. London: Baillière, Tindall & Cox, 1916; 2nd edn., 1917.

—— *Psychology and Alchemy*, trans. R. F. C. Hull. London: Routledge & Kegan Paul, 1953; 2nd edn., 1968. Translation of *Psychologie und Alchemie*. Zurich: Rasher Verlag, 1944; 2nd edn., 1952.

—— 'Psychology and Poetry'. *transition*, 19–20 (June 1930): 23–45.

JUNG, C. G. *The Psychology of Dementia Praecox*. In *The Psychogenesis of Mental Disease*, trans. R. F. C. Hull. The Collected Works of C. G. Jung, vol. 3. London: Routledge & Kegan Paul, 1960. Translation of *Über die Psychologie der Dementia Praecox: Ein Versuch*. Halle a. s., 1907.

——*Psychology of the Unconscious*. New York: Moffat, Yard, 1916; London: Kegan Paul, Trench, Trubner, 1918. Translation of *Wandlungen und Symbole der Libido. Beiträge zur Entwicklungsgeschichte des Denkens*. Leipzig and Vienna: Franz Deuticke, 1912.

KENT, SUSAN KINGSLEY. *Sex and Suffrage in Britain, 1860–1914*. Princeton: Princeton University Press, 1987; London: Routledge, 1990.

KLEIN, MELANIE. *Love, Guilt and Reparation and Other Works*. The Hogarth Press, 1975; London: Virago, 1988.

KLOEPFER, DEBORAH KELLY. *The Unspeakable Mother: Forbidden Discourse in Jean Rhys and H.D.* Ithaca: Cornell University Press, 1989.

KOUIDIS, VIRGINIA M. *Mina Loy: American Modernist Poet*. Baton Rouge: Louisiana State University Press, 1980.

LANG, CAROLINE. *Keep Smiling Through: Women in the Second World War*. Cambridge, UK: Cambridge University Press, 1989.

LASSNER, PHYLLIS. *Elizabeth Bowen*. Women Writers. Basingstoke: Macmillan, 1990.

LEVENSON, MICHAEL H. *A Genealogy of Modernism: A Study of English Literary Doctrine 1908–1922*. Cambridge, UK: Cambridge University Press, 1984.

LOW, BARBARA. 'Mind-Growth or Mind-Mechanization?: The Cinema in Education'. *Close Up*, 1/3 (Sept. 1927): 44–52.

MAREK, JAYNE E. *Women Editing Modernism: 'Little' Magazines & Literary History*. Lexington: The University Press of Kentucky, 1995.

MCNEIL, HELEN. '*Trilogy* and *Four Quartets*: Contrapuntal Visions on Spiritual Quest'. *Agenda*, 25/3–4 (Autumn/Winter 1987/1988): 155–65.

MOLESWORTH, CHARLES. *Marianne Moore: A literary Life*. New York: Athenaeum, 1990.

MONTEFIORE, JANET. *Men and Women Writers of the 1930s: The Dangerous Flood of History*. London: Routledge, 1996.

NEGT, OSKAR and ALEXANDER KLUGE. *Public Sphere and Experience: Toward an Analysis of the Bourgeois and Proletarian Public Sphere*. Minneapolis: University of Minnesota Press, 1993.

OSTRIKER, ALICIA SUSKIN. *Stealing the Language: The Emergence of Women's Poetry in America*. Boston: Beacon Press, 1986.

PETRO, PATRICE. 'Film Censorship and the Female Spectator: *Joyless Street* (1925)'. In *The Films of G. W. Pabst: An Extraterritorial*

Cinema, ed. Eric Rentschler. New Brunswick: Rutgers University Press, 1990, 30–40.

PONDROM, CYRENA N. 'Marianne Moore and H.D.: Female Community and Poetic Achievement'. In *Marianne Moore: Woman and Poet*, ed. Patricia C. Willis. Orono, Maine: The National Poetry Foundation, 1990, 371–402.

PUGH, MARTIN. *Women and the Women's Movement in Britain 1914–1959*. Basingstoke: Macmillan. 1992.

RAY, PAUL. *The Surrealist Movement in England*. Ithaca: Cornell University Press, 1971.

REISS, ROBERT. '"My Baroness": Elsa von Freytag-Loringhoven'. *Dada/Surrealism*, 14 (1985): 81–101.

SACHS, HANNS. 'Film Psychology'. *Close Up*, 3/5 (Nov. 1928): 8–15.

SCOTT, THOMAS L. and MELVIN J. FRIEDMAN with JACKSON R. BRYHER, eds. *Pound/The Little Review: The Letters of Ezra Pound to Margaret Anderson*. London: Faber and Faber, 1988.

SHOWALTER, ELAINE. *A Literature of Their Own: British Women Novelists From Brontë to Lessing*. Princeton: Princeton University Press, 1977; London: Virago, 1978; rev. edn., 1982.

—— ed. *Daughters of Decadence: Women Writers of the Fin de Siècle*. London: Virago, 1993.

SPANIER, SANDRA WHIPPLE. *Kay Boyle: Artist and Activist*. Carbondale: Southern Illinois University Press, 1986.

STEAD, C. K. *The New Poetic*. London: Hutchinson University Library, 1964.

TATE, TRUDI and SUZANNE RAITT, eds. *Women's Fiction and the Great War*. Oxford: Clarendon Press, 1997.

TOLLEY, A. T. *The Poetry of The Forties*. Manchester: Manchester University Press, 1985, 34.

TYLEE, CLAIRE M. *The Great War and Women's Consciousness: Images of Militarism and Womanhood in Women's Writings, 1914–64*. Basingstoke: The Macmillan Press, 1990.

WALKER, CHERYL. *Masks Outrageous and Austere: Culture, Psyche, and Persona in Modern Women Poets*. Bloomington: Indiana University Press, 1991.

WATSON, STEVEN. *Strange Bedfellows: The First American Avant-Garde*. New York: Abbeville Press Publishers, 1991.

WHEELER, KATHLEEN. *'Modernist' Women Writers and Narrative Art*. Basingstoke: The Macmillan Press, 1994.

WILLIAMS, RAYMOND. *Culture*. Glasgow: Fontana, 1981.

ZACH, NATAN. 'Imagism and Vorticism'. In *Modernism: A Guide to European Literature 1890–1930*, ed. Malcolm Bradbury and James McFarlane. London: Penguin, 1961, repr. 1991.

Index